Young Men in Prison

Young Men in Prison
Surviving and adapting to life inside

Joel Harvey

WILLAN
PUBLISHING

Published by

Willan Publishing
Culmcott House
Mill Street, Uffculme
Cullompton, Devon
EX15 3AT, UK
Tel: +44(0)1884 840337
Fax: +44(0)1884 840251
e-mail: info@willanpublishing.co.uk
website: www.willanpublishing.co.uk

Published simultaneously in the USA and Canada by

Willan Publishing
c/o ISBS, 920 NE 58th Ave, Suite 300,
Portland, Oregon 97213-3786, USA
Tel: +001(0)503 287 3093
Fax: +001(0)503 280 8832
e-mail: info@isbs.com
website: www.isbs.com

First published 2007

Hardback
ISBN-13: 978-1-84392-203-2
ISBN-10: 1-84392-203-7

British Library Cataloguing-in-Publication Data

A catalogue record for this book is available from the British Library

Project managed by Deer Park Productions, Tavistock, Devon
Typeset by GCS, Leighton Buzzard, Bedfordshire, LU7 1AR
Printed and bound by T.J. International Ltd, Padstow, Cornwall

For my parents, Tom and Isobel, and my sisters,
Esther and Hannah

Contents

Acknowledgements

The research on which this book is based was funded by a three-year studentship from the Economic and Social Research Council and a three-year award from the Isaac Newton Trust. The research was conducted with considerable help from the staff at HM YOI Brinsford and, especially, HM YOI Feltham, notably Richard Foster, Paul McDowell, Tom Murray, Nick Pascoe, Marion Rayment and David Shelton. I am grateful to the many prisoners who agreed to take part and who were open about their experiences.

Alison Liebling brilliantly supervised the thesis on which this book is based, and I thank her warmly for her sound advice and kindness. My doctoral examiners, Adrian Grounds and Keith Bottomley, gave me useful advice on preparing this book. Thanks to Helen Krarup, Mary Gower and Stuart Feathers at the Radzinowicz Library, University of Cambridge. I would also like to thank Helen Arnold, Deb Drake and Linda Durie for their friendship and their support in my research. Sarah Bruce, Katherine Chapman, Jo Coggins, Julie Colville, Barry Crosbie, Adam Danquah, Paul Stephenson and Andy Thomas have also helped me in different ways.

I am also grateful to my mum for her encouragement and to my dad for his insightful comments. Thanks also to my sisters Esther and Hannah and to my grandmother, Joyce Greenwood. Finally, thanks to Daniel Wakelin. He has provided me with constant support, and I could not have done this work without him.

List of tables and figures

Tables

Figures

Chapter 1

Introduction

In January 2006, there were 8,031 young men aged 18–20 in prison, of which 1,937 were on remand (NOMS 2006).[1] They are housed in the 16 young offender institutions (YOI) and 42 adult prisons across England and Wales (Solomon 2004). They arrive in prison with a variety of early-life experiences and an array of beliefs about themselves, the world and their future. Some of these experiences and beliefs are positive; others are negative and are socially and psychologically damaging. Although much research has focused on the pathways to crime for young men, less research has explored the experience of imprisonment for this age group.

This book provides a detailed analysis of the psychosocial experience of imprisonment for young men within one custodial setting, HM YOI Feltham, a remand centre in London, England. How do they fit in at Feltham? Why do some survive prison better than others? How do they relate to prison staff? Can they feel supported by staff? How do they interact with fellow prisoners? Can they make supportive friendships or are their experiences marked solely by negative intimidating interactions? How can staff and peers help them – and encourage them to accept that help? What happens when they become too distressed and cannot cope? What leads some of them to harm themselves? These are some questions this book sets out to answer.

The physical, social and political worlds of Feltham

To answer these questions, we must first enter the physical, social and political worlds of HM YOI Feltham. The buildings at Feltham are placed within quite a pleasant open area of grass and trees, and Feltham has to some extent the feel of a university campus. Big peacocks roam around the buildings, or stand outside the gates in the corridors, and are seen and heard by prisoners in their cells. Yet these grounds are circled with barbed wire and a wall which cuts each prisoner off from his life outside. The prison itself is a labyrinth of low, red-brick buildings, 21 units in all, connected by numerous long corridors, which are at first confusing. Each of the main residential units is podular in design and split into two self-contained triangular sides, separated by gates, and each side has two levels, the upper level being reached by a middle open plan stairwell. Most of the units have a certified normal accommodation of 56 young men in cells on both levels. Two of the units are on one level: Teal, which accommodates 56 prisoners, and Waite, which accommodates 12 prisoners. The cells are where these men live in prison, sleeping, eating and going to the lavatory all in one space. These are the spaces they must adapt to.

They do, though, leave their cells and enter the wider social world of the wing. They come out three times a day for food, although they take their food back into their cells, eating alone or with a cellmate. Some have jobs serving and preparing the food on the wing, or cleaning the wing. The bottom floor of each wing has an association area, with pool tables, a table-tennis table and arcade machines. One side of a wing has association in the morning, and the other in the afternoon. Here prisoners take showers, make phone calls, put in applications for education and workshops, and talk to other prisoners and staff; for example they may raise their concerns with the staff. On the wing, this is the main arena for social interaction. While the prisoners on one side of a wing have association, the prisoners on the other side leave the wing to enter the wider social world of Feltham as a whole for education or workshops. This ensures that there are only half of the 56 prisoners on the wing at any one time during the day. Outdoor 'exercise' takes place in the mornings for the wing as a whole.[2] Within the prison there is a gym, religious centre, educational facilities and workshops, where some prisoners take part in activities. The gym department is now the largest in the country with over 20 physical education instructors. The wings can sometimes be very quiet and sometimes chaotic. In particular, the social world of the wing is transient in nature, with some prisoners leaving for court in the morning, and others being transferred from other wings of the prison, or from other prisons, with a bag of belongings to be allocated a cell. In the prison as a whole, the average length of stay is only 35 days, although others stay much longer than this average.[3] The flow of people in and out of the prison is fast.

Feltham is a remand centre but also holds people who have been convicted and are awaiting sentencing or who have been sentenced; those who have been sentenced are quickly transferred to other establishments. Feltham is the largest young offender establishment for London and the Southeast with a certified normal accommodation of 712. It holds juvenile prisoners aged 15–17 and young adult prisoners aged 18–21. One side of the prison (residential area 1) is dedicated to juvenile prisoners. The other side of the prison (residential areas 2 and 3) holds both juvenile and young adult prisoners, although prisoners are separately located in different wings. As this book focuses solely on young adults, the world it describes is largely that of the seven young adult units: Kingfisher (the induction unit); Partridge (the unit for vulnerable prisoners);[4] Osprey, Mallard and Raven (normal locations); Teal (an enhanced unit); and Waite (a super-enhanced unit).[5] Feltham also has a diverse population of prisoners: in April 2003, 22 per cent of the young men were foreign nationals, from 20 different countries, and the men as a whole came from many different economic and social backgrounds.[6] They must adapt to living with many different people on their wing and as cellmates. Making friends and adapting socially are challenges for people in the outside world but within the confined space of a prison they can be harder. HM YOI Feltham has a particular reputation for being a hostile world. In fact, the prison has a negative public reputation, which impinges on the way the prisoners interact with their peers (as we shall see in Chapter 2). Many prisoners have heard 'horror stories', passed on through friends or associates who had been at Feltham or on their own previous stays there, which leave them fearful of being attacked by their peers. Over the past few years Feltham had received considerable attention from the media for its difficulties. (The prison has also had a well-known history of cultural, industrial and managerial difficulties.)[7] The reputation is not, though, a fair account of the social world of Feltham. Most staff and prisoners told me that Feltham had changed dramatically for the better in recent years.

In 1998, Her Majesty's Chief Inspector of Prisons (HMCIP) carried out an unannounced full inspection of Feltham and concluded that it was the most disturbing inspection he had made in the last three years as Chief Inspector. David Ramsbotham, the then Chief Inspector, commented in his report that the core of the institution was 'rotten' (HMCIP 1999a). Following this inspection the then Director General of the Prison Service, Martin Narey, set up a task force to implement recommendations made in a prior 1996 inspection and ploughed £11.7 million into the establishment. By September 1999, following a short unannounced inspection, HMCIP (1999b) concluded that the establishment had changed for the better. The establishment had been split into two, Feltham A (for juvenile prisoners) and Feltham B (for young adult prisoners), and the certified normal accommodation had been reduced as units were being refurbished.[8]

By 2000, however, problems had become evident again. In March 2000 Zahid Mubarek was murdered by his cellmate and in September 2000 a juvenile prisoner committed suicide in his cell; as a result, Feltham continued, even throughout 2001, to receive negative attention from the media. (The public inquiry into Mr Mubarek's death was completed in November 2005, and the report was published on 29 June 2006.)[9] HMCIP returned to the prison in October 2000 to carry out a short unannounced inspection that was reported in March 2001. He stated: 'I am forced to conclude from this, my fourth inspection of HM YOI and RC Feltham in four years, that Feltham B – the part of the establishment that now holds young adult prisoners between the ages of 18 and 21 – should no longer be allowed to operate as a Prison Service run Young Offenders Institution' (HMCIP 2001).[10]

Following the completion of this inspection, Nick Pascoe took over as governor, charged with turning the establishment around. Despite the fact that there was much negative publicity for Feltham in the media, especially concerning the 2001 inspection, positive changes were initiated after Mr Pascoe took over as governor. With a short period of time to make improvements, Mr Pascoe came up with a 12-month action plan. He developed a 'core day' for the establishment so that each unit would be carrying out the same activities at the same time. He initiated a rolling programme to install in-cell electricity, enabling prisoners to have televisions. September 2001 brought more tragic events: another suicide by a juvenile prisoner. However, in January 2002 a new Chief Inspector of Prisons, Anne Owers, carried out her first inspection of Feltham and concluded that Feltham had improved. The inspection found 'an establishment whose culture, regime and vision were fundamentally changed' (HMCIP 2002). It was considered to be cleaner, prisoners spent more time out of cell, and there was more and better education and training. Feltham in this year was also to hear that it would remain in the public sector. The threat of privatisation had been lifted, and this reprieve may have brought about a sense of relief among the prison staff.

By the time I arrived at the establishment, in July 2002, the prison was entering a more settled phase. During the ten months I was present, many of the senior management team's efforts were spent building on the work of the previous year. Monitoring and development plans had been put in place (e.g. the core day), aiming for more time out of cell, including evening association and education classes. At a full staff meeting in mid-2003, the governor announced that young adult prisoners now had more time out of cell than juvenile prisoners: this was against the historical trend of juveniles receiving more attention and more activities (from the Youth Justice Board).

When I first arrived, however, there was still a problem with staff shortages. These shortages put staff under considerable pressure and were their main source of complaint. As time progressed, one of the major achievements of the prison was the recruitment and retention of additional staff. In May 2003, just before I left, there were 742 staff working at Feltham, of whom 324 were basic grade officers, who generally appeared content.[11] This increase was achieved through a move to local recruitment and training and putting a freeze on staff, preventing them from moving to different prisons.[12] The local training and recruitment resulted in a large influx of new staff over a short period of time, and it was interesting to consider the perception of staff already working in Feltham. Many considered the increased staffing levels to be a positive step, as new staff coming into this prison brought with them the opportunity to develop a positive culture within the prison. New staff brought with them a greater focus on suicide prevention, which had been emphasised in the prison officer entry-level training, and a willingness to see themselves as part of a supportive profession. It was often said that the 'dinosaurs' were 'a dying breed', and that now the staff were more able to support prisoners with their problems, with less stigma attached to such helping behaviour. (These ideas will be discussed in Chapter 4.)

There was some negative impact, though. Others in the establishment felt that such an increase in the number of newly trained staff put the more experienced staff under pressure, because they had to take responsibility not only for their own work but also for that of the new staff members. Relatively inexperienced staff, once outside their probation period, distanced themselves from the *brand-new* officers. This distance was evidenced in the negative comments they would make about new staff as they performed their duties, or in their agreement with negative comments made by more experienced officers. This stance enabled the relatively new staff to see themselves as more experienced and to position themselves closer to the experienced staff. They feared being seen as inexperienced.

Yet, the overall mood was increasingly positive. During this period, there were major changes to the built environment as part of the Safer Custody Group's Safer Locals Programme. A number of areas in the prison were refurbished as part of Safer Custody investment, including the reception area (November 2002), the induction unit (July 2002) and a new health-care centre (July 2003).[13] At this time a significant amount

5

of money was spent on Feltham, and things were unusually dynamic, after the prison had seemed to stagnate for so long. HMCIP returned to Feltham in February 2004 to carry out a follow-up inspection of education and training. She concluded: 'Feltham had made further progress in developing an acceptable regime for the children and young people in its care' (HMCIP 2004a: 6). A follow-up inspection in 2005 identified problems with the provision of health care at Feltham, but, overall, concluded that 'progress had been sustained, and was continuing. Relationships between staff and young people had continued to improve, and this was confirmed by the young people themselves' (HMCIP 2005: 5). When we consider social support and welfare, we must remember that Feltham had made considerable improvements by the period of this research. The staff of the prison were able to provide a high level of support for those who needed it most: those who felt suicidal, those who were withdrawing from drugs, and those who were distressed. This provision has important implications for the analyses of prisoners' responses to that help.

Prison politics, policy and research

This concern with improving the experience of imprisonment for young men at Feltham has been part of a wider concern among policy makers and politicians with the criminal justice system. The criminal justice system in England and Wales has changed dramatically in recent years, through the Criminal Justice Act of November 2003,[14] and the new National Offender Management Service (NOMS) (Carter 2003: 5). One area within the criminal justice system that has been given particular attention is youth justice (see Goldson 2002; Smith 2003; Bottoms and Dignan 2004). Bottoms and Dignan (2004) noted that one of the main political priorities of the Labour government since its election in 1997 has been the 'reform of the English system for dealing with youth crime' (p. 25). The Crime and Disorder Act 1998 and the Youth Justice and Criminal Evidence Act 1999 brought about a number of key changes. These included a separate system for 10–17-year-olds overseen by the Youth Justice Board, the establishment of youth offender teams, and the replacement of the custodial sentences of secure training order and detention in a YOI with the detention and training order. Bottoms and Dignan (2004) argued that this 'new youth justice' is more correctionalist than before and 'has prioritized the prevention of offending by young people as the principal aim' (p. 167).

Yet, while policy makers have shown much interest in those involved in the criminal justice system under the age of 18, they have given substantially less attention to offenders aged 18–21.[15] In the report *Young Adult Offenders: A Period of Transition*, NACRO (2001) stated that the welcome focus on the under-18 age group 'has tended to deflect attention from offenders in their late teens and early twenties' (p. 2). Anne Owers, HMCIP, concluded that 'for young adults, there is nothing to compare with the joined-up, centrally funded training and resettlement for under-18s' (HMCIP 2004b: 43).[16] The young adult offender has reached the policy agenda primarily with the publication in 1999 of the consultation paper *Detention in a Young Offenders Institution for 18-20-year-olds*. This paper set out to abolish the sentence for young adult prisoners. The Home Office concluded that the sentence of detention in a YOI for 18–20-year-olds was no longer justified, on the grounds that it 'no longer caters properly for the needs of that age group and has practical disadvantages in its enforcement' (Home Office 1999). The command paper *Criminal Justice: The Way Ahead* (HMSO 2001) was then published, and within the Labour Party's 2001 election manifesto, *Ambitions for Britain*, were pledges to improve conditions in prisons for 18–20-year-olds. However, to date, there has been little sign of change at the level of policy for prisoners within this age group.

Despite this lack of progress in policy over recent years, policy-driven research has ensured that the issues faced by young adults in prison have not been forgotten (Lyon *et al.* 2000; NACRO 2001; Neustatter 2002; Howard League 2003a; Solomon 2004; Farrant 2005a, 2005b, 2005c, 2006). Academic research on young adults in prison has considered a number of relevant areas such as suicidal behaviour, coping and psychological distress (Liebling 1992; Inch *et al.* 1995; Biggam and Power 1999a, 1999b; Nieland *et al.* 2001; Mohino *et al.* 2004; Ireland *et al.* 2005). Other areas of research have included bullying behaviour (Beck 1995; Ireland 2002, 2005; Dyson 2005; Smith *et al.* 2005), social support (Biggam and Power 1997), identity (Little 1990) and the socialisation of prisoners entering custody (Dunlop and McCabe 1965, Ericson 1975).

While policy makers have not concerned themselves with young adults in prison to any great extent over the past few years, they have focused a lot of attention upon the difficulties faced by prisoners more generally, when adapting to prison life. One particular area of concern and controversy has been the problem of suicide and self-harm in prisons of all types. In the year 2002/3, the time period during which I carried out my research, the Prison Service recorded 106 self-inflicted deaths, which translates into a rate of 148 per 100,000 of the annual average daily population (ADP). This number decreased slightly in 2003/4 to 93, a rate of 126 per 100,000 ADP (HM Prison Service 2004a). Yet, what proportion of younger prisoners engages in suicidal behaviour? In 1998/9-2000/1, those under 21 years accounted for 19 per cent of self-inflicted deaths (n = 47). In 2001/2-2003/4, this figure decreased to 13 per cent (n = 36). This age group constituted 13 per cent of the total prison population in 1998 (HM Prison Service 2004a).

Beyond the data on actual suicides, which have been available for several years, the data on self-harm have only recently been collated. In 2003, a total of 16,214 incidents of self-harm were recorded across the prison estate in England and Wales. A total of 5,425 people harmed themselves, which translates to a rate of 74 per 1,000 ADP (HM Prison Service 2004b). Although they represented a proportionate number of suicides among the prison population, young prisoners were over represented in the figures for self-harm: indeed, they accounted for 25 per cent of incidents. Female prisoners were over-represented, accounting for 65 per cent of incidents. Moreover, it is estimated that incidents have been under-reported by 15 per cent, so that the estimated actual number of incidents is 18,710. Meltzer *et al.* (1999), in their report, *Non-fatal Suicidal Behaviour among Prisoners*, found that 20 per cent of male prisoners on remand aged 16–20 had attempted suicide (compared with 27 per cent of all age groups). Furthermore, 38 per cent of male prisoners on remand aged 16–20 had thought of suicide in their lifetime (this figure was 48 per cent for all age groups).

These issues are on the political agenda at the highest levels: in 1999, the World Health Organisation (WHO-Europe) established a working group to review suicide prevention policies in prison, and the British government produced a White Paper, *Saving Lives: Our Healthier Nation* (HMSO 1999). This White Paper aimed to reduce suicides by a fifth by 2010; that aim also encompassed suicides in prisons. In 1999, HMCIP carried out a thematic review on suicide in prison and concluded by emphasising that 'suicide is everyone's concern'. The then inspector, David Ramsbotham, also outlined the broader objective of developing 'healthy prisons'; that is, institutions 'in which prisoners and staff are able to live and work in a way that promotes their well-being' (HMCIP 1999c: 59). This holistic approach highlighted the fact that the problem of suicide in prisons will not be tackled effectively if efforts focus solely on the problem within the person; attention must also be directed towards regimes and relationships in general. In April 2001, the Safer Custody Group at Her Majesty's Prison Service put forward a three-year strategy, through which 'an all-round pro-active approach will be developed which encourages a supportive culture in prisons based on good staff–prisoner relationships, a constructive regime and a physically safe environment. There will be improved identification and case arrangements for high risk prisoners' (HM Prison Service, 2001). This strategy was piloted in six establishments with £8 million invested in implementation during the first year. The Safer Locals Programme was intended to improve the early custodial experience: changes included the development of new risk-assessment tools and alterations to the built environment; the Safer Custody Group also refurbished reception areas and first-night centres and created detoxification units. Feltham was a pilot establishment in the project.

Just as there have been important developments in policy, there has also been significant academic research into prison suicide and self-harm. Studies have been carried out in Australia, Austria, Canada, England and Wales, Finland, France, Greece, Italy, New Zealand, Scotland, Switzerland and the USA.[17] The majority of these studies focus solely on male suicidal behaviour, and have included suicidal behaviour among young men. These studies identify the rates of completed suicides; examine risk factors and motives associated with suicide, attempted suicide and self-harm; and examine specific variables in relation to attempted suicide, self-harm and coping. However, only recently has this literature begun to consider the social as well as the individual dimensions of suicide risk. This book sets out to make a further contribution to this area of prison research by focusing not only on self-harm but also on successful adaptation to prison life. It explores how young men, aged 18–21, adapt to prison life. It will concentrate upon the role of social support, trust, locus of control and safety in relation to adaptation. Having examined how prisoners succeed in adapting to life in prison, it will then return to those who have difficulties.

Aims of the book

The first aim of this book is to understand how young men make the transition into prison and how they adapt practically, socially and psychologically within their first month.[18] Why is this transition such an important element in our understanding of distressed prisoners? Adams (1992), in his review of the literature about adaptation, concluded that the stressful moment of entry into prison marks 'the start of a critical period in which inmates may experience difficulties in transition shock as they try to adjust to a new environment' (p. 331). Liebling (1999) also pointed out that the pains of imprisonment are concentrated at particular points in time, and that one of the most important is the period of arrival in custody. Suicidal behaviour and self-harm occur disproportionately in the first month in custody (HM Prison Service 2004a). Previous studies have focused on procedural aspects of entering prison (Brookes 1994; McManus 1994; HMCIP for Scotland 1998) and the effects of imprisonment more generally (Gibbs

9

1982a, 1982b; Zamble and Porporino 1988; Jones and Schmid 2000). These studies have found that prisoners entering custody experience emotional disturbance (Zamble and Porporino 1988), that their personal lives and sense of self are threatened (Jones and Schmid 2000), that they experience heightened uncertainty and a lack of control (Zamble and Porporino 1988) and that they are thrown off balance (Toch 1992). Gibbs (1982a) identified four pains of confinement in jail: withstanding entry shock, maintaining outside links, securing stability and finding activity. Moreover, certain studies have examined suicidal behaviour that occurs at this early phase (Beigel and Russell 1973; Esparza 1973; Fawcett and Marss 1973; Heilig 1973; Liebling 1999).

These studies provide a useful starting point for the research. However, the concept of adaptation at this entry phase has been defined too loosely. Before we consider the second aim of this book, it is necessary to define the concept of adaptation and to consider some factors we might expect to contribute to it. Adaptation is a process whereby people move towards reaching a cognitive, emotional and behavioural equilibrium. They do so by mobilising the internal and external resources that are available to them. People must adapt *practically* in that they must learn about the prison rules, regulations and regime. People must adapt *socially* in that they must become able to communicate and interact with staff and prisoners on a day-to-day basis, and become involved in the regime. Finally, people must adapt *psychologically* in that they must be able to regulate their cognitions and emotions and to manage their level of psychological distress.

One factor that may aid this process is social support, and this book takes time to consider the role of social support within adaptation. The concept of social support has been widely researched in the general community over several decades and has been prospectively associated with physical and psychiatric morbidity, and mortality (see Cohen and Wills 1985). It has been argued to play a stress-buffering role, protecting people from the detrimental impact of stressful life experiences (see Lakey and Cohen (2000) for a review). By contrast, research in prisons has examined the role of social support only to a limited extent and with conflicting findings (Biggam and Power 1997; Singleton *et al.* 1998; Hobbs and Dear 2000; Lindquist 2000; Liebling 2004). The first aim of this book, to study adaptation, therefore prompts further examination of the concept of social support.

Another concept which researchers have found to be important when considering the process of adaptation has been locus of control. Rotter (1966) put forward the concept of locus of control within the framework of social learning theory. He argued that people differ along a continuum in how they perceive control: that is, they differ in the extent to which they believe they are responsible for their own behaviour. Those with a high internal locus of control perceive reinforcements to be based on their own behaviour, whereas those with a high external locus of control perceive reinforcements to be based on chance or luck. It has been argued that an internal locus of control can aid adaptation within prison (Wright *et al.* 1980; Goodstein *et al.* 1984; MacKenzie *et al.* 1987; Zamble and Porporino 1988; Goodstein and Wright 1989; Pugh 1993, 1994; Blatier 2000; Reitzel and Harju 2000). Goodstein *et al.* (1984) found that if people enter prison with a high internal locus of control they 'find ways to maximise their choices, exert control over outcomes, and seek information to enhance the predictability of personally relevant future events' (p. 353). Those with a high internal locus of control have also been found to have lower levels of depression and anxiety (MacKenzie *et al.* 1987; Zamble and Porporino 1988) and to be better at working towards desired ends (Wright *et al.* 1980). In response to these findings, the study of adaptation in this book also considers the concept of locus of control. Another element of the process of adaptation considered here is the role of trust and safety, which previous research has identified as important for both prisoners and staff when assessing the quality of prison life and the experience of imprisonment (Liebling and Arnold 2002; Liebling 2004).

Alongside this analysis, the second aim of this book is to understand supportive transactions between staff and prisoners. Albrecht and Adelman (1987) argued that research should focus on communicative transactions of support. For them, social support is defined as 'verbal and non-verbal communication between recipients and providers that reduces uncertainty about the situation, the self, the other, or the relationship, and functions to enhance a perception of personal control in one's life experience' (p. 19). It is argued that these supportive interactions reduce uncertainty and thereby enhance the recipient's perception of control, 'by reframing a recipient's cognitive perspective, improving the recipient's skill levels, offering tangible assistance, and expressing acceptance and reassurance' (Albrecht and Adelman 1987: 31). Accordingly, the book will explore associations between support, trust, locus of control and safety. Furthermore, the book will examine the extent to which prisoners are willing to enter into a supportive transaction with a member of staff. Previous research among adult prisoners has found that prisoners are reluctant to seek support and disclose personal problems to staff (Hobbs and Dear 2000). How far do young men in prison utilise the coping strategy of seeking support?

Thirdly, this book examines support within prison among peers. It provides a detailed account of social interactions and relationships among prisoners through an analysis of their social networks. Prison sociology offers many studies of prisoners' social life (Clemmer 1940; Sykes 1958; Mathiesen 1965; Irwin 1970). These studies provide a rich source of data on the dynamic processes that take place within penal settings and on many of the problems prisoners face. However, these studies have focused almost exclusively on adult prisoners.

Fourth and finally, this book examines self-harming behaviour among prisoners at Feltham. It considers the experience of prisoners who were finding it difficult to adapt while inside Feltham. Previous research among young adults who had self-harmed has argued that 'imprisonment is directed at vulnerable groups' and that 'these groups are expected to undergo an experience whereby the demands made may exceed the resources available. The result: pain; the outcome: excessive suicide rates' (Liebling 1992: 184). From this research, and a replication of the study with adult prisoners, a theoretical model of the pathway to suicide was formulated based on the notion of vulnerability and coping (Liebling 1999). This model placed suicidal thoughts and behaviour along a continuum, and incorporated vulnerability, prison-induced stress and situational triggers, in an interactive and dynamic manner. Protecting agents were also included in the model, and these covered many aspects of social support (visits and contact with the family, support from prisoners and staff), constructive occupation in prison, and having hopes and plans for the future. The present book will, in part, draw upon this study and will focus particularly on the role of locus of control, support, trust and safety for prisoners who have self-harmed. The study of people who have self-harmed brings together the themes that emerge from earlier chapters, that is, the elements of adaptation and the various forms of support from staff and peers, and seeks to integrate them. This aspect of the study also turns to those elements of life in prison that, as we have seen, are of pressing concern to policy makers, researchers and all those concerned with the welfare of prisoners.

An embedded multimethod approach

In my research I took what I have termed an embedded, multimethod approach. I carried out the research while embedded within one YOI. Most of the previous studies (see endnote 17) have pursued quantitative analyses, although there is a developing interest in more qualitative, exploratory studies. I utilised a number of different methods, which included semi-structured interviews, quantitative measures, social network analyses and observations of key areas in the prison.[19] Utilising different methods allowed for data triangulation, 'the checking of inferences drawn from one set of data sources by collecting data from others' (Hammersley and Atkinson 1997: 230). Before the fieldwork was carried out, these methods were piloted at HM YOI Brinsford from October to December 2001.[20]

In order to understand the transition into prison and subsequent adaptation, participants were interviewed longitudinally at three time intervals: at 3, 10 and 30 days. A total of 70 prisoners were interviewed at three days. Each day that I was in the prison, I randomly selected prisoners to take part in the research from a computerised list. As I was in the prison most days, the sample included people entering prison from Monday to Saturday (no prisoners arrived on Sunday). In order to over-represent people who were on an open F2052SH form, I would sample one person on a form and one who was not each day, if such people had arrived. The F2052SH records that someone is at risk of self-harm and requires monitoring; this form could be opened by any member of staff.[21] These prisoners were still chosen randomly from the list of people on an open form. Those not selected on a random basis were two participants who had self-harmed within their first three days in custody. As most prisoners were first interviewed on the induction unit, none was yet attending education or work and therefore could be interviewed without much difficulty. Only two of the people whom I approached chose not to be interviewed. I interviewed in a private room, and I offered each person a carton of blackcurrant juice and some chocolate biscuits for their help. Table 1.1 presents the background-demographic statistics of the 70 prisoners who participated at three days.

The interview schedule consisted of four parts (see Appendix 1 for a list of the main questions asked). In the first part of the interview, I gathered background-demographic information, such as prior custodial history, ethnicity and sentence status, and information on level of vulnerability (e.g. prior self-harm, drug problems, psychiatric treatment).[22] In the second part, I asked prisoners to complete a number of measures (rated on a Likert scale from *strongly agree* to *strongly disagree*). If the prisoner had difficulty reading, I helped him complete it. Table 1.2 shows the measures used and their respective reliability levels (Cronbach's alpha).

The prison locus of control scale was devised by Pugh (1994) and had a good internal reliability (alpha = .88). The items on outside social support were taken from the study of the Office of National Statistics (ONS) on psychiatric morbidity among prisoners (Singleton *et al.* 1998). These items were modified to refer to outside support only. In the ONS study, the source of support was not specified. The four other measures were derived from a factor analysis I carried out on the data. The items

Table 1.1 Background and demographic statistics of sample

Variable		%	N
Legal status	Remand	71.4	50
	Convicted	20.0	14
	Sentenced	8.6	6
First time in prison		41.4	29
First time in Feltham		61.4	43
Ethnicity	White-British	41.4	29
	White-other	15.7	11
	Black-African	12.9	9
	Black-Caribbean	15.7	11
	Black-British	5.7	4
	Asian-Indian	1.4	1
	Asian-Bangladeshi	7.4	5

Table 1.2 Quantitative measures and reliabilities

Measure	Number of items	Alpha
Prison locus of control	20	.87
Outside social support	7	.85
Psychological distress	11	.87
Perceived adaptability	4	.74
Prison social support	8	.86
Perceived safety	3	.41

that comprised these four measures were taken, with permission, from previous research aimed at measuring the quality of prison life (see Liebling 2004) and from the evaluation of the Safer Locals Programme (Liebling *et al.* 2005).[23] Each of the measures devised had good internal reliability except for perceived safety, which had a low reliability. This may have been because it comprised only three items and is a difficult construct to measure. Specific items within the scale may have taken on different meanings for different people. I decided to include this measure nevertheless, but the results from this scale must be considered with caution.

In the third part I asked questions about each person's social networks and his level of support from people outside prison, and in the fourth section I carried out a semi-structured interview that covered a number of separate but interconnected areas. In this final part of the interview, I began by asking each prisoner to recall his experience over the past few days. I asked him to imagine that I was wearing a virtual-reality head mask and that I was following him from court until this present moment, so that I could see what he saw, think what he thought, and feel what he had felt. The subjects recalled their experience from being arrested to the present time of interview. I then asked a number of open questions that covered their concerns and their willingness to seek support for these problems, the support received from the prison staff and other prisoners, and the extent to which they trusted others.

Of the 70 people interviewed, 40 were followed up at time 2 (10 days) and 28 were followed up at time 3 (30 days). Due to the high turnover of prisoners at Feltham, I experienced a high attrition rate. The interviews took the same format as at time 1, except that at these two subsequent time intervals I asked about each prisoner's retrospective recall over a longer time period. Table 1.3 presents the background and demographic statistics of this subsample followed up at three time intervals.

Secondly, to understand supportive transactions between staff and prisoners and to examine the extent to which prisoners used the coping strategy of seeking support, I drew on a number of different sources of data. These were data from observations, qualitative data from interviews with prisoners in their first month, and interviews conducted with members of staff at Feltham.[24] I also drew on a cross-sectional survey of support seeking among a sample of 182 prisoners.[25] To carry

Table 1.3 Background and demographic statistics of the follow-up sample

Variable		%	N
Legal status	Remand	82.1	23
	Convicted	17.9	5
	Sentenced	0	0
First time in prison		42.9	12
First time in Feltham		57.4	16
Ethnicity	White-British	28.6	8
	White-other	25.0	7
	Black-African	14.3	4
	Black-Caribbean	17.9	5
	Black-British	7.1	2
	Asian-Bangladeshi	7.1	2

out this survey, I distributed questionnaires to each prisoner over five lunchtime lock-up periods in one week. Before doing so, I spoke to prisoners who were on exercise, explaining who I was and asking them if they would take part in the research. I handed the prisoners a questionnaire when they were on their way back to their cells with their meal, and informed them that I would pick up the questionnaires before they were unlocked for the afternoon. I asked them not to put their name on the questionnaire, as it was an anonymous study, and to place the questionnaire in the sealed envelope provided.[26]

The questionnaire was a modified version of the questionnaire used by Hobbs and Dear (2000).[27] In their research, prisoners rated on a scale from 1 to 7 their willingness to seek support from prison officers for eight different types of problems, such as stress related to legal proceedings, and problems related to where the prisoner was located in the prison. Prisoners rated their responses in relation to seeking both practical and emotional support for each problem specified. In my research I decided to look at prisoners' willingness to seek support from different sources rather than focusing solely on prison officers. The sources included gym officers, prison officers, education staff, the chaplain or imam, drug workers, members of the outreach team, doctors or nurses, voluntary workers, prisoners, prisoner listeners, and the Samaritans (by telephone). Rather than specifying particular problems, I asked prisoners to rate on a scale from 1 to 7 their willingness to seek support from these different sources for practical problems and for emotional problems. Examples of practical problems were given including the needs to make a phone call, to find out if they were due a visit, and to find out when they would receive their canteen orders. Seeking emotional support was defined as asking to talk to someone because they were feeling 'stressed out'. As numerous different sources were included in the questionnaire, it would have taken too long to ask them to rate each source for each type of problem. Therefore I decided to gain a general measure of willingness to seek help for practical and emotional problems from different sources of support. Participants also indicated whether they had experienced any practical and emotional problems since being in prison this time and whether they had received any help for each. Table 1.4 shows the background and demographic statistics for those who completed the questionnaire.

Thirdly, to understand the social life of the prisoners and the level of peer support available, data were again drawn from different sources, including observations and interviews with prisoners in their first month. However, I also carried out two social network analyses: this study is the first time a whole-network social network analysis has been carried out in prisons in the UK. The social network approach allows

Table 1.4 Background and demographic statistics of survey sample[28]

Variable		%	N
Sentence status	Remand	45.4	74
	Convicted but not sentenced	33.7	55
	Sentenced	20.9	34
First time in prison	Yes	44.5	81
Ethnicity	White-British	33.5	60
	White-other	7.8	14
	Black-African	12.3	22
	Black-Caribbean	17.3	3
	Black-British	11.7	21
	Black-other	4.5	8
	Asian-Indian	.60	1
	Asian-Pakistani	2.2	4
	Asian-Bangladeshi	1.7	3
	Asian-other	1.7	3
	Other	6.7	12
Length of time	1 day – 1 month	33.3	52
	> 1 month – 3 months	33.3	52
	> 3 months – 6 months	15.4	24
	> 6 months – 12 months	8.3	13
	> 12 months	9.6	15
Received psychiatric treatment	Yes	13.3	24
Self-harmed (inside prison)	Yes	4.4	8
Self-harmed (outside prison)	Yes	8.3	15
On form F2052SH	Yes	3.9	7
Been on F2052SH before	Yes	10.6	19
Arrived with a drug problem	Yes	32.0	58
Receives visits	Yes	76.8	139
Maintains contact with family or friends	Yes	80.0	144

us to analyse individual behaviour within the localised social context, within which people live. It focuses on relationships and the structure of groups: it 'defines specific relationships and then determines how those relationships are organised or structured and how that structure has an impact on individual lives. They describe the structured environment of individuals, organisations and societies' (Trotter 2000: 211). A network consists of a set of actors and a set of relational ties among the actors. This network can be depicted in the form of a sociogram or graph, which is 'a picture in which people (or more generally, any social unit) are represented as points in two-dimensional space, and relationships among pairs of people are represented by lines linking the corresponding points' (Wasserman and Faust 1999: 11–12). Actors in a network are represented by nodes (vertices or points), and the relational ties among the actors are represented by lines (edges or arcs).

Two wings took part in the study: Partridge unit (the unit for vulnerable prisoners) and Osprey unit (a normal unit). I wanted to compare two units that accommodated different populations of prisoners to see if this had any impact on how networks were formed. A total of 53 prisoners took part: 26 on Partridge and 27 on Osprey. Only one prisoner refused to take part, and he was on Partridge wing. I spoke with each prisoner on the wing individually in a private room and, having explained the study more fully, asked him if he would like to take part. Having obtained his consent, I began by asking him the background and demographic questions (those used in the longitudinal part of the study). Following these questions I presented him with a roster of the surnames of everyone on the wing and asked him whom he interacted with the most (by interacting I meant talking to someone or socialising with someone). No limit was given to the number of names he could nominate ('free choice'). For each name he nominated, I asked him to rate on a five-point Likert scale the following questions:

1 I consider him to be a mate of mine.
2 Since I've been here, he has helped me out by telling me something about the prison and how it works.
3 Since I've been here, he has shared something that belongs to him with me.
4 Since I've been here, he has helped me out with a personal problem.
5 Since I've been here, he has helped me out in a fight (or would do if he hasn't already).
6 In general, I feel I can trust him.

Each of these questions yields out-degree and in-degree scores. An out-degree is a value that depicts how many people an individual nominates. For example, if a prisoner states that he socialises with three other prisoners, he will have an out-degree score of 3. An in-degree is a value that depicts how many people nominate a particular individual, For example, if four people nominate a particular individual, he will have an in-degree score of 4. These paired measures thus allowed me to assess the reciprocal ties that were important for my research. I then asked him to indicate where he had met each person: whether outside prison, from a previous time in prison, or from this present time in prison. Having completed the social network section of the interview, I asked each participant to complete a measure of psychological distress (as used in other parts of this research). I finished the interview by asking each person if he had any questions about the research and how he found the interview. Table 1.5 shows the background and demographic statistics of the samples.

The final aim of the study was to explore in detail the experience of young men who had self-harmed at Feltham. For this part of the

Table 1.5 Background and demographic statistics: Partridge and Osprey[29]

Variable		Partridge		Osprey	
		%	N	%	N
Legal status	Remand	37.0	10	65.4	17
	Convicted	22.2	6	23.1	6
	Sentenced	40.7	11	11.5	3
First time in prison		70.3	19	39.1	9
Time in months	< 1 month	38.5	10	39.1	9
	> 1 month – 3 months	26.9	7	21.7	5
	> 3 months – 6 months	19.2	5	30.4	7
	> 6 months	15.4	4	8.7	2
Ethnic group	White-British	33.3	9	39.1	9
	White-Irish	3.7	1	0	0
	White-other	11.1	3	0	0
	Black-African	0	0	17.4	4
	Black-Caribbean	3.7	1	0	0
	Black-British	11.1	3	21.7	5
	Asian-British	3.7	1	17.4	4
	White-other	18.5	4	4.3	1
	Asian-other	11.1	3	0	0
	Chinese	3.7	1	0	0
Activity	Education	37.0	10	42.3	11
	Wing job	18.5	5	7.7	2
	Other job	33.3	9	3.8	1
	Unemployed	11.1	3	46.2	12

research, I carried out a cross-sectional study of 25 people who had self-harmed within the previous three days (due to the potential dynamic nature of distress). The self-harming sample was selected as and when incidents occurred. Each day I was in the prison, I would check records to find out if anyone had self-harmed. Once he was so identified, I would locate the prisoner and ask him if he wanted to take part. None of the prisoners I approached refused. Because I was conducting several different studies while at Feltham, it was not possible to interview everyone who had self-harmed during that time. Furthermore, it would sometimes take time for incidents to be recorded, and I might not find out about the event until several weeks after it had happened. Therefore, I would not interview these prisoners, as their experience may have differed again at this new stage in their imprisonment.

A total of 25 prisoners who had not self-harmed also took part, in order for me to compare their experience with the experience of those who had. These participants were matched to the self-harming participants on the following variables: length of time in prison (current term, measured from their date at reception in Feltham), first time in prison or not, sentence status (remand, convicted but unsentenced, and sentenced) and, finally, ethnicity. I selected the 25 matched participants by two means. Firstly, if the time period was under one month, and a suitable match could be found with the other variables, I would use data from the interviews carried out with prisoners within their first month in prison. A total of 14 people were chosen in this manner. If the self-harm incident occurred at over a month, or a suitable match could not be found from the first-month interviews, I would randomly select a match from the current prison roll. The database of prisoners currently in the establishment yields information on reception date, sentence status and ethnicity. To ascertain whether the person had been in prison before, I consulted his preconviction records. The remaining 11 participants were matched in this way. As it was somewhat difficult to find a perfect match on length of time in prison, a one-week boundary was set, either side of the reception date, for prisoners who had self-harmed after more than a month in prison. It was more difficult to find people who had stayed in the establishment for this longer time period. The interview was the same as when I interviewed people in their first month, except that I also asked questions about the self-harm incident. (These questions can be found in Appendix 1.) Table 1.6 shows the background and demographic statistics on the 50 people who took part.

Using SPSS 11.0 and UCINET 6.0 (for the social network data), I analysed the quantitative data. Descriptive and inferential statistical

Table 1.6 Background and demographic statistics: individuals who had self-harmed and those who had not

		Self-Harm		Matched	
Variable		%	N	%	N
Legal status	Remand	40	10	40	10
	Convicted	32	8	32	8
	Sentenced	28	7	28	7
First time in prison		40	10	40	10
Ethnic group					
	White-British	40	10	40	10
	White-other	16	4	16	4
	Black-African	16	4	16	4
	Black-Caribbean	8	2	8	2
	Black-British	4	1	4	1
	Asian-Indian	4	1	4	1
	Asian-Bangladeshi	4	1	4	1
	Other	8	2	8	2
Activity	Education	32	8	8	2
	Employed	4	1	20	5
	Unemployed	64	16	72	18

analyses were conducted on the data sets. I transcribed the qualitative interviews (interviews generally lasted 45–90 minutes) and then coded the data thematically. The initial transcribing provided me with a good 'overall picture' of what the main themes were in the interviews. I then developed a coding list and coded each interview accordingly. I coded each interview and analysed the data by looking at the material in the different codes, for similarities and differences between people. Each transcript was read on numerous occasions to maximise familiarity with each person's experience.

An overview of the chapters

Chapter 2 describes the early transition into prison and what contributes to psychological distress at this phase of imprisonment. It presents data from interviews carried out with people during their first three days in prison. Chapter 3 is a direct continuation of this account and follows longitudinally a subsample of the prisoners introduced in Chapter 2 to see how they adapted through their first month in custody. Chapter 4 examines the concept of support in detail and concentrates on supportive transactions between staff and prisoners. It also looks at prisoners' willingness to seek support and at what factors facilitate or prevent this. Chapter 5 explores prisoners' peer networks and the extent to which peer support exists at Feltham. Chapter 6 describes the experience of young adult prisoners who have recently self-harmed. The role of support, in protecting prisoners from distress, along with other constructs, is discussed. The final chapter draws together the earlier chapters and uses attachment theory as a framework to understand the psychosocial experience of imprisonment.

Notes

1 There are prisoners aged 18–20 but also 21-year-old prisoners who have been convicted at age 20 or under, and who have not been reclassified as part of the adult population (NOMS 2006).
2 At the end of 2002, association began to take place in the evenings. The senior management team at the time of my fieldwork were attempting to improve their key performance target of time out of cell and succeeded in doing so.
3 Personal communication with the deputy governor at Feltham.
4 Partridge was unofficially a 'vulnerable' prisoner unit in that prisoners who were thought to have difficulties coping with prison life were located there. Prisoners who did not speak English as their first language were also located there.
5 I also spent a considerable amount of time in the joint health-care centre. The health-care centre accommodated both juveniles and young adult prisoners. When I was at Feltham, a new health-care centre was being built. It was completed in July 2003, just after I left. All my interviews were therefore carried out at the 'old' health-care centre. I also occasionally attended adjudications in the segregation unit and would talk informally with staff there.
6 Data obtained from the race relations officer and governor.
7 Drake (2006) discusses the importance of examining the history of a prison.
8 Feltham A referred to the juvenile side of the prison and Feltham B referred to the young offender side. Due to the increase in number of juvenile prisoners, some of the wings on Feltham B were used by the Youth Justice Board, and therefore Feltham B contained both juvenile and young adult prisoners. The prison was then restructured in 2003 into three management areas: residential areas 1, 2, and 3.
9 See the website www.zahibmubarekinquiry.com for full details.

10 Among the many problems reported was the strength of the Prison Officers Association (POA), considered at the time as the 'alternative management' (HMCIP 2001). In July 2001, HM Prison Service threatened to privatise Feltham by March 2002, unless improvements were made, and threatened that no in-house bid would be allowed. At the same time the Director General transferred the then POA chairman, Andy Darkin, to HM Prison Service Headquarters, in order to enable management to retake control.

11 Some 78 per cent of these officers were male and 22 per cent female. Feltham has a large component of non-uniformed staff with many different agencies working within the prison, and Feltham also has an active voluntary sector. These data were obtained from the personnel department.

12 The senior management team also targeted sickness levels, and HM YOI Feltham was the best prison in London in this respect in 2003.

13 The Safer Locals Programme changed not only the built environment but also the attitude of staff. It is difficult to assess the extent to which suicide prevention was a focus for staff before the built changes occurred, but the set of initiatives had, to some limited degree, filtered through onto other units in that it raised the profile of suicide prevention. Feltham also piloted the F213 self-harm form, and members of staff were therefore encouraged to focus on recording self-harm incidents more systematically. The Safer Locals Programme also brought with it the appointment of a full-time suicide prevention coordinator and project manager. Linked with suicide prevention was the work of the outreach team, which had developed more fully in recent years. The outreach team was one of the most effective resources to facilitate the reduction of distress and incidents of self-harm. One further change to have taken place was the development of a Listener scheme that was coordinated by the suicide prevention coordinator and the Samaritans. The listeners were called out, on average, 40–60 times per week and played a 24-hour role.

14 These included changes to 'pre-trial processes, including reforms to police and criminal evidence, bail, charging and disclosure' (Home Office 2003).

15 As mentioned before, prisoners can be held in a YOI up to and including the age of 21. If, however, they are convicted when 21, they are sent to an adult prison. The age band for sentencing to a YOI is thus 18–20.

16 In 1997, the Chief Inspector of Prisons also highlighted the poor conditions for young adult prisoners in his thematic review of young offender establishments (HMCIP 1997).

17 Australia (Dear et al. 1998, 2000, 2001a, 2001b; Dalton 1999; Dear 2000; Austria (Fruhwald et al. 2000); Canada (Green et al. 1993; Wichmann et al. 2000); England and Wales (Liebling 1992; Liebling and Krarup 1993; Inch et al. 1995; Crighton and Towl 1997; Towl 1999; White et al. 1999; Ireland 2000; Maden et al. 2000; Borrill 2002; Snow 2002; Snow et al. 2002; Borrill et al. 2003, 2005; Meltzer et al. 2003; Shaw et al. 2003; Palmer and Connelly 2005); Finland (Joukamma 1997); France (Benezech 1999); Greece (Fotiadou et al. 2006); Italy (Tatarelli et al. 1999); New Zealand (Skegg and Cox

1993); Scotland (Bogue and Power 1995; Biggam and Power 1999a, 1999b); Switzerland (Schaller *et al.* 1996); and the USA (Bonner and Rich, 1990; Ivanoff and Jang 1991; Bonner 1992; Ivanoff 1992; Ivanoff *et al.* 1992, 1996; Lester and Danto 1993; Smyth *et al.* 1994; DuRand *et al.* 1995; Hayes 1995; Fulwiler *et al.* 1997).

18 Although I looked at the first month in prison, I also included prisoners who had been in custody before. The sample consisted of prisoners who had never been in prison (and therefore it essentially was their *very* first month), participants who had been in prison but never at Feltham (so it was their very first month in Feltham), and prisoners who had been in Feltham (therefore their subsequent first month of this particular term). Furthermore, eight participants had transferred from other establishments, and it was therefore not their first month in prison, as they had been in another establishment prior to their arrival in Feltham. Nevertheless, I decided to interview these people, as they randomly appeared in my sample and they seemed to be experiencing many of the same difficulties as less experienced prisoners.

19 I observed adjudications, segregation, visits, education classes, prerelease courses and case reviews; shadowed prisoners from reception to the induction unit; and observed daily life on each of the wings. This gave me the opportunity to have many informal discussions with staff and prisoners. See Harvey (in press) for a discussion on the choice of setting and ethical considerations.

20 The main aims in the pilot work were to familiarise myself with the environment of a YOI and to test the feasibility of my methods. This pilot work, together with my research experience as part of the safer custody evaluation, provided me with an insight into what life was like. More specifically, the pilot study allowed me to gain a detailed understanding of the process of reception and induction and some understanding of the transition into prison. This pilot work sharpened the focus of my research on this phase of imprisonment and the issues surrounding self-harming behaviour in prison. During this time, 17 prisoners took part in a social network analysis, 17 interviews were carried out with people during their first few days in custody, and 14 interviews were carried out with people who had recently been on, or were on, an F2052SH form (for prisoners identified as being at risk of suicidal behaviour). There were also two focus group discussions, and detailed observations of reception, visits, association, the first-night centre, and two F2052SH case conferences.

21 This form has now been changed, and the Assessment, Care in Custody and Teamwork Approach (ACCT) form is now in place.

22 Due to the sensitive nature of these questions, I asked them later in the interview when it was a more appropriate time to do so.

23 The following items constituted the dimension 'psychological distress':
1   I often feel depressed in this prison.
2   I have experienced major feelings of distress in this prison.
3   Life in this prison involves a great deal of suffering.
4   My experience in this prison is painful.

5   My experience of imprisonment in this particular prison has been stressful.

6   I feel tense in this prison.

7   I have many problems at the moment.

8   I have problems sleeping at night.

9   There is nothing I can do to relieve the distress I feel in this prison.

10   I often feel aggressive and hostile in this prison.

11   My mental health is of concern to me.

The following items constituted the dimension 'perceived adaptability':

1   I feel I can handle my emotions in here.

2   I can easily adapt to this prison environment.

3   I find it hard to cope in this prison most of the time.

4   I can relax and be myself in this prison.

The following items constituted the dimension 'prison social support':

1   I receive support from staff in this prison when I need it.

2   Staff help prisoners to maintain contact with their families.

3   I feel cared about most of the time in this prison.

4   I have been helped a lot by a member of staff with a particular problem.

5   Staff in this prison show concern and understanding towards me.

6   I feel I am trusted quite a lot in this prison.

7   I trust the officers in this prison.

8   This prison is good at delivering personal safety.

The following items constituted the dimension 'safety':

1   There is quite a lot of threats/bullying in here.

2   I feel safe from being injured, bullied, or threatened by other prisoners in here.

3   Generally I fear for my physical safety.

24   A total of 20 interviews were carried out with staff. Some of these interviews were carried out as part of the work as a research assistant on the Safer Locals Programme evaluation. These interviews enabled me to develop local knowledge about the prison and systems in operation, and allowed me to appreciate the difficult job that staff carried out.

25   A total of 254 questionnaires were handed out, and 182 were returned, a response rate of 71.6 per cent.

26   This mode of research is problematic, given the literacy problems of many young adult prisoners. This was the only means to obtain a large general sample, given the time constraints that I faced. I endeavoured to keep the language as plain as possible and explained the purpose of the research. I also gave them time to ask questions if need be.

27   Permission was granted by Greg Dear to use a modified version of the questionnaire.

28   Some of the questionnaires were returned with missing data on certain items. The percentages reported here are valid percentages and add up to 100 per cent for each variable, but they relate to the total number of responses per variable.

29 Some of the data were missing on certain variables. The percentages reported here are valid percentages and therefore add up to 100 per cent for each variable, but they relate to the total number of responses per item.

Chapter 2

The transition into prison

This chapter examines the experiences of young men who had recently entered prison and explores the transitions that they underwent at this early entry stage. It is based on 70 interviews with people who had been in prison for three days and examines the common elements that were evident from their descriptions of their experiences at Feltham. They were preoccupied with safety, uncertainty, losing freedom and control, and separation and loss. Finally, it suggests why individuals differed in the levels of psychological distress they experienced after being in prison for three days.

A number of previous studies have examined the transition from 'street to prison' (Goffman 1961; Ericson 1975; Gibbs 1982a, 1982b; Zamble and Porporino 1988; Jones and Schmid 2000; Neustatter 2002: chap. 3) but the majority of these studies were carried out with adult prisoners. Few studies have examined the experience among young adults (Ericson 1975; Neustatter 2002). Consequently, little is known about the experience of young men as they cross the boundary from a free world to an enclosed order.

Generally, the entry phase of imprisonment has been found to be particularly distressing for prisoners and has been identified as a period of heightened vulnerability to suicide and other self-harm (Beigel and Russell 1973; Esparza 1973; Fawcett and Marrs 1973; Heilig 1973; Liebling 1999). Suicides occur disproportionately in the first month in custody. In the financial years from 1998/9 to 2003/4, a quarter of all self-inflicted deaths occurred within a week of arriving at an establishment, and half occurred within the first month (HM Prison Service 2004a). Zamble and Porporino (1988), in their study of adaptation among 133 Canadian prisoners, concluded that 'emotional disturbance is clearly a problem among inmates beginning a new term' (ibid.: 85). They found that over half of prisoners had difficulties sleeping and that the mean score on Beck's Depression Inventory revealed mild depression; a further 8 per cent were severely depressed. The necessity to withstand entry shock, to maintain outside links, to secure stability and safety, and to find activity has been identified as the main pain of imprisonment at this early entry phase (Gibbs 1982b). Entering prison has been argued to threaten an individual's core existence and to lead to a crisis of identity (Ericson 1975; Jones and Schmid 2000).

The transitional process into prison

Before attempting to understand the transitional experiences of young men at Feltham, we first need to look at the actual transitional *process* that prisoners underwent as they entered prison. Most prisoners at Feltham began their transition from the free world to prison at the time of their arrest.[1] After arrest by the police, they spent a night, or often a weekend, in a police station before being taken to court for their hearing. Most prisoners spent a full day at court and would wait for several hours in the court's cells following their hearing, before being transported in the prison van to Feltham. For some prisoners this journey took less than an hour, but for many it lasted longer, even up to four hours, and they often arrived at the prison after 9.00 p.m. On arrival at Feltham, the staff led prisoners from the van and into the prison's reception area. At first they were seen by an officer who checked the relevant paperwork, entered the prisoners' personal details into the computer and asked a number of questions about their background. The prisoners then waited in a holding-room with others before being called for strip-searches. Next they were given back their own clothes if on remand or issued with the prison's clothes (a T-shirt and jeans) if convicted, whether sentenced or not, and they checked in their property. In reception, each prisoner was also given a microwave meal, which he would eat later at a table in the association area. From reception, staff led the prisoners through the corridors to Kingfisher, the induction unit. There it was standard practice for the nurse to see the prisoners and for each prisoner to be interviewed one-to-one by a prison officer and a link worker.[2] Through these interviews, the prison officer and link worker tried to identify any immediate needs the prisoner might have on his first night and to assess whether he was at risk of harming himself or others. The interview on the first night was of particular importance, because it was at this stage that a prisoner was allowed contact with his family. People also conducted an assessment of the risk in his sharing a cell at this point, an assessment that was particularly pertinent at Feltham following the murder of Zahid Mubarek by his cellmate. Then each prisoner was issued with a first-night pack (either a smoker's pack or a non-smoker's pack), in which was £2 of credit for the telephone. He was then allocated to a single or double cell.

The following morning the prisoners on Kingfisher unit began their day by getting breakfast and then going outside for some exercise, which involved standing in or walking around a small yard. Then they attended an induction programme in the induction classroom, a room purpose built as part of the Safer Locals Programme. This induction programme involved a PowerPoint presentation by one of the induction officers that covered the rules and regulations of the prison and the privileges and the facilities that were available. Following the officer's presentation, other staff members then introduced themselves, such as the gym officers, drug workers and education staff. There was also a short presentation by the listeners, prisoners trained by the Samaritans to offer support to their peers. The chaplain also met each prisoner one-to-one and other members of staff, such as the drug workers, voluntary workers, and members of the outreach team, might meet any individual prisoners who had been referred to them. The induction programme took two mornings, and in the afternoons, the prisoners attended association. It was at this point that they made a telephone call home, if need be. Generally, prisoners remained on the induction unit for three nights and two full days, before they moved to one of the residential units. (Some, however, moved slightly earlier, after only two nights, depending on whether or not there were cells available on the other units.)

In summary, within a few days of entering Feltham, the prisoners had endured a number of different processes and transitions. There was the overall transition from the outside world to the prison, but there were also smaller transitions: from the police station to the court, from the court to the van, from the van to reception, from the reception area to the induction unit, and to and from other spaces within the prison. Further transitions continued throughout their first month in prison: they changed cellmates, moved into different cells, and were relocated to other wings within the prison. Perhaps behind the feelings of uncertainty identified in previous studies lie the continual change and transition, from the initial transition into the prison from outside and then within the prison itself.

Common elements of the transition

The main change, though, on reception into custody was leaving one world or life and entering another. This is a common feature of arriving in any institution. Over 45 years ago, Goffman (1961) summarised the experience of arriving in what he called 'total institutions'. He argued that the arrival in an institution involved several processes that mortify the self.[3] The most general form of this mortification involved role dispossession where the individual finds that 'certain roles are lost to him by virtue of the barrier that separates him from the outside world' (Goffman 1961: 25), that is, roles within employment, education or personal relationships. More specifically, Goffman mentioned the admissions procedures in prisons as ones which mortified the self. He characterised the procedures at reception in prison as 'a leaving off and a taking on, with the midpoint marked by physical nakedness. Of course, leaving off entails a dispossession of property, important because persons invest self-feelings in their possessions' (ibid.: 27). This results in 'personal defacement', as the prisoner is 'stripped of his usual appearance and of the equipment and services by which he maintains it' (ibid.: 29). As we saw above, prisoners at Feltham were stripped of many of their personal belongings, often including their clothing, on arrival. For many of these young men, material possessions and clothing served as a symbol of status; being deprived of these things undermined their presentation of themselves.

Besides Goffman's broader study, other studies have addressed entry into prison more specifically. Gibbs (1982a) originally defined the early period of entry into prison as one of shock, an experience which 'like death, may be reacted to with shock and disbelief' (p. 34). He noted that prisoners entering reception in American jails were in a physical and psychological 'limbo': 'A man has just come from the street where he had some measure of control over his life and he has not yet been immersed into the daily routine of doing time. He is between worlds, and has mastery over neither' (Gibbs 1982a: 35). It is interesting that prisoners used similar language: they referred to giving up a life or even to feeling dead when they described their experience of transition to prison. As one prisoner recently remanded into Feltham said:

> Yeah, the first few days, you're trying to get over your life and entering a new life and that's kind of hard to do. I felt really depressed. When you first come in, you had plans for the next day. You had just done something recently and it's one of those, 'Fuck, I could be on road,' and you're not really into the whole bang-up issue there. [Prisoner]

This experience was sometimes described, as by Gibbs, as feeling temporarily dead:

> Prison is like temporary death. It is like you are watching others while you are dead. You feel like life has kind of gone. You feel that your life has stopped but is [also] going on without you. [Prisoner]

Prisoners presented themselves as midway between two separate worlds, as they neither relinquished their hopes for the lives from which they had been torn, nor yet accepted their existence within a new enclosed order. As such, they occupied a place on both sides of a threshold or boundary between two worlds: they had entered something like the state of liminality.

The notion of liminality was applied to rites of passage by social anthropologists. Van Gennep (1960) argued that three phases constitute a rite of passage: separation, margin or *limen*, and aggregation. This process found in the rite of passage also has relevance to individuals entering prison, particularly for those who have never been in prison before. According to Turner, separation 'comprises symbolic behaviour signifying the detachment of the individual or group either from an earlier fixed point in the social structure, from a set of cultural conditions (state) or from both' (Turner 1969: 94). We might consider the removal of the prisoners' outside clothing and possessions, the symbols of identity, as something akin to a ritual of separation. During the ambiguous liminal phase, on the other hand, 'the individual passes through a cultural realm that has few or none of the attributes of the past or coming state' (ibid.: 94). Only later does the individual reach a more stable state where he is expected to behave in accordance with certain customary norms and ethical standards (Turner 1969: 95). Initial entry into prison may be characterised as the middle liminal state. To enter prison is to be separated from one world and moved into another, but during reception the transition is incomplete. Like someone during a rite of passage, in this early phase of imprisonment the individual is 'betwixt and between the positions assigned and arrayed by law custom, convention and ceremonial' (Turner 1969: 95). It is later that the prisoner may reach an equilibrium or stable state following the initial entry period.

Individuals who are in a liminal state are said to be very self-reflective. Yet, prisoners found it difficult to accept this transition. Understandably, they did not want to accept that they were crossing a boundary from the outside world to the world of the prison. When they recounted their experience on the first night in prison, they described disbelief that their incarceration had actually happened. They found entering this liminal zone a strange experience, or one that did not seem real:

> This isn't reality for me and I refuse to accept it as being so. This is not a way of life for me so I am very reluctant – maybe it will hinder my progress, but I am very reluctant to accept this situation to be reality and to be a way of life. Therefore I want to have minimal contact with the prisoners and just keep myself to myself. [Prisoner]

> It feels strange and different. It almost doesn't seem real. I have to think about it. I'll be watching TV at one point and then I'll look and realise I am in the cell and then it kicks in again. [Prisoner]

Prisoners felt disconnected in time and space and so detached from reality. Many prisoners refused to accept the reality that had been forced upon them, as this acceptance would reinforce the fact that their control and freedom had become limited. This reluctance was particularly prevalent among those who had never been in prison before, as I heard from one prisoner:

> [Interviewer: When you were walking through to the wing what was going through your head?]
> I was thinking I see this on TV. I never thought I'd ever see myself walking down here going into a cell. I just thought I only see that on TV. I never thought it would come to this. I couldn't believe it basically. [Prisoner]

Like this prisoner who compared his experience to previous images, many saw themselves from the outside, having a sense of not being their usual self. Many of those who had been inside before also found it difficult to accept the reality of having to survive and endure prison life once again. They said that they knew they would be back in Feltham, but were still thrown off balance by the suddenness of it all. They did not know when they would be re-entering this world with which they were to some degree familiar, a world they had chosen to forget when on the outside.

Preoccupation with safety

Prisoners identified a number of key elements that made this liminal or transitional period of imprisonment difficult. These included a preoccupation with safety, uncertainty, losing control and freedom, and separation and loss. The preoccupation with the safety of this new environment was one important element of feeling like an outsider. Like outsiders, the new prisoners knew very little about the prison and could only rely on information that had been given to them by others they had met outside, or, like the prisoner above, had to rely on information from television or the reputation of prison. This contributed to the sense of fear through disorientation, as was found by Jones and Schmid (2000) in their study of first-time male adult prisoners in a maximum-security prison in the USA. They found that for people arriving in prison for the first time the main concerns were violence and uncertainty and that the dominant emotion was fear. Faced with this, the prisoners would create what the authors termed an 'anticipatory survival strategy' (Jones and Schmid 2000: 45). Prisoners in their sample imagined that prison life would be 'dominated by the idea of violence' (ibid.: 54). In Feltham, too, concern with fear and violence was again prominent among those in the first stage of transition to prison. Although individuals varied in the extent to which they felt safe, most expressed at least some concern over safety.

Those who had never been in prison before had heard stories from their friends outside that Feltham had a bad reputation. Only two years before the research was carried out, the prisoner Zahid Mubarek had been murdered in his cell at Feltham. This appalling incident has been the subject of a non-statutory public inquiry. Prisoners talked about the incident and some were afraid of whomever they would be sharing a cell with. The reputation of prison was also a problem reported by Bartollas (1982) in his study of adolescent prisoners in the USA. He found that the reputation of an institution moulded their initial impressions of it. Many first-time prisoners in Feltham reported that the prison had a reputation as a place where prisoners were bullied:[4]

> I've heard you had to sing out of the windows. I heard you get your head kicked in; from mates who've already been in here. [Prisoner]

> I was just thinking I am going to prison, I am going to prison. That was it, and I thought when I got there I was probably going to be beaten up or something. [Prisoner]

Those prisoners who had been in prison before had thought about whom they might meet. They thought positively about meeting some friends 'from road',[5] but they also feared meeting their enemies. Some individuals had affiliations with a gang, and this network could have some benefits in prison, with a ready-made network of support, but it could also be problematic if rival gangs encountered each other inside the prison gates.

In fact, it was often that these initial fears were dispelled at this early phase of imprisonment. Although people expected a lot of fighting and an intimidating atmosphere, some did not experience such things. Some others did say that their fears had been confirmed, as they perceived the prison to be large, overwhelming and daunting. When, during reception, they were moved among different holding rooms, the ceaseless transitions confirmed their feelings of powerlessness and helplessness:

> I was feeling a bit scared like, knowing that I'm inside. I ain't on the outside world anymore. [Prisoner]

Generally, their social interactions at this transitional phase were defensive. However, this self-induced ostracism made some prisoners feel even more uncomfortable and awkward; they felt that others were staring at them, and they did not know where to look; they were afraid to meet another person's gaze, in fear of confrontation or victimisation. One prisoner commented:

> You don't know them to speak to, so you wouldn't go up and speak to them. If they want to speak to you, you let them come and speak to you. [Prisoner]

However, the concerns over safety went beyond fears of injury or threats by others in the environment. Their feeling of a lack of safety encompassed their feeling that the prison was essentially an unpredictable place, where uncertainty was rife. One prisoner stated:

> I don't want none of this. It doesn't feel a secure place. It feels like anything can happen at any time. I don't like it here. [Prisoner]

Because many of the young men did not want to accept the reality of imprisonment, and did not want to attach to the world that they had been forced to join, this maintained their sense of uncertainty and fear. Because they did not engage with the new environment, they could not master it and feel safe; they felt uncertain, detached and out of control, and so they felt unsafe.

Uncertainty

So besides the more visceral varieties of fear, prisoners experienced a more generalised uncertainty. This uncertainty has been identified in previous studies. For example, Gibbs (1982b) found that the first phase of imprisonment was marked by uncertainty and that what individuals desired was predictability, which Gibbs argued to be a fundamental need for psychological survival. The reputation of the prison can, again, contribute to the feeling of uncertainty, as it can to fear. Ericson (1975), who interviewed young prisoners in the UK, found that uncertainty surrounded the new prisoner because 'others have told him about the detention in relation to how they wanted it to appear to him rather than how it would appear to him' (ibid.: 51). In Feltham, people who had never before spent time in prison were unsure about their immediate future in relation to the generic aspects of any prison, rather than about Feltham in particular. They were unsure about their cellmate, about the staff, about whether they would cope and about whether they would be bullied. As prisoners stated:

> The first few days I felt alone, like, I didn't know what to expect or nothing like that. I didn't know what to expect. I didn't know what the cell was going to be like. I didn't know what the staff were going to be like. I didn't know what the routines were. [Prisoner]

> I didn't have a clue what was going on. [Prisoner]

> I thought, Oh my God. Where am I going? What are they going to do with me now? I was thinking: will I stay in the cell in the court, or will I go? I just didn't know. [Prisoner]

They knew that they would only be on Kingfisher, the induction unit, for a few days before making the next transition to a normal unit. This scheme designed to help them – and it is a good scheme which eases the transition – in fact also brought with it uncertainty about their subsequent move and a feeling of not being able to settle. This could in fact be predicted. Jones and Schmid (2000) found that prisoners in their sample spent one week on induction and that by the end of it, not having moved onto normal location, they 'still possess only a vague, uncertain conceptualisation of prison life' (p. 54). I also found that prisoners did not feel able to settle until they were more certain about where they would be placed. I asked one prisoner:

[Interviewer: Do you find the longer you are there in one space
the more you make it your own space?]
Yeah, but here, because I know I am not staying on this wing, I
haven't put up any pictures or cards or taken stuff out, so I feel
lost sort of. I can't get settled on this wing. [Prisoner]

To some extent, the staff within the prison had made attempts to reduce
the uncertainty that prisoners felt. Over half of the prisoners (55.7 per
cent) strongly agreed or agreed with the statement that 'the induction
process in this prison helped me to know what to expect in the daily
regime and when it would happen'.

Those who had been in prison before were of course more certain
about the practical aspects of life in the prison such as the rules and
regulations, and the daily regime. However, 61.4 per cent of prisoners
interviewed had never been in Feltham before, while others had been
in Feltham, but not on the 'adult side'.[6] Even those who had been in
Feltham in the past found changes in the social networks of prisoners;
in the staff, some of whom had moved on; and in the systems and
procedures that had been altered. Many of these prisoners noticed
the improvements to the built environment of the reception area and
induction unit, and most of them thought that these changes were
positive. However, a limited number of these returning prisoners
thought that the changes were unsettling, because they were used to
the old arrangements. Again, things designed to help them did not
necessarily have the desired effect. These individuals sought continuity
and a status quo and thought that any change, even an improvement,
was a disruption of a base that was already insecure.

However, there were three other aspects of the prison experience that
caused uncertainty and elicited an array of negative emotions. Firstly,
many prisoners expressed uncertainty over their court case. They were
mostly concerned about when they would be back at court, how long
they would be kept in prison before possible sentencing (if they were
on remand), and what the outcome of their court case would be. As
one prisoner commented:

I want to know what's going on. That's my main problem. I want
to know what's going on with me. I don't know how long I am
here for. Er, I don't know when I'm going to court. I just don't
know. [Prisoner]

The difficulties of being in prison were here exacerbated by lack of
knowledge about the length of his confinement. How would others
control his fate outside prison? When would he be moving back from

prison once again to the world outside? Uncertainty also surrounded the prisoners on remand over the prospect of being granted bail. Some believed that they would receive bail when next in court and desperately clung to this hope, which was a false one for many. The overall experience of being unsure how long they would be in prison was referred to as being 'on remand mode'. It altered their whole approach to the situation they found themselves. As some prisoners commented:

> I'll be on remand mode. Going through the motions of remand. I'll get a bit used to it. I know at the moment I can't think of nothing. Got to go through it day by day. When I get sentenced I'll get used to it and get my mind sorted and that's it. [Prisoner]

> Being on remand is harder than being sentenced because you don't know what is going to happen to you. Once you are sentenced, you know. Then you know that you are looking forward to that certain day of getting out. On remand you are thinking about what is going to happen to you, but you don't know. [Prisoner]

Secondly, many prisoners felt uncertainty about their families and loved ones. In previous studies, the problem that seemed to surface the most for prisoners within their first two weeks was the separation from their family and friends. Zamble and Porporino (1988) found that within the first two weeks in prison, most prisoners 'were troubled by the separation from loved ones on the outside, and for most of them the problem of missing someone ranked near the top of their lists' (p. 91). To counteract such feelings, Gibbs (1982b) noted the importance of family contact at this stage of imprisonment and argued that social support from outside ties could serve as an 'equilibrating' factor, aiding prisoners' adjustment to their new social world. The concern over separation from family and friends was also common to prisoners in Feltham, and links to these people were important here too. This uncertainty over the separation was felt both by the first-time prisoners and by those who had been in prison before. The prisoners found it difficult to be removed from their family and friends. They were often concerned about the possible negative reaction of their families and also about their families' ability to cope with the situation the prisoner had created. Those with partners expressed anxieties about their partner's fidelity while they were separated, and those with children expressed anxieties about whether the children would forget them. One prisoner stated:

They took my bail away and I just had to go downstairs and wait for the van. On my way to prison I was stressed out in that box. Basically I just wanted to cry. My eyes were hurting, my belly was hurting. I was just thinking, driving, seeing people walking past, just thinking about my mum and my sister, how my family would be. If any of my family would phone from abroad and my mum would say I am in jail, how would they feel? Aw, I'm stressed out. [Prisoner]

Imprisonment generated uncertainty in these relationships: Do they know I am in prison? What are they thinking now? Will my family disown me? Will my girlfriend leave me? Will she be faithful? So many questions remained unanswered during the first few days and remained problems for the weeks or months to come. Those who had a 'secure base' outside prison were set adrift from it and found this unanchoring extremely painful.

Thirdly, many people felt uncertainty over their short-term future *outside* the prison. That was why retaining links to one's loved ones was so important. The experience of prison was a severely disruptive one, a transition that affected most major facets of their lives. Prisoners were worried about what would happen to them when they got out of prison: about their accommodation, about debts building up while they were inside, about relationships breaking down, about friends disowning them and about losing their jobs. These needs at resettlement, identified by research carried out by Farrant (2006), were consuming prisoners' thoughts even at this early stage of imprisonment. Maintaining any links with the outside world was of paramount importance to help reduce this uncertainty. The prison staff did give the prisoners opportunities to contact their families and friends outside, by issuing them with PIN numbers for the telephones and by making a call for them on the first night. Yet, despite these attempts by staff to reduce uncertainties of this sort, there was a limit to the contribution that could be made: the reality of being in prison could not be changed. At this early stage of imprisonment, these young men had to think not only about their survival inside prison but also about their survival upon release. They had to survive being in a liminal state, resting between two worlds both of which concerned them, and not being attached to either.

Losing control and freedom

Along with uncertainty, the transition into prison brought with it a loss of control and freedom. One of the pains of imprisonment documented by Sykes (1958) was the deprivation of autonomy. Toch (1977) also identified autonomy as one of the main environmental needs prisoners had. Prisons necessarily limit one's control and deprive one of freedom. Goodstein *et al.* (1984) identified three aspects of personal control that imprisonment may serve to reduce: outcome control (the ability for individuals to influence outcomes in their environment), choice (the opportunity to make choices in their environment) and predictability (knowing what will happen in their environment in the future). They argued that these three aspects of personal control are associated with one another and should not be viewed as separate (Goodstein *et al.* 1984: 344–5). Unpredictability was akin to uncertainty, just as predictability and certainty were related, as discussed above. It has been argued in previous studies that if individuals cannot, or perceive that they cannot, exert control over their world, they may develop a 'learned helplessness' where they no longer use their agency and become despondent (Seligman 1975).

In Feltham, too, the prisoners who had recently entered prison found it difficult to come to terms with a reduction in personal control and being deprived of their freedom. This loss was initially felt in the court cells after being informed that they were going to prison. One prisoner commented:

> I was thinking about my freedom. I was thinking, please let me go home, I want to go home. I was thinking about being locked up in a cell and being claustrophobic. [Prisoner]

These feelings continued on their way to the prison, and many prisoners found the journey in the van particularly difficult. Some of them passed the places where they lived, and these sights reinforced their lack of freedom; one prisoner passed the scene of his crime and had feelings of guilt and remorse. All the prisoners in the van had time to reflect, and, for many, being able to see outside but not being in that world was very difficult for them. The lack of freedom 'hits you', as one prisoner stated, when he saw the outside world, which was now out of reach:

> [Interviewer: What was it like coming in the van?]
> It was such a depressing feeling 'cause I knew I can't do nothing about it. You can see people are free and enjoying themselves. Even if they're not enjoying themselves, at least they are free. And you are going to prison. Ah, that feeling is not a good thing. [Prisoner]

The prisoners felt this lack of freedom most acutely when locked inside their cells. This feeling bothered not only the first-time prisoners, but also those who had been to prison before. Prisoners described their experience of being locked in a cell:

> When they bang that door, it is different. It is weird. Everywhere you turn, you see the same thing. It is not like you can turn around and see a completely different part of the room or walk down the stairs and go into a different room. Everything is in the same room. It's like being trapped really. I can see why people harm themselves and try and kill themselves, but I am stronger than that really. [...] It is like being in a lift and you can't open the door, but people open it from the outside. [Prisoner]

> I couldn't cope in that cell. I was feeling stressed out and weak. I just couldn't do nothing no more in that cell. I was just feeling alive but dead at the same time. [Prisoner]

Others felt trapped even when they were in the yard for exercise. Although they were outside in the open air, this slight change reminded them that they were nevertheless still not in the free world:

> It's not even a playground in a school, you get me? It's your freedom taken away. You are walking around in a little space. The sun is on your head and you're thinking if you were at home you could just go to the shop and buy a drink. In here you've got to take what's given to you. [Prisoner]

One prisoner commented that even animals were given more freedom. The freedom of which they had been deprived represented to them a feeling that society had behaved in an inhumane manner towards them. I asked one prisoner about this:

> [Interviewer: Did you feel any better the second night?]
> Everyday I feel just the same. A dog gets more freedom than this. At least he goes to the park and gets to run about and that. Run down the street and that. You can't even do that. You just have to sit and wait.

A total of 61.4 per cent prisoners strongly agreed or agreed with the statement, 'most of what happens to me in prison is out of my hands'. Many prisoners perceived that they had no control over their immediate situation due to the uncertainty that surrounded them and also due to the imbalance of power between staff and prisoners. This loss of control and freedom brought with it the desire to escape and rumination over what they could be doing 'on the out'.

Prisoners found their reduced control inside prison difficult, then, but also hated the reduced level of control they had over aspects of their lives on the other side of the boundary. Prisoners found it difficult not being able to control what was happening 'on the out' and feared the impact that this might have when they were eventually released. This inability to control the world they had left dominated their thoughts on their first night and contributed to their feelings of uncertainty:

> When you are in your cell, you are always thinking, not about yourself but about other people. I will be thinking about my girlfriend most of the time, what she is doing, who she is with. She could be banging away with some other bloke, and I am in here and don't know nothing about it. [Prisoner]

Imprisonment caused many problems in their personal relationships and attachments; but it also prevented them, through the loss of control, from solving these very problems. One prisoner told me that he was concerned about whether his girlfriend would leave him if he received a long sentence. He had no control over the situation, however, and felt helpless. He did not know when he would be back in court and could not control when he called his girlfriend to inform her of what was going on. He told me:

> I've never had a proper girlfriend before, and as soon as I met her, that was it. I felt happy all at once. Then all this shit happens. [...] She said if I get a long sentence, then she won't be there for me when I come out. She said it is not that she doesn't love me, just that she has to get on with her own life, and that is really scaring me. [...] The thing is I don't know what will happen to me. I haven't had that date through. [...] I can't do nothing. I am powerless. [Prisoner]

Surviving this sudden lack of freedom and control over life outside prison, and in relationships with those on the other side, was a major problem during the transitional or liminal stage of imprisonment.

Separation and loss

As they moved from one world to another, separation and loss pervaded the thoughts of prisoners. Prisoners felt they had lost their 'whole life', their identities and, more specifically, their relationships; there was a feeling of having 'thrown it all away'. Recalling his initial reaction to the news that he was going to prison, one prisoner said, 'I thought, fuck, I've lost everything'. He also expressed a sense of loss when he looked out of the window of the prison van. One prisoner recalled his journey to prison in the van:

> Coming from the courthouse, it was just about finishing the end of the working day, and I could see various people in suits, in office clothes, and I thought of myself three days prior being one of them and what I would be doing at this time of the evening. I remember seeing various shops, Clinton Cards, Addeco job agency, and T Mobile, and thinking will I ever see these shops again? I was thinking, I've lost my job now – in terms of income how am I going to support myself? I have a flat at the moment – what is going to happen to that? Have I lost everything? Have I really lost everything? Have I really thrown it all away? Would I ever be able to get a job again? [Prisoner]

They recalled that they felt their life had gone and that they felt disconnected with the world they had just left. There was a feeling that life was going on without them; they were no longer part of their own life. One prisoner commented:

> You feel that your life is going on without you. You feel you want to be in the race, but you've got a knee injury. You know what it's like to sit on the sidelines and watch the game, and you say, if I had the ball right now, I could have dodged this guy and gone through and scored, but you can't do it. You are close but you can't do it. You kind of feel away. [Prisoner]

They felt that part of the self was missing now that they had been brought to prison. This was associated with a sense of uncertainty and a fear of the unknown. Prisoners stated:

> There is confusion, there is a sense of uncertainty, and you feel, it is hard to explain, it feels like there is a big abyss in your life. You standing on the end of this abyss and you know you can see something on the other side, but you don't know how to get there. [Prisoner]

> Sometimes it's like you are a prisoner and society doesn't want you. […] I am still a person though. Because I did it doesn't make me less of a person. [Prisoner]

Not only did part of the self appear to be missing but also there was a change in how they felt other people perceived them. Others perceived their social identity differently, and this perception in turn made some prisoners question their identity and reassert it, as they feared that their identity would be lost.

The most acute sense of loss, and separation, that the prisoners experienced at this transitional phase was the sense of loss and separation from their loved ones outside the prison. When I asked people to recall their experiences in the court's cells, they said that although they had many thoughts about the prison itself, thoughts about separation from their loved ones predominated. Many reported that they felt they had lost their families. Prisoners stated:

> My mind went blank. I was thinking, I've lost my family. What is my little brother and sister going to think? I was thinking about my family and after that what was going to happen. [Prisoner]

> I was thinking, oh my God, I am going to prison. I am leaving my mum, my girlfriend, and everyone I know. I was thinking I am leaving. I am gone. [Prisoner]

Some also commented that they were worried that someone in their family might die while they were away and that this loss would therefore be permanent. One prisoner said:

> I was thinking madness about my family. The funny thing that passed through my head was what if someone passed away when I was in prison? Imagine if someone died in my family. [Prisoner]

It is interesting that they connected these general forms of loss, as they were separated from their loved ones through entering prison, with the loss of bereavement. This connection revealed the destructiveness and permanence that they perceived in their loss at this transition.

The most important ties individuals had were with their mothers and their partners. These were the individuals from whom they found it most difficult to be separated. A total of 28.6 per cent of them (20 participants) lived with their mothers before entering custody, and 34.3 per cent of them (24 participants) reported that they felt closer to their mothers than to other members of their social or familial network. Fathers were not cited as a close tie within their social networks. A total of 41.4 per cent of them (29 participants) had a girlfriend; 12.9 per cent of them (nine participants) lived with their girlfriend and

14.3 per cent of them (ten participants) reported that they felt closer to their girlfriends than to other members of their social network. Some prisoners had children, and some of these fathers found it difficult being apart from them. Separation from loved ones was the major concern of the prisoners in the transitional stage of imprisonment. At the same time, however, these relationships on the other side of the boundary were often vital sources of practical and emotional support, and it was difficult for prisoners to manage this aspect of their lives. As Toch (1977) stated, 'the absence of contact (outside) can create a psychological vacuum; its presence can be a mood modulator or safety valve' (p. 71). Most prisoners were motivated at this early entry phase to contact their families, friends and partners, and 62.9 per cent of them (44 participants) had done so within three days. A total of 61.4 per cent of them (43 participants) reported that they had been 'helped out in the past week' by someone outside prison: over one-third had not been. Generally, the level of support was perceived to be high. Table 2.1 shows the percentage of prisoners that strongly agreed or agreed with seven statements which formed the dimension, 'outside social support'.

Although the prisoners were concerned with the separation from their loved ones, the majority of the prisoners had in fact made contact with them. As stated previously, the staff at Feltham attempted during

Table 2.1 Percentage of prisoners who strongly agreed or agreed with items relating to outside social support

Variable	% Strongly agreed or agreed	N
There are people I know outside who do things to make me happy	70.0	49
There are people I know outside who make me feel cared for	74.3	52
There are people I know outside who can be relied on no matter what happens	74.3	52
There are people I know outside who would see that I am taken care of if I needed to be	68.6	48
There are people outside who accept me just as I am	81.4	57
There are people I know outside who make me feel an important part of their lives	71.4	50
There are people I know outside who give me support and encouragement	72.9	51

the early phase of imprisonment to ensure that prisoners maintained contact with people outside. Still, due to many practical difficulties, establishing this contact was cumbersome. Often the prisoners did not know the right telephone numbers, as they no longer had their mobile phone containing the number. The officers would have to obtain these numbers, and this could take time. At Feltham, the visitors' centre provided a lot of support to visitors, aiding this difficult adjustment that they, too, had to make to their loved one's being in prison. However, the people visiting the prison often had difficulties travelling across London, or from a further distance, and would arrive late and miss the visiting times. Solomon (2004) also found that distance from home was a major problem for young adults in prison.

The difficulties of establishing and maintaining contact with loved ones must be overcome, because outside contact is fundamental to the survival of many prisoners. As Toch (1992) wrote, with reference to jails in the USA, 'some of the resources needed for psychological survival in the detention setting must be supplied by significant others in the community' (p. 182). Moreover, it has been argued that maintaining contact with the family can help to prevent reoffending and help prisoners to resettle upon release (Home Office 2004). Yet, such contact was emotionally difficult. One prisoner recalled his first telephone call home:

Words cannot explain how you feel. It hits you. You miss them so much and you can't do nothing. You just want to be with them. You want to cuddle them and kiss them, but it is all took away from you. But then I thought there ain't no point in thinking that 'cause I am going to be out there. [Prisoner]

One of the most important forms of contact was through prison visits:

[Interviewer: How did you feel at your visit?]
I was so glad. I sat down and I was shaking. I was so happy. Then my mum come in. She come like a bullet, ran over, and she was just crying. I said, 'Don't cry, you'll make me cry'. My mum was just hugging me all the time. She wouldn't let go of me. [Prisoner]
[Interviewer: What was it like at the end of the visit?]
I didn't want to leave [my mum] but you've got to. [Prisoner]

Although prisoners frequently explained that visits were beneficial at the time, they also explained that once the visits were over, and their families or girlfriends walked off the other way, they became even

45

more upset. At this sight they realised that they had to continue to exist in a separate, restricted environment. Walking down the corridors of the prison, I often met prisoners returning to their cell after a visit: the expressions on their faces told the story of the separation they had just re-enacted once again. Prison visits were a double-edged sword; events that produced a conflict of intense emotions that prisoners often found difficult to understand and contain.

Despite these difficulties, the distress of separation was in fact most evident for the individuals who had failed to make contact with their family members or with friends. Some had been ostracised by their families immediately after they had entered prison. One prisoner said:

> Since this has happened, they don't want to know. I phone them and they don't want to chat to me and shit. I try phoning them, trying to get a bail address, but my mum won't provide it. [Prisoner]

Others chose themselves not to contact people outside prison: they feared a negative reaction by family members, and this fear led to self-induced ostracism. They were often very ashamed, and the guilt that they felt prevented them from making contact. For others, in order to adjust to the prison world, cutting off communication seemed a necessity. Generally, these prisoners employed blocking out the outside world as a coping strategy, in order to leave one world behind before they could immerse themselves in their new one. This avoidant coping strategy is arguably a maladaptive one in the long term but one that must be adopted by some people in making the transition. (The difference between thought suppression and thought regulation will be examined in Chapter 3.)

Psychological distress and entering custody

Different themes were evident from the accounts given by young men of their prison experience at three days. This phase of imprisonment was not experienced in a uniform manner. From interviews with prisoners and from the self-completed measure of psychological distress, it emerged that people at three days differed in their levels of psychological distress. Table 2.2 shows the items that constitute the measure of psychological distress and the percentage of participants who strongly agreed or agreed with each item.

The dimension scores ranged from 1 to 5. Scores on the dimension of psychological distress ranged between 1.36 and 4.82 (on a scale from

Table 2.2 Percentage of prisoners who strongly agreed or agreed with items relating to psychological distress

Item	% Strongly agreed or agreed	N
1. My experience of imprisonment in this particular prison has been stressful	54.3	38
2. I feel tense in this prison	52.9	37
3. I have experienced major feelings of distress in this prison	50.0	35
4. I often feel depressed in this prison	57.1	40
5. My experience in this prison is painful	40.0	28
6. I have many problems at the moment	65.7	46
7. I have problems sleeping at night	57.1	40
8. There is nothing I can do to relieve the distress I feel in this prison	52.9	37
9. My mental health is of concern to me	31.4	22
10. Life in prison involves a great deal of suffering	54.3	38
11. I often feel aggressive and hostile in this prison	42.9	30

1 to 5 where a higher score indicates higher distress) with a mean score of 3.34 (SD = .82). The data on this dimension were normally distributed, although with slight negative skewness (–.178), indicating that the data were slightly skewed towards individuals being more highly distressed.[7]

Why did these individuals differ in their levels of distress? In order to explore this question, I first conducted two *t*-tests to look for differences between first-time prisoners and those who had never been in prison before, and differences between individuals who had one or more vulnerability factors and those who had none.[8] Table 2.3 shows the results. There was no difference in the mean levels of psychological distress according to past imprisonment. Experiencing prison for the first time brought with it particular concerns and led to some more uncertainty in some regards, but those who had been in before experienced similar levels of distress. Indeed, the shock of re-entering prison at a fast rate brought with it its own difficulties.

There was no significant difference in mean levels of psychological distress according to imported vulnerability. Although people who were severely withdrawing from drugs had a particularly distressing experience (physically and psychologically), overall levels of imported vulnerability did not increase levels of distress. The experience of withdrawing from drugs will be discussed in Chapter 6, in the context of self-harming behaviour.

Table 2.3 Summary of *t*-test for differences in mean level of psychological distress

Variable	Yes		No			
	Mean	SD	Mean	SD	T	Significance
First time in prison	3.23	.89	3.41	.76	.91	.365
One or more 'vulnerability factors'	3.45	.82	3.27	.81	−.91	.366

(N = 70).

Table 2.4 Summary of standard multiple-regression analysis for variables predicting psychological distress

Variable	B	SE	β	T	Significance
Locus of control	−.627	.57	−.371	−4.17	.001
Prison social support	.129	.09	.123	1.41	.163
Outside social support	−.020	..08	−.097	−1.18	.242
Perceived adaptability	−.445	.075	−.509	−5.91	.001
Safety	−.166	.089	−.163	−1.87	.066

Adjusted R^2 = .59. (N = 70).

Next I carried out a standard multiple-regression analysis.[9] Table 2.4 shows the regression model. I had to limit the number of 'predictor' variables included in the regression model due to the sample size of 70 (hence I carried out *t*-tests with the other variables above). Five 'predictors' were entered into the model. These were locus of control, prison social support, outside social support, safety and perceived adaptability.[10] The model was significant; $F (5, 64) = 18.50$, $p < .001$.

A total of 59 per cent of the variance in psychological distress was accounted for in the model. The variables that significantly accounted for variance in psychological distress at three days were locus of control and perceived adaptability. Safety also showed a trend towards significance. As this concept was of importance in the qualitative data, I will also consider it.

The finding that an internal locus of control predicted lower levels of psychological distress is in line with previous research (MacKenzie *et al.* 1987; Zamble and Porporino 1988; Reitzel and Harju 2000). Individuals with an internal locus of control perceive outcomes in their environment to be contingent upon their actions. Despite the fact that prison limits control over outcomes, limits choices and increases uncertainty, individuals who are internal in their locus of control may nevertheless be able to find means to exert more control than those who are external in it; this, in turn, may enable them to feel less distressed. They attempt to make environmental changes: they may create niches (Seymour 1992) or become active 'gleaners', for example (Irwin 1970). They are able to seek out resources in their environment when they need them most (Pugh 1993). As they feel that they are able to control the environment, the environment has less of a controlling impact on them. In Feltham, although losing control was a common element of the transitional process, it appeared that some individuals were able to deal with this differently and counteract that loss.

Perceived adaptability also appeared significantly to predict variance in psychological distress. Individuals who reported that they found it difficult to adapt to life in prison, or could not cope with the experience, were also more distressed. These individuals may have been less able to regulate their thoughts and emotions. Individuals were often aware of their ability or inability to cope, and they thought about whether or not they would be able to adapt to prison life, whether or not they would 'hack it'. The role of meta-cognitions may be of importance in examining how individuals adapt psychologically. Meta-cognitions are the reflections individuals have about their own ability to adapt: individuals who think about their inability to adapt, and the reasons for this inability, may engage in rumination (see Papageorgiou and Wells (2004) for a collection of papers on depressive rumination).

Finally, safety appeared in the model as an important variable, showing a trend towards significance. These findings must be considered with caution, however, due to the lower reliability of this measure than that of the other measures in the study. Individuals who scored higher on the dimension of safety reported lower levels of psychological distress at this early phase of imprisonment. Again, although concerns over safety were a common element of the process of transition, individuals differed in the extent to which they felt safe. I also found a small, but significant, correlation between locus of control and safety ($r = .28$, $p < .05$). In their study of prison violence, Edgar *et al.* (2003) found that safety comprised five elements, one being 'a sense of control over one's environment' p. 90). This sense of control may be enhanced when individuals import with them into prison an internal locus of control. This sense of control, in turn, may help to reduce their concerns over safety and alleviate their level of psychological distress. Due to the cross-sectional nature of the study reported here, and the small sample size, it is not possible to attempt causal modelling, but the conceptual links between these constructs are still of interest.

In summary, this aspect of the research set out to explore the early period of entry into prison and examined prisoners' experiences as they made the transition into the prison world. Many common themes emerged from the interviews: a preoccupation with safety, feelings of uncertainty, the loss of control and freedom, and separation and loss. Individuals differed in the degree to which they experienced these aspects of transition and in their level of psychological distress; the effects of imprisonment were not uniform. What appeared to be the most important construct measured here was locus of control. This emphasis is in line with previous research on the period beyond the first three days. It seems that, at the period of entry into prison, an individual's internal locus of control, his perceived ability to adapt, and his perception of safety helped to alleviate the level of distress. Crossing the boundary was a demanding task for young adults, one that required resilience within themselves in the face of adversity.

Notes

1 Five prisoners in the sample had court dates and were therefore more prepared for this experience. Eight more were transferred from other prisons, although they had also attended court before arriving at Feltham.

2 The link worker on the first night offered to make a telephone call to a family member or friend on the prisoner's behalf. These link workers were employed by a charity, the Foundation Training Company. Only a handful of prisons have involvement by the voluntary sector at this early and crucial stage of custody. The link worker's role was to provide connections between prisoners and their families and between prisoners and prison staff.

3 Total institutions contained several features: 'First, all aspects of life are conducted in the same place and under the same single authority. Second, each phase of the member's daily activity is carried on in the immediate company of a large batch of others, all of whom are treated alike and required to do the same things together. Third, all phases of the day's activities are tightly scheduled, with one activity leading to a prearranged time into the next, the whole sequence of activities being imposed from above by a system of explicit formal rulings and a body of officials. Finally, the various enforced activities are brought together into a single rational plan purportedly designed to fulfil the official aims of the institution' (Goffman 1961: 17).

4 For a study of bullying among young offenders, see Ireland (2002) and Edgar et al. (2003).

5 The term 'on road' is the prisoners' frequent phrase for life outside prison.

6　Prisoners at Feltham referred to the juvenile side of the prison and the 'adult' side of the prison, that is, the young adult side (those aged 18–21).

7　To examine the distribution, I used the Kolmogorov–Smirnow (K–S) test. This test 'compares the set of scores in the sample to a normally distributed set of scores with the same mean and standard deviation' (Field 2000: 46). I found that there was no significant difference between the distribution of the sample and a normal distribution (K–S (1) = .094, p = .254).

8　Imported vulnerability was a composite measure of a number of factors that prisoners may have imported with them (self-harm history, psychiatric treatment, and a problem with drugs). The scale was coded 0 = no factors; 1 = one or more factors. A total of 37.1 per cent (26 participants) arrived in prison with at least one vulnerability factor (self-harm, psychiatric treatment or substance misuse), 7.1 per cent (five participants) had two of the three, and 1.4 per cent (one participant) had all three of the vulnerability factors.

9　'In the standard, or simultaneous, model, all IVs [independent variables] enter into the regression equation at once; each one is assessed as if it had entered the regression after all other IVs had entered. Each IV is evaluated in terms of what it adds to prediction of the DV [dependent variable] that is different from the predictability afforded by all the other IV's (Tabachnick and Fidell 1996: 149). Brace et al. (2003) argue that 'if you have no theoretical model in mind, and/or you have relatively low numbers of cases, then it is probably safest to use Enter [standard regression]' (p. 213).

10 The five measures (locus of control, prison social support, outside social support, safety and perceived adaptability) were recoded so a higher score denotes a more positive outcome; for psychological distress, a higher score denotes a negative outcome.

Chapter 3

Adapting to life in prison

As we saw in Chapter 2, several factors contributed to prisoners' difficulties as they made the initial transition to prison from the outside world. Preoccupation with safety, uncertainty, deprivation of freedom and control, and feelings of separation and loss were all part of the negative experience of the first three days in prison. Individuals differed, however, in how distressed they felt, and those who were internal in their locus of control and who felt safer were less distressed. Chapter 3 now follows a subsample of 28 of the original 70 prisoners through the following month, and is based upon interviews with them after ten days and 30 days in prison. (The background descriptive information of this smaller sample of 28 can be found in Chapter 1.) How did they adapt over the full length of the first month in prison? How and why did some prisoners adapt to life in prison while some did not?

Previous research into prisons has variously defined the concepts of adaptation and coping. Much of the early sociological work focused on how prisoners adapted socially to life in prison and how this adaptation in turn served to reduce the pains of imprisonment (Sykes 1958). The work concentrated on factors that individuals were deprived of when they entered prison. Research was also conducted on the concept of prisonisation, examining the role of importation factors that led to adherence to the inmate code (Clemmer 1940; Wheeler 1961; Irwin and Cressey 1962). Later it was found that both deprivation and importation models had an additive relationship to prisonisation (Thomas 1977). Although this body of research was useful in looking at the socialisation of prisoners, it did not examine how prisoners adapted psychologically. It did, however, alert researchers to the importance of the interaction between the individual and their environment.

Toch (1977) examined the psychological consequences of the interaction between individuals and their environment. His ecological model of how to survive prison posits that there should be a match between the individual's needs and the environment in order for successful adaptation to take place. Toch put forward seven needs that individuals differentially aim to fulfil: safety, privacy, structure, emotional feedback, support, activity and freedom. If there is a fit between the individual's needs and the environment's ability to satisfy the needs, then this fit increases the likelihood of successful adjustment. These transactions 'mark the difference between psychological survival and non-survival; between growth and discomfort or maladaptation' (Toch 1977: 4). Goodstein and Wright (1989) found that the person–environment fit, as measured by Toch's measure of environmental concerns, was associated with internal adjustment, as measured by level of distress. Toch and Adams (2002) also argued that the degree of congruence between the individual's needs and the ability of the environment to meet those needs was a critical factor in determining adjustment.

Besides the transaction between the individual and the environment, Adams (1992) identified a second line of research: the appraisal-coping approach. Lazarus and Folkman (1984) put forward a process model of coping that comprises two main stages of appraisal. The first of these stages is primary appraisal, which involves perceiving the situation as stressful. Once this perception has occurred, secondary appraisal is enacted, involving an evaluation of the individual's ability to cope. Two main types of coping are put forward: problem-oriented coping and emotion-oriented coping. Problem-oriented coping occurs if a 'person obtains information on which to act and mobilises actions for the purpose of changing the reality of the troubled person–environment relationship'; emotion-focused coping, on the other hand, involves 'regulating the emotions tied to the stress situation' (Lazarus 2000: 204). It is argued that emotion-focused coping is used more if the environment is not changeable, while problem-oriented coping attempts to bring about change in the environment itself. What is crucial to this theory, an idea which Zamble and Porporino (1988) favoured, is that it is not the situation *per se* that is of importance but the appraisal of the situation by the individual. As Snyder (2001) states, 'the most productive approach to understanding a stressor is to understand *how* it is construed by the individual' (p. 9).

Within the literature on prisons, the role of using effective coping strategies has been found to ease psychological distress (Zamble and Porporino 1988; Greve *et al.* 2001; Ireland 2001; Mohino *et al.* 2004;

Ireland *et al.* 2005), while the inability to employ them has been associated with self-harming behaviour (Liebling 1992, 1995, 1999; Liebling and Krarup 1993; Dear *et al.* 1998). These findings corroborate studies of stress and coping in the community. Appraisals, and coping styles, vary (Lazarus 1966, 2000; Lazarus and Folkman 1984), and it is important to understand what impact these varying coping styles may have on subsequent adaptation. Zamble and Porporino (1988) examined the coping strategies of prisoners in their longitudinal study. They examined individuals' concerns and their ability to enact effective coping strategies to deal with these problems. They found that the most common strategy was reactive problem solving, although the use of escape strategies was also fairly common. Seeking social support as a coping strategy was used by only 21 per cent of participants in prison (compared with 32 per cent when outside prison). Although prisoners generally did not employ effective coping strategies, those who did were able to adapt psychologically over time. However, although Zamble and Porporino tell us that most individuals adapt over time, more needs to be known about the different pathways of those who adapt and those who do not.

Ireland (2001) found that 'although the early use of emotional and avoidant coping may be beneficial to psychological health, the *prolonged* use of the strategies may not be' (cited in Ireland *et al.* 2005: 414). In a more recent study, Ireland *et al.* (2005) examined coping styles and psychological distress among juvenile prisoners (15–17-year-olds) and young adult prisoners (aged 18–21). They found that young adults reported using more emotional, avoidant and detached coping styles than juveniles. Emotional coping predicted increases in psychological distress among young adults and juveniles, and rational coping predicted a decrease in psychological distress among the young adults. Mohino *et al.* (2004) found, in their study of young male adults imprisoned in Spain, that approach coping strategies were used more than avoidant ones and that the main method of coping was cognitive rather than behavioural. Interestingly, they found that during the first months of imprisonment first-time prisoners made greater use of the strategy of emotional discharge (behavioural attempts to reduce tension by expressing negative feelings). This was used less as the length of time in prison increased. During the first months the strategy of positive reappraisal was used less (cognitive attempts to construe the problem in a different way while still accepting the reality of the situation). Although this study was cross-sectional, it provides some useful information on how coping strategies may vary as the length of time in prison increases.

Finally, there are some studies that have examined levels of psychological distress in prison and factors that may contribute to it (Wooldredge 1999; Gover *et al.* 2000; Nieland *et al.* 2001). Wooldredge (1999) found that background demographic factors and institutional factors such as activity visits, and victimisation were associated with adjustment. Gover *et al.* (2000) found that age, race, perceived activity and perceived justice were associated with a measure of anxiety. They thus argued for the importance of including both importation and deprivation variables in research design.

These studies, however, are solely based on quantitative measures, and it is difficult to understand the meaning of individuals' experiences when individuals are restricted to responding to particular measures. In examining adaptation to prison life, it is important to recognise that prisons differ in their moral performance (Liebling 2004), and no two prison environments are the same. The interaction between one individual and an environment will differ from that of another individual *within* the same institution. It is important to recognise that within one prison there will be differences between individuals within that environment. As I have chosen to examine adaptation within one establishment, I am interested in the process of differential adaptation *within* one prison and over time.

Types of adaptation: practical, social and psychological

Within the first month in prison, young men had to adapt in three different ways. Firstly, they had to adapt *practically* to life inside. There were a number of aspects of the prison about which they had to learn: they had to learn what they were entitled to and what they were not; what they were allowed to keep in their cells and what they were not; and what time different procedures of the regime occurred, such as when they would be unlocked and for how long. They needed to know where to apply for employment within the prison or how to attend education, how to attend the gym or a church, or other religious services (for example, Friday prayers for Muslims). The canteen was another essential aspect of prison life: how much money could they spend and how did they go about spending it? They needed to know when they could shower, and how and when they could receive visits. How would those with special dietary requirements for medical or religious reasons get their needs met? Prisoners needed to know how they could find out about the progress of their court case and when they would be returning to court. So there were numerous transactions that took place within prison in order for an individual to adapt practically to his surroundings. This process began within the first few days on the induction unit, but it continued to take place throughout the first month in prison. Although the induction programme taught prisoners many of the basic rules of prison life, most of the transactions had to be experienced personally in order for practical adaptation to succeed.

Secondly, prisoners had to adapt *socially* and interact with staff and with fellow prisoners on a day-to-day basis. They had to learn how to relate to the staff in order to receive their entitlements and perhaps to benefit from the staff's discretion. They had to be able to seek support from staff for a particular question, problem or concern. They had to know when it was appropriate to ask staff for things and how to do so in an appropriate manner, and with respect, an important aspect of social adaptation. When was it appropriate to ask for an extra telephone call? When was it acceptable to press the cell bell to ask a question that had been preying on their mind? Prisoners had to learn to maintain a balance in the amount of support sought, not becoming too dependent upon staff nor being too distant. Prisoners also had to begin to trust staff and interact with them. They also had to be able to interact with their peers. This peer interaction was an aspect of prison life that was also learned: there were norms and language for interacting with fellow prisoners and for integrating with them. An important part of social adaptation was becoming involved with activities which required people to adapt to social transactions. Finally, in order to adapt socially within prison, the prisoners also needed to be able to maintain contact with significant others outside prison. These bonds, if they existed, were part of an individual's social self, and maintaining links was important in determining adaptive outcomes. Moreover, individuals who had more support outside prison were more likely to interact with staff and prisoners inside prison. (This finding will be discussed more fully in a later chapter.)

Thirdly, young men had to adapt *psychologically*. Psychological adaptation involved both problem-based coping as well as emotion-based coping (Lazarus and Folkman 1984). Adaptation is a process whereby individuals move towards reaching a cognitive, emotional and behavioural equilibrium. Prisoners had to learn to deal with potentially stressful situations in an effective manner, but they also had to manage the different emotions they continued to experience. Prisoners had to be able to reach a state where their level of psychological distress was at a manageable level. All prisoners found the experience of imprisonment difficult to some degree, but they had to learn to manage this distress internally as well as externally. This regulation of emotions has been established as an important part of the coping process (Snyder 2001).

Young men had to regulate their emotions about stressful situations, both those situations within the prison and those without. Indeed, managing the emotions associated with outside contact was an essential aspect of psychological adaptation. (As will be argued in a later chapter, outside support was extremely important for psychological well-being.) Prisoners also had to regulate their behavioural responses towards others, exerting a high degree of self-control. The stark reality of imprisonment was not going to change for these individuals, but their appraisal of the situation could be altered. Psychological adaptation involved the enactment of effective coping strategies to deal with a myriad of highly emotive situations.

An interaction between practical, social and psychological adaptation

Moreover, the three types of adaptation interacted with one another. Firstly, practical adaptation assisted social adaptation and psychological adaptation. For example, if an individual knew practically how to apply for a place on education, he would attend education more quickly and be involved socially in the regime earlier than someone who did not know how this system worked. Having purposeful activity served as a distraction and thus aided psychological adaptation. If an individual knew what the regime was like and when he would be unlocked, this could allow more certainty, which, in turn, would aid psychological adaptation. A further example is knowledge of how to apply for a visit. Knowing how to apply for visits ensured that contact was maintained with those outside prison, which, in turn, aided psychological adaptation. There are numerous other examples that could be given, but the point to note is that these practical considerations had profound implications for the prisoner's social and psychological life. For prisoners who had been to Feltham before, practical adaptation was easier than for those who were in prison for the first time.

Secondly, social adaptation affected practical and psychological adaptation. The formal rules were taught during the induction course, but fellow prisoners could also assist one another by providing informal information about the prison's regime and systems. Gaining this information enabled prisoners to make the most out of the prison world and helped them learn how to be in prison. Peers also distracted one another from negative thoughts by providing one another with conversation and laughter. Fellow prisoners also provided some advice that helped reduce their levels of anxiety and depression. Social adaptation also involved interacting with prison staff and knowing whom to seek support from and in what circumstances. The social support derived from peer and staff relationships will be discussed more fully in later chapters.

Yet, the benefits worked both ways. Psychological adaptation also affected practical and social adaptation. Indeed, this mode of adaptation enabled the other modes to come into effect. Individuals had to be able to regulate their thoughts and emotions to a sufficient degree before they could *fully* undertake practical and social adaptation. Those individuals who entered prison unable to regulate their emotions, who felt they could not adapt to prison life, and who had an external locus of control suffered from acute levels of psychological distress and found it difficult to adapt within their first month. There appeared to be a hurdle of psychological distress, and if this hurdle was not jumped, they were unable to proceed further with adaptation. There was a vicious circle: a certain level of psychological adaptation was needed *first* before an individual could adapt practically and socially; social and practical adaptation, in turn, assisted psychological adaptation.

Stages of adaptation: liminality, acceptance and equilibrium

Besides the three types of adaptation, there were three stages of adaptation that one could pass through within the first month in prison. These stages I have labelled liminality, acceptance and equilibrium, and each stage marks a progression from the previous one. Within each of these stages, the three types of adaptation described above interact with one another. Just as individuals differed in their level of psychological distress at three days, individuals differed in their progression through the first month. Although I gathered quantitative data, using the same measures that prisoners completed at three days, no statistically significant differences were found on any of these measures, for the subsample of 28 individuals. Therefore the results will not be included. However, qualitative interviews with prisoners over time revealed that young men did differ in their ability to adapt. The longitudinal design of the research provided a means of following through the same group of individuals over time and was essential to tracking their adaptation. Furthermore, because I was based in the prison for ten months, these changes were apparent in my day-to-day observations of behaviour. I could see how some prisoners changed socially over time.

By the end of the first month, some people remained in the liminal zone (described in Chapter 2) while some had moved towards acceptance and some had moved towards reaching equilibrium. Moreover, this adaptation was a dynamic process, with some individuals moving backwards as well as forwards. Although, to some extent, the time so far spent in prison was important when considering the process of adaptation, in fact what was more important was the ability of the individual, no matter how long he had been incarcerated, to draw on internal and external resources available to him. This created the differential experience of prisoners of the following three stages of adaptation.

Remaining in the liminal zone

Liminality was the first stage of adaptation. Upon arriving in prison, although the experience of imprisonment was not uniform, all of the prisoners experienced the common transitional preoccupations with safety, feelings of uncertainty, loss of control and freedom, and feelings of separation and loss. However, although this liminal state was, to greater and lesser degrees, difficult for all of the prisoners at three days, some 13 individuals remained in the liminal zone after ten days and five remained there for the entirety of their first month. What was the experience like for those who remained in the liminal zone?

Some individuals remained on the Kingfisher unit and did not move on to normal locations within the prison, because there were safer cells on Kingfisher and prison staff deemed it necessary for them to remain there in this liminal world. Because it was an induction unit, it lacked a regime and although these prisoners did begin to adapt practically, and to some extent socially, they still had to experience life practically as it was lived on the normal units, as one noted:

> [Interviewer: What are you used to and what aren't you used to?]
> I am used to the routine, waking up, breakfast, lunch, sleep [...] but I am not used to prison on the whole. I am not used to being banged up all day. I am used to freedom, you know? [Prisoner]

Accordingly, in some respects, their adaptation had not yet begun properly. Psychologically, they continued to be swamped with excessive thinking, were plagued by the feelings of uncertainty and of separation, and could not cope with being locked in their cells. They did not attend education, although two were given jobs on the wing to allow them more time out of their cells. They continued to find it difficult to deal with the lack of freedom, and for those who were most acutely distressed, the reality still remained extremely painful and shocking, as one prisoner described:

> [Interviewer: So if you were to sum up your experience so far, what has it been like?]

Terrifying really. You are locked up all day, you are away from everything. You are looking out the window, and all you can see is the one thing all the time. It is pretty terrifying. Believe me, when I see myself walk out these gates it'll be like a miracle. It's like I'm dreaming, being in here. I'm waiting for someone to pinch me and wake me up. [Prisoner]

Another prisoner related how he felt depressed and that he felt that he was not in control of his thoughts and emotions, but was at the mercy of them. This feeling of helplessness prevented him from taking active steps to improve his situation:

Your head is you, you know, it's a horrible feeling. Like your head is just, you know, like your head is out, you don't know where your mind is. You feel like you've lost your mind. It is just hard. [Prisoner]

Those who were most distressed found the experience of remand most difficult, and they told me that they could not adapt until they were sentenced. They felt continually unsettled:

I won't be settled 'cause now you are worrying how long am I gonna get? Like when I get sentenced tomorrow, they'll move me from this prison to the next prison, innit? That's what they do, innit? They only keep me here 'cause this is a basic remand prison. Some sentenced prisoners do stay here, certain selected ones, but most are shipped out. [Prisoner]

Although over time these prisoners had to some extent become oriented towards the practicalities of the regime and system on Kingfisher, this unit was not representative of other units in the prison, and, overall, they could not deal with being locked in their cells. They felt out of control and unsafe, unable to trust others around them. They could not jump over the hurdle of distress and so could not begin to adapt psychologically. Although individuals who imported higher levels of vulnerability did not differ *statistically* in their level of distress, from those who imported lower levels, many of the people who remained in the liminal zone had previous psychiatric treatment or problems with drug misuse, or had self-harmed in the past. The prisoners who were withdrawing from drugs suffered both physically and psychologically in acute ways. These individuals, along with the others who remained on Kingfisher, were far from accepting the reality and adapting socially and psychologically to life in prison.

Others remained in the liminal stage despite being moved onto a normal residential unit. They still found imprisonment difficult, albeit not as difficult as those who remained on Kingfisher. These people, who had been struggling psychologically on Kingfisher, reported that moving made them feel as though they had to start the process of adaptation all over again. The move onto another unit was marked by increased unpredictability, less perceived control and less safety. One prisoner found it particularly difficult and overdosed on the first night after the move. This one of the prison's many further, internal transitions was for him a major trigger and escalated his level of distress, which was already high. This young man was socially withdrawn and felt unable to approach the staff for help. Another prisoner told me that he felt so unsafe on his next wing that he had smashed his cell in order to be taken to the segregation unit. He also felt angry and reacted strongly to being moved, and this angry behavioural response was his coping strategy, one that may be termed maladaptive, but one which changed his social situation nevertheless. He thought that the segregation unit would be safer, a place where he could withdraw further from the rest of the prison community. However, these young men's behavioural reactions brought with them additional points of transition, which in turn further increased their levels of despair and tested their ability to adapt.

Individuals remaining at the liminal stage found it difficult to comprehend the regime. They found small tasks arduous: for example, they often did not remember to bring their towel and shower kit to the showers during association. They found it difficult to take control of their environment and felt out of their depth: they were overcome by the feelings of uncertainty and anxiety that ensued. Socially, they were withdrawn and did not interact as readily. Many of them found it difficult to initiate interactions and were annoyed that they had been split from others on Kingfisher with whom they had worked towards associating. Worse still, one individual who found his situation difficult even when he was located with his co-defendant, found it even more distressing once he had been split from him when moved off Kingfisher. Individuals now had to work towards interacting with new people, and the instability of the social world of Feltham, which is a remand centre, made social adaptation difficult: some suffered from the breaking of preliminary associations they had made, even since moving to their new unit. One prisoner commented:

> People move. Every time I start talking to people they move like. Everyone keeps moving. There is someone that I know who lives in my area. He came in last night, and now he has gone to a different wing already. [Prisoner]

These forms of transitions occurred throughout the first month. Individuals who shared a cell often found that their cellmate would attend court and then fail to return; or if he did return, he would be relocated in another cell. One prisoner said:

> It's a bit stupid in a way, getting to know someone for a couple of days, thinking, 'Yeah, it'll be all right, I'm getting to know him better.' As soon as I get to know them better, they've got to move. [Prisoner]

These transitions were most difficult for individuals who perceived less control over their environment and who felt less safe. The social world was perceived as turbulent and ever changing, so that they could not rein it in, nor keep a hold on it. This perception of the social world differed for those who perceived *more control* over their world, those who recognised the transitions but did not let them influence their feelings of uncertainty as much as others did. Indeed, some of these prisoners saw it as an opportunity for people that they knew to arrive on the unit.

Individuals who found it hard being moved also commented in interviews that staff treated them differently on their new unit compared with Kingfisher.[1] First-time and returning prisoners alike made similar comments. One prisoner stated:

> Kingfisher is more of an introduction, more of a caring, finding out who you are, and what you are, what you are about, before you get moved on to a normal unit. The normal unit is more like, 'All right, you've had your induction shit, get down to it'. It is harder on the normal units. [Prisoner]

These prisoners wished they did not have to move and would rather have stayed on Kingfisher, where life was beginning to feel slightly calmer. Perhaps these prisoners now realised that their perception of safety was relative. One prisoner, who did not feel particularly safe when located on Kingfisher, stated with hindsight:

> The prisoners were more calm at Kingfisher. I don't know why, but there is not so much shouting on Kingfisher like here. The vibe is more calm on Kingfisher. [Prisoner]

The induction unit did indeed have a calmer feel to it than the other units. At first, many prisoners expected there to be a lot of 'window warriors', prisoners who shout abuse out of the windows at one another.

This did not happen on Kingfisher because safer windows that could not be opened had been installed during the refurbishment. This was not the case on the other units, where abuse was regularly hurled out of windows in the evenings. Although the reputation of Feltham was dispelled for most, for others, it was confirmed once they had moved onto a normal unit:

I've learned that there's a lot of bullies inside here who try to, you know, see how weak you are. They try to bully you. There are guys who act like they control the block. They act like they run it, they control the prison and things like that. [Prisoner]

[Interviewer: How did you feel when they were all shouting?]
I felt intimidated. Why are they intimidating? Why are they saying that? They have no reason. They are acting like they want everything. They want to be the ruler of the block. They want to run it themselves in their own way. [Prisoner]

Since being moved, two prisoners reported that they had been victimised, and this victimisation confirmed their feelings of insecurity. Experiencing victimisation disturbed an individual's ability to adapt socially and was a reminder that adaptation was not a linear process. Situational triggers, such as being bullied, could reverse any progress that may have been initiated. Individuals who had begun to adapt, albeit in a slow and fragile manner, could easily regress if a negative life event was experienced.

However, psychological adaptation was difficult for all the people who remained at the liminal stage of adaptation. They found it difficult to regulate their thoughts and emotions. Individuals who remained in the liminal stage continued to experience difficulties in managing the emotions associated not only with the prison, but with the outside world they had left behind. An avoidant coping strategy was apparent: blocking out the prison world and failing to accept the reality they faced. Furthermore, this avoidance was also used to block out the outside world in a desperate hope to find life inside prison more bearable. Cohen and Taylor (1972) noted that, for many, maintaining relationships outside prison may be an emotional strain that is too much to bear. Indeed, 'there may almost be fatalistic relief in reducing the emotional reliance on outsiders. It increases the individual's autonomy; ensures that the absence of visitors or letters is not a recurrent worry, and that such absences do not provide opportunities for patronizing sympathy by officers' (Cohen and Taylor 1972: 68). For prisoners remaining in the liminal stage, this blocking was only a half-successful attempt at regulating their thoughts and emotions and was often an extreme approach to take. However, some felt that prison life would have been even more distressing if they had not attempted it:

> It depends if you think about outside road. When you are inside, you have to get adapted to it. You have to. You have to stop thinking about outside. [Prisoner]

This strategy of blocking out the outside world thus affected whether they wanted to contact their families. Although the level of family contact had generally increased for all individuals as their time in prison increased, individuals who were finding it most difficult to adapt found the separation from their families the hardest. Some prisoners wanted to wait until they were sentenced, as they were not psychologically strong enough to manage their outside lives as well as their life within prison until the situation was fixed. One prisoner, who said that he was trying to 'block out the out', said:

> I don't really want my family to come and visit me because, as I told you, it's just gonna hurt them more and when they see me they're just gonna start crying. It's just gonna be a big circus and I don't want them to go through that, but I am gonna write to my sister, one of my older sisters. I should write to my mum, but I don't know. I'll write to my older sister. I haven't done that yet but I will. I'll just wait till tomorrow till I know when I'll come out, 'cause it's sentence-day then, you know. You are settled, you know, when you are coming out. [Prisoner]

On the other hand, some failed to get the visits they had expected and felt rejected:

> When you are in here, you realise a lot of things, like who your friends are and this and that, who comes to visit you and this and that, if they care about you, your so-called friends. [Prisoner]

This ostracism had a profound impact on the individual's sense of self-worth at an already difficult time. The role of outside contact was complex and important. (It will be discussed in more detail in Chapters 6 and 7.)

Although, to some extent, time eased the situation for some of these young men, in that they had at least moved towards some form of practical adaptation, they still had profound difficulties adapting socially and psychologically. These prisoners continued to have a profound lack of acceptance of their situation. One prisoner said that he still could never accept his reality and he could not come to terms with it:

> To me it's like a nightmare. I'm waiting for someone to pinch me and wake me up. It's not real like. I don't think this is real. I think this is a nightmare. It's a dream. [Prisoner]

This denial had a profound impact on the ability of many of the individuals to adapt practically and socially and left them feeling disoriented, displaced and dazed.

Moving towards acceptance

As the length of time in prison increased, some prisoners began to move towards the second phase of adaptation, the stage of acceptance, and these prisoners showed a marked change in their ability to adapt. By ten days, 15 prisoners showed signs of reaching this stage. By 30 days, eight more of the 13 prisoners who were in the liminal zone at ten days had moved towards acceptance. At this stage, some prisoners had accepted the reality of the situation with which they were faced and, to some extent, had begun to adapt practically, socially and psychologically. This stage was marked by feeling more settled and attached to the institution in which they were forced to reside. Acceptance thus enabled adaptation to occur.

Individuals who had moved towards this stage reacted positively to the transition from the induction unit onto one of the residential units. Although they had some initial anticipatory anxiety when leaving Kingfisher unit, this anxiety was dispelled after a few days on the new unit. For these individuals, comprising both first-time and returning prisoners, this move represented an opportunity to get on with their prison term and marked the beginning of becoming settled in it. As one prisoner commented:

> Induction is not the beginning. It is an in-between coming in and starting. I didn't settle in there. I settle in better here. I didn't try and settle in there or try to get into the routine, but I am trying here. [Prisoner]

Settling in was seen as a conscious choice that people had made for themselves: something that they controlled. Moreover, this transition represented entering a new world over which they could begin to exert control. They had left the acute liminal zone and were becoming more embedded within the social and psychological world of the prison.

They had oriented themselves towards the regime and the routine, and they knew when things would happen, what they were entitled to, and how the system operated more generally. As one prisoner said:

> I think it took about a week before I started getting used to it. I got a hang of the routines, the dinner routines. I got the hang of the routines of everything. I mean, even till now, it's taken me till now to get used to everything. But there's still a few bits I still need to get used to. [Prisoner]

The complex world of the prison brought with it something different to learn each day, and these prisoners recognised that. Generally, though, at this stage, they had 'got the hang of the routines' and had progressed practically in their adaptation. Individuals at this stage began to take what limited control they could over the situation they faced.

At the stage of acceptance, prisoners also had begun to adapt quite well socially. They recognised the benefits of a more structured regime having moved from Kingfisher. Some had found jobs and were attending education, or had submitted an application and were eagerly awaiting a response. They had also been involved in some form of social activity, be it gym, football or visiting the library. They were involved in activities on association too. For example, one main means of interacting at Feltham was through playing pool, a game which facilitated interaction and aided social adaptation. One prisoner said:

> I played pool. That's how you get to know people in here. It is through pool. [Prisoner]

Instead of standing around the side of the association areas, prisoners who had reached this stage were beginning to make some choices about how to use this time. They had become more integrated within the prison world, rather than remaining on the literal boundary, and they interacted with prisoners and staff. Although this interaction was difficult, they felt better for it:

> It's got a lot better 'cause I got to know people. In the first few days I didn't know no one. I couldn't get to sleep properly. Probably be a bit shyer speaking to people, not knowing who they are. Now I can go and speak to everyone. They'll probably come and speak to me 'cause I know them now. [Prisoner]

At this stage, they felt more secure in the prison, and because they felt safe they were able to interact more. As one prisoner commented:

You are not scared to go up to people and speak to them. You know them a lot better. You speak to them if you need something. [Prisoner]

At this stage, there was also an increase in social confidence: for example, prisoners were more proactive in initiating conversations, and interactions with peers were less defensive. Perhaps a reciprocal relationship existed between their acceptance of the situation that they faced and the perception that others in that situation were beginning to accept them.

I feel more stable like here, I feel more taken into the place. I am accepted more. They recognise my face. [Prisoner]

This sense of belonging and acceptance brought with it the benefits of social support (which I will discuss fully in later chapters). Feeling safer enabled them to interact, and this interaction, in turn, enhanced their feeling of safety.

Another form of social adaptation at the stage of acceptance was continuing to maintain links with families and loved ones. At this stage, young men had begun to establish a routine of contacting people outside. They began to accept the separation to some extent, even though it was difficult, and were eager to maintain contact as much as they could. Accepting this separation and loss was extremely difficult, but, rather than feeling controlled by it, they attempted to appraise the situation differently and to generate alternative thoughts such as 'I may be in prison but they can't keep me here forever'. Accepting the situation allowed the separation to be managed more effectively.

At the acceptance stage, individuals had begun to adapt psychologically too. Although these prisoners continued to face problems like those they had faced at three days, when prisoners reached the stage of acceptance, they displayed a greater ability to regulate the thoughts and feelings that these problems elicited. However, this regulation was difficult and had not quite reached a state of equilibrium. As one prisoner said at his third interview:

The second time [of interview] I was on and off. There was times when I could handle it and times when I couldn't. Now I can handle it better. [Prisoner]

In order to adapt psychologically, there was a fine line between thought blocking or suppression and thought regulation. Thought blocking or suppression was an ineffective coping strategy that could increase disruptive cognitive activity. Indeed, as Snyder (2001) stated, 'contrary to becoming a useful self-regulatory approach for coping with stressors, cognitive avoidance often backfires and makes the stressor even more problematic' (p. 13). Research has shown that avoidance is accompanied by an increased level of self-awareness that, in turn, may 'amplify any negative self-referential thoughts and feelings' (ibid.). This self-focused attention 'sustains emotional distress and interferes with cognitions and behaviours that are necessary for adaptation' (Hamilton and Ingram 2001: 186). To avoid and suppress thoughts could have negative consequences, for this suppression is different from regulation. Individuals who were able to regulate their thoughts and emotions did not seem to engage in avoidance or suppression. Instead, when thinking about the stressful events in their lives, they were more equipped to deal with the negative affect that arose. At the stage of acceptance, these prisoners were also aware of their ability to cope with prison life and noticed changes in their own level of distress. I questioned one prisoner, who felt that he was coping better, as follows:

> [Interviewer: What do you mean by saying that you are coping?] I've learned to down-size my stress. I've learned to know where my limits of my stress are. I can think of my freedom and not go into detail. Just think of it as freedom and not go into I could be there doing this or that. That makes me stressed. If I start to define it, it becomes a bigger problem. [Prisoner]
> [Interviewer: When were you first able to do that?]
> I don't know – it comes gradually. The first night after our interview, I wouldn't say till after three or four nights. I fell asleep earlier than I normally would. And I woke up and it felt normal for me to go out for breakfast, wait up till twelve, go out for lunch, you know, three o'clock 'sosh,[2] four o'clock go into your cell, five o'clock dinner, TV, do a couple of things, do my press-ups, write a few lyrics, go to bed. You kind of just learn to get through the day. [Prisoner]

As Hamilton and Ingram (2001) state, 'while emotional reactions to difficult life events are linked to the thoughts that greet their occurrence the continual rumination that follows these events amplifies and extends the negative emotional reactions to such events' (p. 182). Individuals must therefore be able to regulate the negative affect that was produced by a stressor in the first place. Both types of coping (emotion-focused and problem-focused) complement each other and are necessary in order to cope effectively. As so many problems within prison cannot be solved, due to the actual loss of control, it is plausible to suggest that emotion-focused coping is at least as important as problem-focused coping in order to survive psychologically. The existing situation is unlikely to change substantially, and therefore those who are able to manage their emotional distress may be more likely to manage their lives in prison better.

Accepting the reality of the situation was a key aspect of psychological adaptation. They had now experienced 'psychological arrival' (Gibbs 1982b) and worked towards regulating their distress. Another prisoner stated:

> It changes. When you first come in, you're thinking about everything. You are thinking about all the bad things like it's the end of the world or something, but after a while you don't care. You just forget about it. You can't keep going on, you have to get on with your sentence, you're gonna have to do it. [Prisoner]

To reach acceptance, the young men had jumped the hurdle of distress and had begun to sleep more easily:

> I can sleep a lot easier at night. I've got to know a lot more people in here. I don't feel stressed out anymore. [Prisoner]

Acceptance was an important stage to have reached within the process of adaptation. It marked a turning point, and appraisals of the reality of imprisonment became somewhat more positive. Individuals at this stage had adapted practically, and they had begun to adapt socially and psychologically. From the qualitative data, it was evident that those who entered prison with moderate, as opposed to high, levels of psychological distress were the individuals who were able to move towards acceptance. Having reached this stage was evident in their narratives at ten days, but more so at 30 days. Prisoners who had been in prison before did benefit from this experience in that they could adapt practically to the prison regime. Prisoners who had reached acceptance had moved beyond the liminal stage of imprisonment. In order to exert control, it seemed necessary first to accept the situation, then to evaluate it and finally to work out ways to cope with it.

Moving towards equilibrium

The third stage of the adaptation process was the move towards equilibrium. Unlike the stage of acceptance, which prisoners could reach at ten days as well as 30 days, reaching the stage of equilibrium was only apparent from accounts given by prisoners at the end of their first month. Only five of the 28 young men reached this stage within the time period over which I interviewed. This final stage of adaptation showed continuity with stage 2, but the key difference was that a balance was reached in their adaptation. At stage 2, in the stage of acceptance, the individual was still attempting to adapt socially and psychologically to some extent; at stage 3, the move towards equilibrium, social and psychological adaptations showed a more consistent pattern over time. Moreover, at this stage, the prisoner had become an active participant in his world and had begun to glean from the environment, in order to make the most of the difficult situation with which he had to contend. He felt more familiar with the regime and increased his level of social interaction.

The stage of equilibrium was marked by a continued acceptance of reality and an increased level of self-efficacy. At this stage, prisoners had begun to experience positive emotions more readily. Rather than just enjoying an absence of negative emotions, these young men appeared more positively at ease in the prison and had a higher degree of optimism than before. They became more active participants in their world and had often gleaned enough knowledge from their experience to be able to improve their own conditions. As one prisoner observed:

> I started to interact in different ways. I started going to rugby, started going to gym. I started doing all those little things I did at one point or another. I thought, instead of me being depressed and keeping it to myself and being a bitch and a half, I thought, why not try and get involved in things to help me out, to keep me busy, and help me interact? I have learned to give the governors the respect they wish to deserve in order to get the respect I expect to get, and that has led me to get onto enhanced, a different wing, and more gym sessions. [Prisoner]

Another said:

> The past two weeks I've started feeling better about myself. I've nothing to fear. I ain't thinking about the things I was thinking of. I can sleep. I can talk to people. I don't feel worried at all now. [Prisoner]

At this stage, individuals regulated their thoughts and emotions further and had begun to reach a cognitive-emotional equilibrium, albeit a fragile one. Although this was part of the stage of acceptance, this regulation was much more manageable. External negative events could happen and the individual would still retain a high degree of cognitive-emotional regulation. Zamble and Porporino (1988) reported in their study that individuals were better at regulating their thoughts at the 16-month follow-up than at the initial period of entry. Indeed, 'the majority of long-term prisoners had become more self-controlled in their thoughts parallel to the way they had also become socially more self-contained' (Zamble and Porporino 1988: 123). Jones and Schmid (2000) also recognised the importance of the ability to regulate thoughts and stated that 'coping with their imprisonment required them to regulate their own thoughts, about their situation, about the outside world, and about time itself' (p. 94). As mentioned previously, being able to regulate one's own thoughts and emotions has been recognised as an essential requirement for psychological survival, but this regulation can itself be problematic (Liebling 1999). Gallo and Ruggiero (1991) argued that in prison a certain amount of distress is caused by 'the effort to keep distress itself under control' (p. 323). At the stage of equilibrium, prisoners had become adept at keeping distress under control; it was less effortful, and they appeared more skilled at it. They had worked out which coping strategies suited them best and which circumstances required the use of particular strategies. At this stage, prisoners were able to use an array of coping strategies (both problem-oriented and emotion-focused) to deal with an array of difficulties.

It was apparent that some young men had reached equilibrium, or a balance, in their expectations, learning not to be too positive and then be disappointed, but not to be too negative either, sliding towards depression. Uncertainty continued to surround the prisoner. When would the next court case be? Will my visitor get across London on time for the visiting hours? Will my cellmate return from court or will I be allocated someone new? However, what differed at this stage were the appraisals made of the uncertainty and that some perceived control was attached to it. It was also important to be balanced in one's trust. Too much trust in prison was foolish, but too much caution and the refusal to trust anyone could also be psychologically detrimental. A balance had to be reached in social interactions too, not becoming too dependent upon a particular officer or prisoner due to the transient nature of the prison world, yet not being too independent either, and becoming a social isolate.

Some prisoners that were aware of the Incentives and Earned Privileges (IEP) scheme were eager to obtain the enhanced status (see Bottoms (2003) for a review of the IEP policy). This status could be granted only after being in the prison for one month. In some ways, this incentive served as a means to motivate them to regulate their feelings and behaviour:

> Certain prisoners will get crazy and start smashing their TV and this and that, but I don't get too stressed 'cause that's just fucking my own self up. If I smash my TV up, I'm gonna go to basic; I'm gonna go to block. I'm not going to block 'cause I've been there and I don't like it. You get me? [Prisoner]

Very few young men provided accounts that were like this, but some did. Perhaps if I had followed up these young men to three months, this form of resilience would have been more evident. Equilibrium was a difficult stage to reach within the adaptation process. However, if prisoners successfully reached this turning point, their practical, social and psychological adaptation would be sustained more easily. Although negative life events could still occur, at this stage, the individual would be less likely to be thrown off balance. These events, such as failing to receive canteen items when they were ordered, could be put into perspective. Realistic expectations had been formed along with realistic optimism. From the qualitative data, it was evident that those who had reached equilibrium had a less distressing experience on entry and appeared more willing and able to make use of the support that was available at Feltham. Although prior prison experience may have been helpful, it was not the most important factor in ensuring equilibrium was reached.

Being thrown off balance and moving backwards

Adaptation was a dynamic process. Although prisoners could progress in a positive direction from liminality to acceptance and then to equilibrium, they also could move backwards. Although it is not possible to say whether individuals who reached equilibrium found life more difficult after one month, some individuals who reached the stage of acceptance were thrown off balance and moved back into the acute liminal zone. One individual smashed up his cell and was relocated in the segregation unit because it all became 'too much' for him. He was expecting a visit from his girlfriend, but she had failed to attend. A young man who had been in prison before, and who had begun to feel more settled, had relapsed into a state of despair. His accounts given at the second interview indicated that he was beginning to get to know some prisoners, to recognise some staff from before, to sort his cell out, and to get involved in the prison regime. However, he did not have the capacity to sustain this level of social and psychological adaptation. He was thrown off balance by failing to receive a visit. Understandably, his ability to manage his sense of separation and loss was insufficient at this point in time.

Another individual was physically attacked on association. He was stabbed with a fork in the mouth, and this caused him a great deal of distress. He had previously reported that he felt safe, more settled and familiar with life on the wing; he was beginning to sleep better. He had been taken to a hospital outside the prison to receive stitches and found retuning to the prison difficult. The attack jolted him psychologically and made him see the world in a different way. He felt fearful and was withdrawn.

Finally, one individual, who had also been progressing well in his first month, went to court and had received a sentence of two and a half years. Although he expected to be found guilty, the length of the sentence was unexpected: he could not accept how long he would be in prison. Prior to this decision, he was beginning to accept the reality of imprisonment but this sentence forced him to come to terms with yet another element of his reality, the duration of his stay in prison. He found it very difficult to regulate his thoughts and emotions and did not know which way to turn. It appeared that his level of distress was too high and had smothered any effective coping strategies he previously could have employed.

Resilience and surviving the first month

In summary, within the first month in prison, individuals differed in their levels of adaptation. As Adams (1992) stated, 'adjustment varies across individuals and settings […] and varies for the same individuals across time' (Adams 1992: 282). It has been argued that there are three modes of adaptation: practical, social and psychological, and it has been argued that prisoners have the potential to pass through three stages in the process of adaptation: liminality, acceptance, and a move towards equilibrium. Most individuals improved in some ways practically, socially and psychologically as time progressed. However, only a small number of individuals managed to progress to equilibrium within 30 days; this group included both first-time and returning prisoners. Time in prison brought with it, to some extent, the ability to adapt practically, but it did not secure social and psychological adaptation. For these adaptations to occur, the prisoner had to rely on the social and psychological resources he had imported with him into prison and to seek and receive the support that was available to him in the prison. Adapting to prison life was not a linear and simple process. It was not predictable, given that positive and negative life events, internal and external to the prison, continued to affect prisoners in different ways. Although individuals who had achieved some equilibrium might have been less likely to be thrown off balance, they might still have been susceptible to this.

Those who were able to progress to equilibrium showed resilience in the face of adversity. These individuals were more able to draw on whatever resources they had available to them and were able to exert some control over their environment. On the other hand, those who were less fortunate and who remained in the liminal zone had less resilience, were more vulnerable, and had fewer internal and external resources available to them. These individuals experienced more troublesome interactions with the environment and personnel of the prison. Although they, too, were surviving, their existence was more painful than that of those who adapted more positively. The concept of resilience is a useful way of thinking about how people differentially adapt over time to life inside. The concept of resilience has been applied extensively to studies of human development (Masten and Powell 2003; Yates *et al.* 2003; Schoon 2006). Masten and Powell (2003) defined resilience as 'patterns of positive adaptation in the context of significant adversity'. They proposed that resilience requires two fundamental judgements: firstly, that the person is doing 'okay' (which they define as social competence) and, secondly, that 'there is now, or has been, significant risk or adversity' (p. 4). The prison would qualify as a context of 'significant adversity' (Sykes 1958; Johnson and Toch 1982) and as we have seen, some prisoners were more competent than others in their ability to adapt to it.

Schoon (2006) drew upon Bronfenbrenner's (1979) ecological perspective to development and Elder's (1998) life-course approach, and put forward a developmental-contextual model for the study of resilience. Although this is a model of human development over time, it may offer a useful framework for understanding how young men adapt to prison life, an additional transition that these young men have to make within their lifespan. Schoon's (2006) model includes a number of multilevel spheres (individual, family, neighbourhood, institutions and socio-historical context) that interact with one another and that influence an individual's ability to adjust over time. Masten and Powell (2003) also identified three major categories of protective factors for positive adaptation: personal qualities, relationships, and community resources and opportunities. Personal qualities which act as protective factors include cognitive abilities, self-efficacy, self-esteem, sociability, self-regulation skills and a positive outlook on life. Relationships which do so include the quality of parenting which the individual received, close relationships with competent adults, and connections to pro-social peers. Finally, the helpful community resources and organisations include access to good schooling, the quality of the neighbourhood, and the quality of social services and health care. Schoon (2006) also takes into account the 'transactional nature of development over time [and focuses on] the reciprocal interactions between risk experiences and individual adjustment, which are embedded within the wider social-historical context' (pp. 25–6). This model stresses the importance of understanding the individual within context. When understanding how young men adapt to prison life, it is essential that a contextual account is provided. I have examined adaptation within one social context, HM YOI Feltham, and have done so by examining the adaptation process over a period of one month. However, it must be recognised that this month was only a small moment of time in the developmental path of these individuals through life. To understand more fully why some young men adapt more successfully than others, it would be beneficial to explore what point in his life trajectory each individual is at, to understand what his experience of life has been up until his entry (or re-entry) into prison, and to understand what resources he has accumulated along the way. The later chapters of this book will further suggest the importance of understanding what young men bring with them into prison in the way of early familial experiences and social and psychological resources.

Notes

1   Interviews with staff members on different units confirmed that staff on the induction unit were especially sensitive to prisoners' problems. Staff who worked on the induction unit described their task as preparing prisoners for the rest of their custodial experience and acknowledged that they had to be more patient and understanding, because these prisoners were newly received into the establishment.
2   The term 'sosh was used by staff and prisoners to refer to *association* by abbreviation.

Chapter 4

Supportive transactions between staff and prisoners

Chapter 3 outlined three different modes of prisoner adaptation: practical, social and psychological. Social adaptation comprised many different factors. Prisoners had to learn to interact with staff and with their peers, to become involved in the regime, and to manage relationships outside prison. In this chapter, I focus on one aspect of social adaptation in particular: the transactions between prisoners and staff. How is support provided? How is it perceived? And what factors facilitate and inhibit prisoners' willingness to engage in such supportive transactions? The chapter draws on observations, qualitative data from interviews with prisoners within their first month, and a survey of prisoners' willingness to seek support.

It is important to study social support in relation to adaptation and maladaptation because it has been associated prospectively with mortality, and psychiatric and physical morbidity. It has been argued that it plays a stress-buffering role, protecting individuals from the detrimental impact of stressful life experiences, allowing people to adapt and change (Cohen and Wills 1985; Albrecht and Adelman 1987; Lakey and Cohen 2000). The stress-buffering role of social support is one of the most important consistent hypotheses to emerge from previous studies.

Social support has been examined to a limited extent among people in prison. The study, *Psychiatric Morbidity among Prisoners in England and Wales*, by the Office of National Statistics (ONS) found that the level of perceived social support was lower among prisoners than among adults in private households (Singleton *et al.* 1998). Lader *et al.* (2000) carried out further analysis of the ONS data but in relation to young offenders aged 16–20. Over a quarter of them had a severe lack of social support, while just over a tenth of 16–21-year-olds in the general household survey did. In prison, 13 per cent of young offenders had a primary group of less than three; this figure was 6 per cent in the general household survey; 23 per cent received no visits.

Biggam and Power (1997), in their study of young male prisoners in Scotland, argued that support was a protective factor. Indeed, 'social support could be considered as an important psychological and social variable that contributes to adjustment in prisons and the amelioration of stress'; social support, they suggest, acts as a 'coping assistant' (1997: 214). The authors found that inmates displaying psychological distress wanted more support from both their fellow inmates and officers. In fact, 'vulnerable inmates show a desire for a more "therapeutic" relationship with staff' (Biggam and Power 1997; see also Liebling and Price 1999). Biggam and Power (1997) found that perceived deficits in support from officers 'were the major predictors of anxiety, depression and hopelessness' (p. 226).

In broad contrast to these findings, albeit with a different population, Lindquist (2000) found a negative relationship between *outside* social support and mental well-being among jail prisoners in the USA. It was found that married prisoners were more depressed and anxious than single prisoners, and that prisoners with more close relationships in jail reported higher levels of hostility. It may be that the closer one feels to those left behind. the more painful the experience of imprisonment becomes. (The role of *outside* social support and family ties will be considered in more detail in Chapters 6 and 7.)

Most recently, Liebling (2004) examined support in her study of the moral performance of five prisons in the UK. She found that support was positively correlated with other dimensions in her study, including humanity, respect, trust, relationships and fairness. Prisoners made distinctions between staff they found supportive and those they did not. She used a number of items to define the dimension of support, some of which I have used in this research. She found that 'as with the dimension "humanity", notions of "concern and understanding" may be a stronger test of the notion of support than our other questions' (Liebling 2004: 254). The qualitative data about young adults in Feltham support this proposition.

Sources and types of support

Within Feltham, there were a number of different individuals who provided support to prisoners: prison officers, gym officers, link workers, drug workers, probation officers, psychologists, psychiatrists, nurses, doctors, chaplains, counsellors, education staff, workshop instructors, volunteers/prison visitors, and outreach workers. On some occasions, senior managers had a supportive part to play too. These different sources of support functioned through both informal and formal channels. Informally supportive exchanges occurred on an *ad hoc* basis. For example, support was provided during cell checks, during wing movements, when unlocking cells, when escorting prisoners to and from visits, or when chatting in the association period. These situations might be seen as windows of opportunity during which supportive exchanges could flourish within the custodial setting. Prisoners frequently asked different questions to different people whenever they saw them on the wing. On a daily basis, I saw numerous supportive exchanges between prisoners and different members of staff. More structured, formal support was also available at Feltham. Firstly, if problems were revealed during the interview on the first night by a prison officer and a link worker, the individual would subsequently be referred to different staff members. They included the medical staff, the outreach team, drug workers, the counselling service, or one of the agencies that formed part of the voluntary sector (e.g. the group Supporting Others through Volunteer Action (SOVA), who gave one-to-one tuition to individuals who had difficulties reading and writing). A prisoner that arrived on an open F2052SH was automatically referred to the outreach team, who saw him immediately or within 24 hours. The identification of problems became more difficult at a later stage when prisoners were on the normal units, but support was formally available then through the referral process. This process, which had been improved as part of the Safer Locals Programme, enabled prisoners to be seen by different members of staff if particular problems had been identified or if prisoners actively sought such help.

Laireiter and Bauman (1992) stated that not every person can satisfy every support need, and that some types of support can be only provided by certain people. We must therefore consider the precise source of support in our questions. Individuals had different needs in prison, and different modes of support were required to meet these needs. Support has been conceptualised in terms of the functions it is thought to play in various different ways. For example, Weiss (1976) identified six basic needs that social support can provide: attachment, social integration, opportunity for nurturance, sense of reliable assistance, reassurance of worth and guidance. From their review of a number of different multidimensional models of social support, Curtona and Russell (1990) postulated that five basic support dimensions appear in most of them. These include emotional support, social integration and social network support, esteem support, tangible aid and informational support.

In Feltham, I identified four main types of support that the staff provided: informational, material, emotional and physical. These forms of support also corresponded to forms of peer support (delineated in the next chapter) but also differed somewhat. Informational support was the provision to prisoners of the information that they required in order for them to become familiar with the regime and regulations of the prison; it generally took the form of an induction programme and thereafter of answering any questions that the prisoners had. Material support was the provision of the basic essential commodities, such as access to clean clothes or essential material possessions, and the ability to contact family and friends. Emotional support was the provision of opportunities to discuss concerns or feelings, and to listen effectively to them, in a safe, private and confidential environment. Finally, physical support denoted the provision of a safe environment for the prisoner. As Chapter 2 showed, the prisoners did not always perceive Feltham to be a safe place, and this perception was the cause of considerable distress. Staff played a major role in securing prisoners' perceptions of safety.

Understanding perceptions of support

How did prisoners perceive this support? A key finding in previous studies has been that *perceived support* is more important in buffering the effects of stress than *received support* (Cohen and Wills 1985). *Received* support is defined as 'real interactions between people who exchange support', while *perceived* support refers to 'the generalised experiences of being supported from the social environment and the general perception of availability of supporting persons and actions' (Laireiter and Bauman 1992: 37). Indeed, 'the data suggest that whether or not one actually receives support is less important for health and adjustment than one's beliefs about its availability' (Cohen *et al*. 2000: 5). It is *perceptions* of social support which may lead an individual to appraise the situation as less stressful, and it is this perception that will lead to a stress-buffering effect. This model is related to the theory of Lazarus and Folkman (1984) about the appraisal of stressful events and coping, discussed in the previous chapter.

My own quantitative data in Table 4.1 provide a general measure of perceived support at Feltham. This table shows the statements that constituted the dimension 'prison support' and details the percentage of prisoners who strongly agreed or agreed with the statements about the support that they perceived to be available. As Table 4.1 shows, the dimension of prison support included an item pertaining to safety and

Table 4.1 Percentage of prisoners who strongly agreed or agreed with items relating to prison social support

Item	%	N
I feel cared about most of the time in this prison	25.7	18
I have been helped a lot by a member of staff in this prison with a particular problem	35.7	25
I receive support from staff in this prison when I need it	58.6	41
Staff in this prison show concern and understanding towards me	45.7	32
Staff help prisoners to maintain contact with their families	38.9	27
I feel I am trusted quite a lot in this prison	28.6	20
I trust the offficers in this prison	40.0	28
This prison is good at delivering personal safety	41.4	29

N = 70

two items pertaining to trust. These quantitative responses show that perceptions of support are bound together with perception of safety and trust. Just over a quarter of the people felt that staff trusted them, over 40 per cent of them felt they could trust the officers in the prison, and over 40 per cent of them strongly agreed or agreed that the prison was good at delivering personal safety. In general, a total of 58.6 per cent of participants perceived that they could receive support from staff when they needed it, and 45.7 per cent felt that staff showed them 'concern and understanding'. However, there appeared to be a difference when the word 'care' was used: then only 25.7 per cent of prisoners strongly agreed or agreed that they felt cared about most of the time in this prison at three days. The word 'care' has emotional connotations with which prisoners may have been uneasy when describing how supported they felt.

These figures provide some insight into the construct of perceived support within prison and into prisoners' global perceptions of that support. However, the picture presented thus far is limited. In order to understand support in prison more fully, it is essential to examine it within the social interaction in which it was embedded to see what moulded prisoners' perceptions of support. Many researchers have argued that it is essential for social support to be understood within the context of social relationships (Pierce et al. 1990; Kessler 1992; Reis and Collins 2000). Pierce et al. (1990) argued that attention must be paid not only to the intrapersonal context (stable and unique patterns of perceiving social relationships) but also to the interpersonal context (quantitative and qualitative features of relationships and networks) and the situational context (the event to which the relationship is responding). Indeed, Reis and Collins (2000) stated that relationships are the 'context for the development of social support' (p. 138). Leathman and Duck (1990) called for attention to a fine-grained analysis of the transactions of social support. They stated that 'any emphasis on the transactions of social support aims to tell us *how* social support is offered, how it is received, and what it means to a given person in the relational context' (p. 1). They proposed that social support should be seen to be 'embedded in relational, communicative, and, to some extent, phenomenological processes of everyday life' (p. 8). The day-to-day conversations and transactions of individuals should be examined in order to understand stress, social support and personal relationships. The nature of the social relationship between the interactants is thus of direct significance. In measuring supportive communication, the manner of the supportive message and that relationship should be included in the analysis (Albrecht and Adelman 1987).

What appears to be necessary when studying the process of social support is to consider not only the perceptions of social support but also the distinct *manner* of supportive behaviours or 'transactions', as they are embedded within interpersonal social relationships. We must understand how these relationships are structured, and the support that is derived therein. On the whole, research in the field of social support has concentrated more on the impact of global perceptions of social support and has somewhat neglected 'the interactional and relationship processes that foster or inhibit the expression and reception of support' (Reis and Collins 2000: 138). According to Eckenrode and Wethington (1990), research had failed to examine the process and outcome of mobilising social support adequately. What have not been fully appreciated are the 'personal and situational contingencies surrounding the activation of potentially supportive social ties, the patterning of supportive transactions over the course of adjustment, and how these factors may in turn be related to the efficacy of support mobilisation as part of the process of coping with stressful experiences' (p. 83). In order to understand these supportive transactions I asked prisoners about their experience of support provision at Feltham and they provided examples of when they felt supported and what constituted this support.

The importance of trust

Just as the quantitative data revealed that trust was bound to perceptions of support, trust also lay at the centre of accounts of supportive transactions given within the qualitative interviews. When I asked about trust, many prisoners reported that it was an extremely important aspect of life:

> [Interviewer: What does the word *trust* mean to you?]
> That is a serious word. That is a serious word. It is not a game. [Prisoner]

Prisoners provided various definitions of *trust*. Some prisoners defined *trust* as 'basically putting my life in someone else's hands'. Others used money as an analogy to describe what they perceived as trust:

> [Interviewer: What does it mean to trust someone?]
> I reckon trust is if I have £50,000 and put it down, and my brothers are around, and I come back a month later and it is still there. You get me? [Prisoner]

The prerequisites to prisoners forming a trusting relationship with prison staff were that the staff should respond in a timely manner and that they should not break promises or make promises they could not keep. Often trust was developed from responding to prisoners' practical concerns. If the members of staff demonstrated that they were listening to the more minor concerns (for example, the request for a brush to clean their cell), then prisoners became more willing to approach them with emotional problems in the future. The response of staff to practical problems served as a testing ground for trust to be established or distrust to be confirmed. Trust in a member of staff therefore required them to fulfil what they said they would do. The discussion below, from a section of one interview, reveals this point:

> [Interviewer: What is it about him that is decent?]
> I appreciate what he did yesterday, the servery thing. When I first got moved, they asked, 'If you lot want a job in the laundry or cleaning...'; and, basically, I want a job in the servery – or get moved to Teal wing; that's where all the food gets made. Could you get me moved to Teal? 'Cause that is enhanced – I'd rather be there. They said, 'Yeah'. 'And if not, can you get me a job in the servery?' So he said, 'I'll bear you in mind,' and he did, 'cause some of the govs say they'll do it for you, and they then forget. [Prisoner]
> [Interviewer: So did he come back?]
> Yeah, he did. [Prisoner]

[Interviewer: And how did you feel?]
I thought, yeah cool, at least someone's listening to what I was saying. Some of the govs will say, 'Yeah, yeah', and then don't do it. He did. It was only for a day but I can see what he did. [Prisoner]

Prisoners recognised when officers showed a genuine concern with their problems. They trusted staff who did show such concern and felt supported by them, as this example illustrates:

[Interviewer: Do you trust the staff?]
So far they have been kind. I trusted someone on Kingfisher. I told him my personal problems 'cause, like, my dad wasn't speaking to me, and, like, after about a week my mum must have been crying, and my dad must have felt sorry for her, and then I spoke to my dad and I chatted to him, and I told the governor, and he was so happy, happier than me! He was, I thought, he was more happier than me. He was all smiling and everything and said, 'I am very happy for you,' and even shook my hand. [Prisoner]
[Interviewer: Which one?]
Mr X. Even on Christmas Day, he finished work at 5.30, and, you know, everyone wants to go home on Christmas Day, but he weren't doing that. After he finished he come to my cell and was chatting to me, and said, 'You've got to learn from your mistakes,' and he was talking to me for about half an hour and I was thinking, boy, at least he can go home for his dinner, but he is not, he is talking to me! [Prisoner]

The most frequent way of describing trust in prison was by referring to confidentiality: the ability to tell someone something and know that he would not tell anyone else. Trust in staff entailed telling them something in confidence and being certain that they would not tell other people. As one prisoner commented:

They tell me it's in confidence, and then a couple of days later some other people come to see me about my problems, and then someone else, and then someone else, and they already know the information I told a certain member of staff. I'm thinking: how is that possible if I'm told it's confidential? [Prisoner]

Prisoners found it difficult to disclose personal problems to staff, as they had little trust in them.

However, many prisoners expressed a distinct lack of trust in other situations, regardless of which individual they were describing and regardless of the institution or social setting. Many felt that they could not trust anyone in their lives, often including their own peers and families:

> [Interviewer: Why don't you trust people?]
> That will get people fucked up in life if you trust too much people. I know that for a fact. My brothers have told me that. Sometimes you can't even trust family. [Prisoner]

> I don't really trust no one in here. I don't trust no one. You never know. People, like, people are like snakes. They are all smiley-smiley with you. If you are playing pool and you beat them at pool, they could just turn sour and could be plotting against you. [Prisoner]

> [Interviewer: So, is there anyone here you can trust?]
> No. [Prisoner]

When a prisoner entered prison with an already low level of trust, the staff had a difficult task to engage with him and develop a trusting relationship. At the same time, young men at Feltham wanted staff to provide them with certainty, to let them know what was happening, to give straight answers, to be reliable and not to make false promises. For many prisoners in Feltham, there was a tension between not being able to trust staff and realising that being able to trust staff could be beneficial.

The importance of manner

Nevertheless, staff could have an influence on the extent to which prisoners trusted them. One prisoner described how he trusted a member of the outreach team, because of the *manner* in which he dealt with the prisoner, beyond the specific solution offered to the problem:

> [Interviewer: What does the word *trust* mean to you?]
> To trust someone, I don't really… Make sure it is confidential. With X, when I first spoke to him, I knew I could trust him. It was by the way he put himself over to me. He understood what I was saying. Some of them can't be fucked. [Prisoner]
> [Interviewer: What way did he put himself across?]
> He sat there and listened to what I had to say. He sat there and listened.

Word for word, he sat there and listened, and he come back with answers for me. These I can't trust. I will be able to trust them, but it will be hard. They need to listen and understand what I am saying, and then I can trust them. It don't just work like that. [Prisoner]

I asked another prisoner:

[Interviewer: What makes you not trust an officer?]
It depends on how they are with you. Some people are moody. If you see they are moody, you can't go up and speak to them. Others invite you by cracking jokes. You can tell by their body language. They are more open. [Prisoner]

As he puts it, 'It depends on how they are with you'. 'How', or manner, is what matters. In order for prisoners to feel supported, they also expected a number of other qualities from staff. Prisoners were aware of the moods of officers and often commented upon their facial expressions: they perceived some as 'moody' and others more favourably, as having a relaxed, easy-going manner.

[Interviewer: What about the older woman you mentioned?]
She is good, man. She has a laugh and relaxes the mind, you get me? Ease off the mind. You get me? [Prisoner]
[Interviewer: You said she is caring person. What is it about her that is caring?]
She is always nice and polite. She is not rude or nothing. If you are nice to her, she'll be nice to you. She's always got a nice smile on her face, not a screw face, and this and that which is good. [Prisoner]

Officers who were able to demonstrate a sense of humour were rated highly by prisoners, and this manner of interaction supported prisoners on a day-to-day basis. Humour enabled staff to get to know prisoners and encouraged prisoners to feel less intimidated when interacting with them. Humour, when used appropriately, was an effective vehicle to make prisoners feel supported. Support in prison did not have to be elicited in an emotional and gentle manner; in fact, that offering of emotional care could be counter-productive. They wanted human contact without obtrusive intimacy, as shown in the following comments:

[Interviewer: How supportive have the staff been here?]
They support you in a different sort of way. They don't support

you as in sit you down and make you worry about your mum, but they make your life in Osprey humorous. They crack jokes with you, they play games with you, not games, but like games, as in things that you say, they will turn it around and make you sound stupid, which is funny. [Prisoner]

[Interviewer: The ones that are all right, what is different about them?]
They just speak to us and make jokes. They are all right. If you were to say something to them, they'd listen, and if you were to ask for something, or can I use the phone, 'cause I ain't had no time to use the phone, they let you out. [Prisoner]

To be supported, the prisoners also wanted to be understood. One prisoner explained to me that he would talk only to one member of staff, a member of the outreach team. I asked him why, what was different about him, and he explained:

He is down to earth. He is real. He is not talking what he has been taught to talk. He is talking what he feels and what he actually thinks, and not what he is told to think. [Prisoner]
[Interviewer: What is his approach?]
His approach is one of the best I've seen. He is cool and he's calm. [Prisoner]
[Interviewer: How does he act towards you?]
He is relaxed. He takes me into a room, asks me what's wrong; I tell him. If it is to do with my mum, he'll make me call my mum. He'll crack jokes with me as well, which eases it, and if he says he is going to do something, he does it as well. He doesn't say it and then wait till the door is closed, and it goes out the other ear. [Prisoner]

Overall, the prisoners felt supported when the manner of staff was approachable and familiar, rather than formal, and when they seemed to demonstrate personal concern rather than simply meeting needs grudgingly. As well as valuing staff members who met their informational and material needs, they also valued and trusted staff members who understood and listened to them.

Prisoners perceived support when staff engaged with them personally, for one deprivation of prison life is the restricted opportunity to communicate with others. Many prisoners valued it when staff took time to talk and felt supported when staff listened to them during their interactions. Of course, the busy staff often stated that they found it difficult to take time to talk and listen to prisoners, but they simultaneously recognised the importance of such interactions. I asked one prisoner:

[Interviewer: Have you been helped out by staff since being here?]
Well, they make me feel good. Other prisons, yeah, from what I've experienced, even when you've got a problem and you go and confront them, they don't even want to listen. They just say 'Get up, get up', but over here it is different. They talk to you if you've got any problems. They listen to you. [Prisoner]

Prisoners also felt supported when a staff member himself initiated the supportive exchange and was able to recognise that they may have particular problems. This initiative from the staff was of particular importance, given the reluctance of the prisoners to seek support. Prisoners commented that they were surprised that staff detected when they felt worried or were experiencing particular problems. This proactive manner of interaction symbolised that staff had an interest in them and affected their perceptions of support:

[Interviewer: What do you mean by support?]
Coming round to your cell and saying, 'Are you all right?' Not just opening your flap and closing it again. What else? At least one person, like, say, three people a day speaking to an officer one at a time. That would help. [Prisoner]

The governor come to my cell and he goes to me, 'Come to association,' and I said, 'No, I am proper tired,' and he said 'Are you all right?' If it was some of the other governors, they'd be like, 'Fuck it,' and slam the door, but he asked if I am all right, is there something wrong, and I said, 'No, I am just tired'. And he said, 'That's cool'. [Prisoner]

[Interviewer: Did you appreciate that?]
Yeah, 'cause he asked me if I am all right, you get me? He cared for me a bit, asking me about my welfare, you get me? [Prisoner]

The prisoners valued staff who were proactive, as they perceived it, when a particular incident was preying on their minds. For example, one prisoner recalled an argument in the servery when he had not been given any ice cream because another prisoner, working in the servery, told him that the ice cream was not halal. After the argument, he returned to his cell with an orange to eat and ruminated upon his difficulties, grave to him. He was not left alone, however:

The next governor doesn't give a toss, but this one, he came to my cell and said, 'You all right?' [...] The officer came up and explained to me why they didn't give me the ice cream, 'cause I walked off, and said, 'You lot are trying to stitch me up'. So I just walked up and took my dinner and ate it, and I was laying on my bed, and he come and he explained about the thing and I said, 'That's all right, if that's the case as long as I know'. [Prisoner]
[Interviewer: How did that make you feel?]
It was all right. He was showing some concern. It was cool. [Prisoner]

He really appreciated the fact that the officer came back to his cell and talked to him privately about it. It highlighted to him that the member of staff had paid attention to him as an individual. Overall, prisoners said that they felt 'wanted', as they put it, when staff initiated supportive exchanges. One prisoner recalled:

Well, I was emotional in my cell and the members of staff said, 'We are going to get outreach. You are emotional and in a state of stress, but you could [harm yourself], not saying you are going to do something, but you could.' So I spoke to outreach and they were really helpful. They are polite and that, and they are experienced, they know what to say to make you feel better. [...] It makes you feel wanted and that. [Prisoner]

The word 'wanted' was one that was used by several prisoners: it suggested that there was a desire to be accepted by prison staff; there was a need to belong. Although many prisoners stated that they did not like the staff, at the same time some said that they were eager to be liked by the staff; they wanted to be seen favourably in their eyes. There was a curious tension between the negative attitudes of prisoners towards staff and their wish that staff should hold positive attitudes towards them.

Another important aspect of enhancing an individual's level of perceived support was for prisoners to be treated with respect (Liebling 2004). One prisoner stated:

The ones who are level-headed talk to you like you are human. Some of them talk to you like you ain't nothing. You're in prison so you ain't nothing. [Prisoner]
[Interviewer: What are the ones who talk to you like you are human like?]

When you come off association, you can sit down and talk to them for a minute, yeah, talk to them for a minute, rather than just staring at you. [Prisoner]

They'd have to be on a level with me if you know what I mean. Someone that, an officer that I get along with obviously. I wouldn't go to one I didn't do, you know what I mean? [Prisoner]

Respect was also linked to trust. If a member of staff talked to the prisoner with respect, listened to him and responded in a timely manner, he would be more likely to trust the staff member:

[Interviewer: What would it take for you to start trusting an officer?]
For them to respect you more. To respect you more, listen to you more. When you ask for something, they say, yeah, in a minute, and they forget about it. [Prisoner]

Associated with being treated with respect was the manner in which staff used their power. Prisoners were aware that staff held more power than they did and were sensitive to officers who used their power disproportionately. This dislike of others' power might explain the prisoners' common wish that staff approach them in a humorous, down-to-earth or 'real' manner. As folk psychologists, the prisoners made their own observations and drew their own conclusions about the world of the prison. They felt unsupported by staff who treated them in a childish manner, as they wanted to be treated like adults and would only perceive support if this occurred. Prisoners' perception of support was also influenced by how they perceived the officer to view his or her role. Prisoners who felt that the officers viewed their role as punitive felt less supported by them. Officers who aimed to facilitate an improvement for the prisoner were perceived as more supportive:

They deal with you nicely, you know? That they want to look after you, they want to help you. It's not like they want to lock you down and say, 'That's the end of your life'. They maybe want to make you a changed person or something like that. [Prisoner]

Perceptions of support were thus intertwined with perceptions of trust and the manner in which a prisoner was addressed. The manner in which a problem was solved was as important as solving it. Perceived support was complex and covered many different aspects of an interaction. Prisoners had a clear view of how they wanted to be treated by staff, and at the heart of this view was the desire to be treated as a human being.

From these detailed interviews with prisoners within their first month, it became apparent that to offer social support did not just require staff to meet prisoners' needs by solving or managing their problems. The perceptions, and so the efficacy, of social support differed according to the *manner* in which staff interacted with them and the extent to which prisoners felt they could *trust* staff. When I asked prisoners what would make them feel more supported, many of the responses related to specific issues such as the fulfilment of their material needs, more activities to occupy their time, or help with maintaining contact with their loved ones outside prison. However, the majority of responses pertained not only to the needs being met but also to the *manner* in which staff interacted with them. This *manner* was at the core of what was perceived to be supportive and what was not. The prisoners most frequently responded that they wanted staff to talk to and listen to them more. They wanted staff to show an interest in them, to take time to understand, to be more approachable, and to show and feel concern.

Willingness to seek support

However, every supportive transaction by definition requires two social actors: the person giving support and the person receiving it. The prisoners' willingness to seek support adds complexity to the relationship between social support and distress. This willingness has been examined by Hobbs and Dear (2000). In their study, a sample of 187 male prisoners in a maximum-security prison in western Australia completed measures on their willingness to seek practical and emotional support for eight different types of problems.[1] The authors found that prisoners would rarely seek social support and that, if they did, they would more likely seek support for a problem relating to placement in the prison. Hobbs and Dear (2000) concluded that 'prisoners appear to be least willing to approach staff for those types of problem that are most important from a suicide prevention point of view, and are generally reluctant to seek emotional support from officers' (p. 136). The authors found that prisoners would hardly ever approach officers for problems relating to family, personal problems or conflicts with other prisoners. In this final section of the chapter, I turn to the prisoners' willingness to seek support from staff and prisoners at Feltham. I adapted a questionnaire devised by Hobbs and Dear (2000) and surveyed a total of 182 prisoners about their willingness to seek support from different sources for both practical and emotional problems. Responses were rated on a seven-point Likert scale from 1 (= not at all) to 7 (= definitely would). (The background and demographic information of the sample are detailed in Chapter 1.)

Seeking practical support

Table 4.2 shows the percentages of respondents who scored above a cut-off point of 5 for each of the sources of practical support (in descending order). A total of 55.8 per cent of prisoners were willing to approach the chaplain, and 50.8 per cent of prisoners were willing to approach an officer. Respondents rated all other sources under 50 per cent. Table 4.3 shows the ranking of different sources of practical support according to their mean scores. Prison officers appeared to be the first choice for prisoners when they had a practical problem, followed by the chaplain, fellow prisoners, and a member from the outreach team. Telephoning the Samaritans was rated the lowest for practical support, an unsurprising finding, as Samaritans were unlikely to be able to solve practical problems, as they had no direct contact with the prison itself. I carried out one-way ANOVAs with Scheffé post-hoc comparisons in order to reveal any significant differences between the officers and other sources of practical support. Prisoners were statistically more willing to turn to an officer for practical assistance than to eight other sources (namely, education staff, workshop instructors, drug workers, gym officers, medical staff, volunteers, listeners and the Samaritans).[2] There were no differences between officers and other prisoners, the chaplain and outreach workers as sources of practical support.

Table 4.2 Percentage of prisoners scoring above 5 for each source of practical support

Source	% scoring over 5
Chaplain	55.8
Officer	50.8
Drug worker	40.4
Outreach worker	37.1
Education staff	34.3
Prisoner	34.3
Listener	30.3
Gym officer	25.6
Volunteer	23.7
Doctor or nurse	23.2
Workshop instructor	22.9
Samaritans	20.8

Table 4.3 Ranking of sources for practical support

Rank	Source	M	SD
1	Officer	4.56	2.1
2	Chaplain	4.47	2.1
3	Prisoner	3.57	2.2
4	Outreach	3.56	2.1
5	Drug worker	3.50	2.4
6	Education	3.46	2.3
7	Listener	3.29	2.3
8	PE instructor	3.17	3.2
9	Nurse or doctor	3.14	3.1
10	Voluntary sector	2.89	2.9
11	Workshop instructor	2.85	2.9
12	Samaritans	2.56	2.6

Seeking emotional support

The situation differed when the prisoners considered *emotional* support, however. Table 4.4 presents the percentages of respondents who scored above a cut-off point of 5 for each of the sources of emotional support in descending order. All percentage scores were lower for emotional support than practical support, except for the chaplain. A total of 58.4 per cent of respondents were willing to approach the chaplain with a personal problem. The prison listeners were the next most popular category of sources, followed by drug workers and members of the outreach team. Table 4.5 shows the ranking of different sources for this emotional support according to their mean scores. As in the percentage results, prisoners were most willing to speak to the chaplain, followed by a prison listener, a member of the outreach team, and a drug worker. They were least likely to report a willingness to speak to a gym officer.

Again, for emotional support, I carried out one-way ANOVAs with Scheffé post-hoc comparisons in order to reveal any significant differences between the chaplain and other sources of support. Prisoners were statistically more willing to seek support from the chaplain than *all* other sources.[3] Furthermore, although prisoners were most willing to turn to an officer for practical assistance, when emotional problems arose, officers were ranked only sixth out of 12 sources. The chaplain remained a reasonably popular source, regardless of whether the problem was practical or emotional. (Of course, the heading of 'chaplaincy' refers to religious leaders of various religions,

Table 4.4 Percentage of prisoners scoring above 5 for each source of emotional support

Source	% scoring over 5
Chaplain	58.4
Listener	30.9
Drug worker	30.7
Outreach worker	29.4
Prisoner	27.3
Officer	24.7
Samaritans	24.1
Medical staff	22.0
Education staff	17.2
Volunteer	14.6
Workshop instructor	11.8
Gym officer	10.4

Table 4.5 Ranking of sources for emotional support

Rank	Source	M	SD
1	Chaplain	4.52	2.4
2	Listener	3.20	2.1
3	Outreach worker	3.10	2.3
4	Drug worker	3.07	2.3
5	Prisoner	2.98	2.1
6	Officer	2.93	2.1
7	Samaritans	2.79	2.2
8	Doctor or nurse	2.65	2.1
9	Education	2.39	1.9
10	Volunteer	2.36	2.0
11	Workshop instructor	2.09	1.8
12	Gym officer	1.99	1.6

as the population of Feltham is diverse in its religious beliefs.) Many commented that they would speak to the chaplain because the chaplain was connected to religion and God. I asked one prisoner:

[Interviewer: Why would you choose the chaplain?]
Chaplaincy cause they work in the church and they have a society of listening to people, their sins and sorrows and the things they've been through. They are the next thing to family out of all the people in the prison. They are the next best thing to family. [Prisoner]

However, besides religious authority, it was again the manner of interaction which mattered: as the previous prisoner said, 'they have a society of listening to people'. Others commented that the chaplains were good listeners and gave good advice:

> He is a very nice guy. A helpful guy. He is one of the few people that will listen to all your problems. He will listen and advise you on what he knows, just like a normal person. He will give you advice that comes to his head. He is not an expert but he will give you advice still. [Prisoner]

Some prisoners said that they would prefer to speak to chaplains about personal problems because they were non-judgemental. They thought that other staff members might judge them for what they have done, as the staff members were part of the penal system. The chaplain, on the other hand, was described as follows:

> Chaplain, he was good. I've never really thought about religion before. He said people who get into trouble doesn't make them a lesser being. You shouldn't make other people judge. They are still human, 'cause a lot of people who do get in trouble, a lot of people will look at your criminal record, like when you go for an interview and say forget about it. They should think of the person. [Prisoner]

Once again, as in the previous discussions of officers' manner of interaction, we hear the concern with respect and being treated as a human being. As we have seen, the officers were perceived to offer greater practical support, but the manner of the chaplains made prisoners more willing to seek emotional support from these figures.

Seeking practical and emotional support from different sources

I conducted t-tests to ascertain whether, for each source of support, there were any significant differences between prisoners' willingness to seek practical assistance and their willingness to seek emotional assistance. Figure 4.1 shows the mean scores for each source in relation to practical and emotional support. Table 4.6 reveals that there were no statistically significant differences between their relative willingness to seek practical or emotional support from the chaplain, listeners, outreach workers, drug workers and the Samaritans. The most significant differences, between the willingness to seek practical as opposed to emotional support, emerged in relation to prison officers,

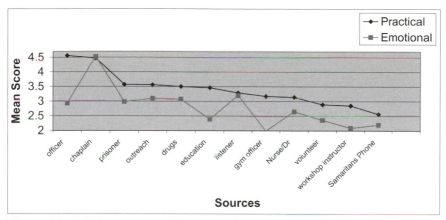

Figure 4.1 Willingness to seek support for practical and emotional problems

Table 4.6 Differences between willingness to seek emotional and practical support from each source

Sources	Practical		Emotional			
	Mean	SD	Mean	SD	T	Significance
Officer	4.56	2.1	2.93	2.1	7.01	**
Gym officer	3.17	3.2	1.99	1.6	5.59	**
Education	3.46	2.3	2.39	1.9	4.61	**
Workshop	2.85	2.9	2.09	1.8	3.41	**
Chaplain	4.47	2.1	4.52	2.4	−.19	NS
Drugs worker	3.50	2.4	3.07	2.3	1.68	NS
Outreach	3.56	2.1	3.10	2.3	1.78	NS
Nurse/doctor	3.14	3.1	2.65	2.1	2.13	*
Volunteer	2.89	2.9	2.36	2.0	2.33	*
Prisoner	3.57	2.2	3.98	2.1	2.45	*
Listener	3.29	2.3	3.20	2.1	.37	NS
Samaritans	2.56	2.6	2.79	2.2	−.87	NS

*p<.05; **p<.001.

gym officers, education workers and workshop instructors. From each of these people, prisoners were more willing to seek practical help than emotional. For some sources, their role as support provider was more differentiated than for others. Laireiter and Bauman (1992) noted that some types of support are best met from particular support providers. So, too, in Feltham, although practical assistance may have been sought from prison officers, gym officers, education workers and workshop instructors, those people were not the relatively favoured sources of emotional support.

The difficulties in seeking emotional support

Moreover, besides these differences in the types of support which prisoners were willing to seek from different agents, there was a general reluctance to seek support of an emotional sort. In interviews with prisoners in their first month at Feltham, many stated that they had not actively sought help from a member of staff, and they gave a number of reasons for this unwillingness, particularly in relation to emotional support. Many prisoners chose not to enter into a supportive transaction with the officers because they held a negative attitude towards them. This negative perception of authority figures was a theme that pervaded numerous interviews. The perceived role of the officer was fundamental to whether prisoners felt supported by staff. Likewise, their perceived role influenced prisoners' willingness to seek support from them. Many prisoners said they saw the role of the officer as solely one who opened and closed doors: a keyholder, not a support provider. Various prisoners stated:

> [Interviewer: Why can't officers help?]
> They just can't, man. What can they do? All they've got is keys to open doors and lock doors. Me personally, they can't help me. [Prisoner]

> [Interviewer: Can you tell the officers?]
> No. I don't know if it's the uniform or what. I just don't like them. I don't know. They kind of think they are police but not. They think they've got the same authority. It is weird. People who work in this jail with no uniform are more easy-going and down to earth and have a sense of humour and know what to say to you. [Prisoner]

There was also some resentment of their position in comparison with the perceived freedom of the staff:

> But if I talk to someone, say, a prison officer, I feel as if – as if I am talking to someone I dislike but at the same time I am pretending to get on with, you know? I have to live with this person for most of the time I am in here. Tomorrow they may go home and him or her, and him or her husband may not get on, he or she might not get fucked, and she or he will come back with

their problems and take them out on me. I'd rather not deal with someone like that. [Prisoner]

For these prisoners, talking to officers was out of the question. If prisoners were fundamentally opposed to the prison's staff, they would not seek help from them.

However, regardless of their current situation, for many prisoners, seeking support was not their usual coping strategy; they would not seek help from anyone. When they talked about their lives, they reported that they had been forced to be self-reliant throughout childhood and so had developed without enacting help-seeking behaviour. Many found it difficult talking about their problems because they were not used to doing so:

It is hard to say I am not all right, I am feeling shit. It is easier to say I am all right, I am all right, don't worry about me [Prisoner]

Moreover, as it was not a usual coping strategy, the perceived gain from seeking support was often seen as minor or temporary. Many prisoners felt that taking an independent stance had been necessary for survival through their teenage years. Many had been rejected by their family many years before; they had often spent time in children's homes or secure settings, and had had to learn to adapt to this way of life with independence and without support. At least, that is how they saw themselves:

I am a person that is independent. I really don't talk about things. I'd rather keep them to myself. I think I can manage by myself. It is one of them things I learned to cope with even when I was 13. On my thirteenth birthday, I ran away from my house. It is nothing to boast about, but I've been through that life. I know it is like a one man to me. [Prisoner]
[Interviewer: Did you choose this?]
Choose? I suppose. If you do a crime, that's the way it goes. When you go to the police station, no one is with you, your mum is not with you, no one is with you, you are by yourself, all by yourself. [Prisoner]

In particular, those who felt hopeless thought that talking to other people would not help, or rather that nothing would help. One prisoner stated:

> Talking can't help. I wouldn't talk to no one cause I don't think nothing can help you from thinking, you know? [Prisoner]

This feeling was understandable given the insoluble nature of many of their problems. Prisoners wanted solutions and often did not appreciate that seeking social support may not have provided a solution to their problems but may have helped them to manage their own problems more effectively. Seeking support might have helped these individuals to regulate their thoughts and emotions to greater effect. Particularly when prisoners felt distressed, they found it more difficult to seek help. (This is discussed more fully in Chapter 7.)

Not only was the perceived *gain* low; many perceived the *cost* of seeking support to be high. Indeed, receiving social support may lead to stigmatisation, a lowered sense of self-worth, and a feeling of guilt, burdening others with one's problems (Rook 1992). These risks may have a special dynamic in the prison environment. Rook (1992), stated 'contemporary work has been dominated by nearly unwavering enthusiasm for the consequences of social support' (p. 157). It is important that research include the possible negative perception of seeking support: as Vaux (1992) observed, many of the scales fail to include the negative aspect of the social support process (Vaux 1992). So, too, in Feltham, prisoners perceived that there were many costs in seeking support. In their social interaction, they perceived one cost to be the impact it had on their self-presentation towards other prisoners: seeking support seemed to be a revelation of weakness to others or, perhaps worse, to themselves. If a prisoner asked directly for help, he was obviously presenting himself as vulnerable in front of his peers:

> It is more of a losing-face sort of thing if you do. It is showing weakness, being depressed, and some people, unfortunately, do take advantage of weaknesses. [Prisoner]

Being able to 'stand on your own two feet' was respected in prison, and this prejudice may have served as a further barrier to seeking support and so losing respect:

> When it comes down to it, you've got your friends from road, but you are by yourself at the end of the day. If you can stand on your own two feet, people will respect that and want to be with you. [Prisoner]
> [Interviewer: So who doesn't get respect in prison?]
> Like that boy who came there. [...] He doesn't stand up for himself

and lets people push him about and his respect drops. Being able to stand on your own two feet. [Prisoner]

Another perceived cost to seeking support was the notion that this transaction would provide staff with more power. Officers had to exercise their power in a fair manner in order for this barrier to be weakened. I asked one prisoner about whether he was honest about his feelings when questioned by staff at Feltham:

> I was pretty honest but I guess I was just trying to get off the report thing to start work. That's all that was going through my head. Not the total truth, 'cause, like, I punched the wall on Saturday and they asked me why and I said, "Cause I was pissed off,' but it was because someone used the credit on my phone, and it was my girlfriend's birthday as well. Think I left my PIN number in my cell. [Prisoner]
> [Interviewer: And did you speak to anyone in health care about how you were feeling?]
> No. If you speak to anyone down there, they'll just keep you down there longer. I was telling them I was perfect. If you tell them what was really wrong with you, they'll keep you down there. [Prisoner]

A further cost of seeking support was that this behaviour symbolised an affiliation to the institution. The connection implied in such transactions was undesirable to prisoners who were struggling to accept the temporary world, as they saw it, in which they were forced to live. This was particularly the case when the young men first arrived in prison. Prisoners summed up this point well:

> Because they are strangers to me and I am also reluctant to fall into prison life where I'm relating to inmates and laughing and joking and carrying on as if they are my friends outside of prison and I'm relating to staff as if they are friends of mine. They're not: they are here to do a job. Those around me are not friends – they are people I have to encounter on a day-to-day basis. So, on that basis, I am reluctant to relate to staff, reluctant to relate to inmates, and reluctant to trust either. [Prisoner]

> They were telling me, can't really remember basically, it was going in one ear and passing through the other 'cause I was just thinking: what am I doing here? Why am I here? Why do I have

to be hearing this? I was just stressing out and couldn't wait to get in the cell. I was feeling ill too. I just couldn't believe basically I was in here. [Prisoner]

Because they did not want to accept their situation, prisoners often chose not to make use of any support on offer. However, the loss of control inherent in being in prison (as was discussed in Chapter 2) in fact forced prisoners to depend on others, and this forced dependency acted as a further barrier to seeking and receiving help. These individuals did not feel that they were in a position where they could choose to depend on the staff or not. As they were forced to depend upon the staff, accepting help was perceived not as positive choice but as further sign of their lack of control over themselves. To accept help seemed to strengthen their feelings of uncontrollability and uncertainty:

[Interviewer: What do you mean about depending?]
In prison you depend on – OK, you don't really depend, but you more or less do, on the governors. For example, when you come out on association, we have to sign up for pool and table tennis and it's up to them who they shout out who's on the table next. They become the big guys. For them to open your cell, you depend on them to turn the key. [...] I just don't want to fall under that regime. [Prisoner]

Moreover, those people who felt least in control over the outcome of their behaviour were also those who perceived less support. I found a small positive correlation between an internal locus of control and the perception of support within prison ($r = .30$, $p < .05$). It could be suggested that individuals who were more external in their locus of control were those who would be least willing to seek help, because they were less able to see the benefits that support may bring. As they felt that control lay in the hands of others, they were wary of relinquishing any more by asking for another's assistance. On the other hand, those who were more internal in their locus of control were more able to recognise the benefits that support could provide and also more willing to relinquish some control as part of a calculated transaction. These individuals felt more in control and perceived themselves able to elicit help from others, rather than perceiving themselves to be under the unswayable control of others.

Finally, the lack of trust that many individuals brought with them into prison was another core factor influencing their decision to seek help or not. There were four significant statistical findings. Firstly, there was a significant correlation between trusting staff and the willingness to seek support from officers for a *practical* problem (r = .52, p < .001). There was a second significant correlation between trusting staff and willingness to seek support from officers for an *emotional* problem (r = .65, p < .001). Thirdly, those who in the past had a *practical* problem and had received help for it were more likely to trust staff and felt more supported (than those who had a problem but did not receive support).[4] Fourthly, the same result appeared in relation to *emotional* support, although less markedly.[5] A likely explanation is that trusting staff was connected to a willingness to seek support, while having received assistance with a problem was important in developing trust and enhancing perceptions of support.

In summary, although there were barriers to seeking support, many individuals within Feltham did seek it, albeit with caution. They were more likely to seek help with practical rather than emotional concerns, as found by Hobbs and Dear (2000); they were also more likely to seek help from specific members of staff. A match between the mode of support and the source of support was essential in order for prisoners to perceive that they had been given assistance and to begin to benefit from it. An individual's perception of support was bound together with his perception of trust (as evidenced from the factor analysis and qualitative data analysis). The manner in which a member of staff dealt with a problem was crucial in determining how supported prisoners felt. In Chapter 6, I will examine differences between individuals in their perceptions of support, but before doing so, I will consider the role of peer support in prison.

Notes

1   The eight different types of problems included:
    1 stress related to legal proceedings, bail or parole;
    2 conflict or problems with other prisoners;
    3 conflict or problems with prison staff;
    4 problems relating to placement within the prison or the prison system;
    5 dissatisfaction with management decisions or regime restrictions;
    6 stress related to the general routine;
    7 family problems (including relationship problems);
    8 other personal or emotional problems.
2   $F_{(11, 2070)} = 12.45$, p < .001.
3   $F_{(11, 1958)} = 15.70$, p < .001.
4   A total of 45 individuals had a practical problem and received help for it (group 1); 37 had a problem and did not receive help for it (group 2). The mean score on 'trust' for group 1 was 3.76 (SD = 2.46); the mean score on 'trust' for group 2 was 2.54 (SD = 2.03), $t_{(80)} = 2.40$, p < .05. The mean

score on 'support' for group 1 was 4.20 (SD = 2.84); the mean score for 'support' for group 2 was 2.24 (SD = 2.01); $t(80) = 3.51$, $p < .01$. Individuals rated 'trust' and 'support' on a scale of 1–7.

5   A total of 41 individuals had an emotional problem and received help for it (group 1); 37 had an emotional problem and did not receive help for it (group 2). The mean score on 'trust' for group 1 was 3.82 (SD = 2.44); the mean score on 'trust' for group 2 was 3.08 (SD = 2.47), $t(77) = 1.35$, $p < .10$. The mean score on 'support' for group 1 was 3.81 (SD = 2.63); the mean score for 'support' for group 2 was 2.16 (SD = 2.14); $t(77) = 2.99$, $p < .01$.

Chapter 5

Peer interactions and relationships in prison

This chapter sets out to examine another aspect of social adaptation: how prisoners interacted with one another and formed relationships. It uses data from several different sources and includes observational data, two social network analyses, and qualitative data from interviews with prisoners within their first month. It looks at the level of peer interaction, the structure of these interactions, and some factors that may influence an individual's position on a wing. This chapter explores the difference between a social interaction and a social relationship and examines factors that facilitate and inhibit the formation of friendships in prison.

Some classic studies carried out several decades ago still provide a rich source of data on the dynamic processes that take place within penal settings and on many of the problems that prisoners face (Clemmer 1940; Sykes 1958; Mathiesen 1965; Irwin and Cressey 1962; Irwin 1970; Slosar 1978). In perhaps the most famous study, Sykes's (1958) ethnographic research attempted to uncover the structure and function of social relationships within prison and proposed that an 'inmate code' was the 'major basis for classifying and describing the social relations of prisoners' (Sykes and Messinger 1960: 9). He proposed that 'as a population of prisoners moves in the direction of solidarity, as demanded by the inmate code, the pains of imprisonment become less severe' (Sykes and Messinger 1960: 16). The postulation that solidarity can lead to a decrease in the pains of imprisonment is important: it implies that social relationships are somehow supportive in nature, protecting prisoners from the psychological distress that results from the pains of life in prison. More recent research in the community has argued that belonging, a similar concept, is a fundamental human need and, if threatened, can lead to a decrease in self-esteem and meaningful existence (Leary 2001). Goffman (1961), in his study of total institutions, stated that in order to reassemble themselves prisoners engage in a 'fraternalisation process' whereby 'socially distant prisoners find themselves developing mutual support' (Goffman 1961: 57). Through forming, prisoners can regain a sense of self and feel more in control of their environment.

In reality, however, Sykes (1958) noted that the reaction to the pains of imprisonment was not always that of coming together as a group. Rather than being collectivist, social relations in prison may also be highly individualistic: the inmate 'can enter into a war of all against all in which he seeks his own advantage without reference to the claims or the needs of other prisoners'; 'the society of captives lies balanced in an uneasy compromise', and this uneasy state leads to an imperfect solution to the pains of imprisonment (Sykes 1958: 83). Although Sykes saw the potential for social relationships to be supportive in nature, this potential was not always borne out in reality. On the contrary, one set of rules within the inmate code 'have as their central theme the maintenance of the self: Don't weaken' (Sykes and Messinger 1960: 9). Indeed, he argued that 'the rigors of the inmate's world are to be met with a certain self-containment and the excessive display of emotions has to be avoided at all costs'. Such behaviour is embodied in the prototypical 'right guy', the man who can 'take it' and so 'wins the admiration and respect of his fellow captives' (Sykes 1958: 100–1).

It appears that the inmate code would function to decrease the pains of imprisonment only for those who are more resilient in the first place. What is the fate of the prisoner who is suffering from more acute psychological pain, who cannot 'take it', and who exposes his vulnerability or weakness? Surely, the inmate code becomes dysfunctional for him? If he follows the rule for self-maintenance, what may result is an inverse relationship between the need for support and its availability. Those who need support less may actually be able to seek and obtain it more easily, whereas those who are more in need of social support are the least likely to access it. The vulnerable prisoner may be determined to mask his weakness and refrain from seeking support in order to prevent a detrimental impact on his position within the hierarchy of inmates. This barrier to help-seeking behaviour was identified in the previous chapter, where some people worried that seeking help from staff, in particular, would make them vulnerable among their peers.

Clemmer (1940), on the other hand, in a study of a maximum-security prison in the USA, was less concerned with how the code was formed in the first place, and instead explored the extent to which prisoners embraced this inmate code. Clemmer described the prison as an atomised society in which impersonalisation was the general rule: 'that the majority of inmates themselves do not share the rather common impression that consensus in groups is strong behind the penitentiary walls' (Clemmer 1940: 123). Mathiesen (1965), in his study of a medium-security, treatment-orientated correctional institution in Norway, also found that 'though cohesive groups could be observed, a surprisingly large number of inmates appeared to live in relative isolation from others. Furthermore, the cohesive groups appeared quite unstable and subject to sudden disruptions' (Mathiesen 1965: 122–3).

These studies provide many insights into the social life of prisons and, through examining the structure and function of social relationships, they have provided a wealth of information on both solidarity and its lack. The findings of these studies imply, even if they do not state, a beneficial role for social support in reducing the pains of imprisonment (Sykes 1958). These studies, however, do not account for the presence of different levels of individual distress or sociability, nor for the impact that these differences have on the formation and maintenance of social relationships. Also, these studies do not fully articulate what the psychological significance of social relationships is for particular individuals, or what these relationships are like; nor do they examine the potential detrimental psychological impact of social ostracism. Moreover, it is not clear what role single dyadic ties play in the experience of imprisonment.

Social networks at Feltham

Firstly, we must obtain an overview of the social networks among prisoners at Feltham. As described in Chapter 1, each unit generally comprised cells that collectively held 56 prisoners. These were separated onto two sides with locked gates. Much social life occurred on these units. Prisoners interacted with one another on exercise, where they went out on the yard, and on association indoors. Prisoners interacted, and formed ties, with one another in a number of other locations within the prison too: on the wings, at workshop placements, at education or the pre-release programme, at the gym or football, waiting in reception, at health-care outpatients, at the chapel and in the library. They had further opportunities to interact with people from their unit when going to, or returning from, education, workshops, or a visit. Prisoners who had jobs on the unit had more time to interact with fellow workers as they were out of their cells most of the day.

They also on occasion had time to interact with prisoners who were still in their cells through passing items under their cell doors or taking an item from one cell to another. Interaction also took place between cellmates and through the cells' walls and windows.

Observing interactions on the wing

During my fieldwork, I spent time in the different parts of the prison and on each unit, carrying out observations of the prisoners' social life. In addition to these informal periods of observation, I also systematically spent a full day on each of four units from the time when the prisoners were unlocked for breakfast until the time when they were locked up after dinner (from 0730 until 1730; or until 2000 if they had evening association). I carried out full-day observations on Kingfisher, Partridge, Osprey and Mallard, and these observations provided some insight into prisoner social life. Life on the units was silent when the prisoners were locked behind their doors. Apart from the odd sound of music or shouting from a cell window, it was almost as if nobody else was in the prison except the officers. Prisoners came out of their cells to collect their meals, for exercise and association, and when being escorted to education, work, the gym, the visiting hall, or the chapel. They also emerged when an officer or another member of staff wanted to talk with them or when they were being moved within the prison or transferred to another prison. The opportunities to interact in prison were thus limited and structured by the regime or the transitions. Mathiesen (1965) argued that the lack of freedom to interact within prison was a contributing factor to a lack of solidarity among prisoners. Indeed, Cloward (1960) argued that 'the official system plays a vital part in regulating the types of inmate roles that emerge, the social functions they serve, and the relationships between them' (p. 35).

Prisoners at Feltham had most freedom to interact with one another and the officers on association. It is during this one hour of the day (1500–1600) that life on the wing was at its liveliest. From observations and interviews, it was evident that prisoners used their association time differently. Some participated in the activities that were offered on the wing during this time, such as playing pool, table tennis and arcade games, others were only concerned with making a telephone call and having a shower, while others would just sit throughout this period and not interact at all. Some individuals who had been in prison before, or were less distressed, managed their time on association well. They would come out, put their names down on all the lists straightaway (for pool, showers and telephone calls) and then interact with others, put in applications for a job or education, or sort out practical problems with the officers (for example, visits or money for the canteen). These individuals were the most proactive and within an hour could achieve a number of different tasks. They were the individuals more likely to have moved towards reaching the stage of equilibrium in their transition to prison. Those who lacked the social confidence and the practical skills struggled to achieve as much. The practical, social and psychological experience of association differed.

The peer networks that were formed revealed a complex mosaic of interactions. Although groups of three or four would be gathered, these groups did not remain static throughout the association period. Individuals would move from one area of the unit to another, perhaps talking to people playing pool and then moving over to others, sharing 'burn' or standing chatting. Others would sit throughout the entire time period, maybe talking to only one person, or none at all. These individuals also tended to sit near the officers, who would oversee the list for the pool table. There were other prisoners, however, who were not able to become group members within prison. Some were socially connected while others remained more isolated, talking to only one individual, or none at all: again, a variety of experiences.

Social ties on two wings

In order to provide a more systematic picture of these interactions, I gathered social network data from individuals from two sides on two units (Osprey and Partridge). As described in Chapter 1, each individual was asked to nominate from a list of names the people with whom he interacted the most. It must be remembered that these network analyses were based on the wings only, and, as explained, other ties might have been formed elsewhere in the prison, with people not from their own unit. (The background and demographic information of the samples are detailed in Chapter 1.)

Between the two wings, a total of 178 ties were nominated: 86 on Partridge and 92 on Osprey. The range of ties nominated did differ between the units. The number of ties nominated by the prisoners (whether reciprocated or not) ranged from 1 to 6 on Partridge and from 0 to 9 on Osprey. The range for reciprocal ties (mutual nominations) was 0 to 4 for Partridge and 0 to 6 for Osprey. Yet, the density of both networks was also very similar: .13 for Partridge and .14 for Osprey. Density ranges from 0 to 1 and gives a general measure of the level of interaction or activity in a network.[1]

This low level was confirmed by an analysis of the percentage of reciprocal ties. Of the 86 ties nominated on Partridge, only 42 were reciprocal (48.8 per cent) and 44 were non-reciprocal (51.2 per cent). Of the 92 ties nominated on Osprey, only 44 were reciprocal (47.8 per cent), and 48 were non-reciprocal (52.2 per cent). Both wings were therefore similar in the reciprocity of relationships. It is evident that although some people nominated an individual, in many cases the other individual did not nominate them back. Previous studies in the general community have concluded that reciprocity is important in forming relationships which can offer support. Antonucci and Jackson (1990) suggested that 'individuals take a long-term developmental view of their social exchanges' and thus develop a 'support bank', keeping tally of 'the amount of support or various benefits they have given to or received from others' (p. 178). However, it seemed that within the two wings examined in Feltham, individuals did not readily develop reciprocal ties. It also emerges from data below that they seldom saw these ties as ties that would endure beyond the immediate social world of the prison.

Table 5.1 shows the mean out-degree and in-degree dichotomous scores for the question, 'Do you consider him to be a mate of yours?' As can be seen, the mean out-degree (number of ties nominated) was 3.27 for Partridge and 3.46 for Osprey.[2] The mean out-degree for reciprocal ties only was 1.62 for Partridge and 1.58 for Osprey, similar results for both wings. Gillespie's (2003) study of prisonisation found that the mean number of close friends nominated was 1.52 (although he did not use social network analysis as a tool). These data, then, reveal a similar figure for the reciprocal ties.

Table 5.2 shows that every person on Partridge nominated at least one other person, but that on Osprey four individuals (15.4 per cent) did not nominate anyone. Gillespie (2003) found in his study that 15.5 per cent of individuals did not nominate anyone. For reciprocal ties, 50

Table 5.1 Mean out-degree and in-degree scores for 'mate'

| | Partridge | | | | Osprey | | | |
| | All | | Reciprocal only | | All | | Reciprocal only | |
	M	SD	M	SD	M	SD	M	SD
Mate out-degree	3.27	1.61	1.62	1.13	3.46	2.70	1.58	1.62
Mate in-degree	3.15	2.67	–	–	3.46	3.17	–	–

Table 5.2 Distribution of nominations

| | Partridge | | | | Osprey | | | |
| | All ties | | Reciprocal only | | All ties | | Reciprocal only | |
	%	N	%	N	%	N	%	N
0	0	0	19.0	5	15.4	4	19.0	5
1	19.2	5	31.0	8	15.4	4	50.0	13
2	11.5	3	19.0	5	7.7	2	12.0	3
3	26.9	7	0	–	19.2	5	0	–
4	19.2	5	31.0	8	7.7	2	8.0	2
5	11.5	3	0	–	11.5	3	4.0	1
6	11.5	3	0	–	7.7	2	8.0	2
7	0	0	0	–	3.8	1	0	–
8	0	0	0	–	7.7	2	0	–
9	0	0	0	–	3.8	1	0	–

per cent of individuals on Osprey had one reciprocal tie compared with 31 per cent on Partridge. On Osprey, however, three individuals (12 per cent) had between five and six reciprocal ties compared with none on Partridge. The distribution of reciprocal ties is therefore different on each unit.

Observations of life on the units revealed that many ties were dyadic rather than clique based. Most of the research examining social relationships between prisoners has placed an emphasis on whether individuals belong to groups or not (Clemmer 1940; Sykes 1958); little focus has been on dyadic relationships. Sykes's (1958) argument was focused at an intergroup level of analysis. He was primarily concerned with group solidarity, with inmates presenting a unified front against the officials. Is it possible that the pains of imprisonment can be managed through building single friendships with fellow prisoners? As Cohen and Taylor (1972) found from their ethnographic research conducted at a maximum-security prison in the UK, 'a single personal relationship may be called upon to sustain the various functions which would be spread across several friends in the outside world' (Cohen and Taylor 1972: 75).

Although individuals did stand together within groups of three or four, as discussed, they would also move between groups and individuals. Although some groups remained stable – for example, a group of Kosovan prisoners who played table tennis at the furthest corner of the wing on most days – many individuals migrated between different sets of individuals. In order to understand the extent to which interactions on the wings were dyadic or clique based, I generated digraphs from the two social network analyses. Then, in order to examine more closely the extent to which individuals were connected to everyone else in the network, I created digraphs that plotted reciprocal ties only. The network presented in Figure 5.1 is Partridge. As seen in this digraph, only one clique had formed, comprising three individuals (participants 1, 2 and 5). These individuals were all from Kosovo, all had been on the unit for more than one month, and all had jobs on the wing. There were also a number of dyadic relationships; however, some were isolated from the rest of the unit, and others were in a more central position within the network. For example, participants 9 and 10, who were cellmates, were isolated from the rest of the network, communicating with each other only on the wing. However, participant number 6 had three dyadic relationships, and each of these individuals also had other dyadic relationships. He therefore had more opportunity to come into contact with them. Others in the network had no reciprocal ties (participants 11, 12, 13, 15, 16 and 21). (Participant 16 was not included, as he did not take part in the study.)

Figure 5.2 shows the social network of reciprocal ties on Osprey wing. This digraph shows that four cliques existed. These groups

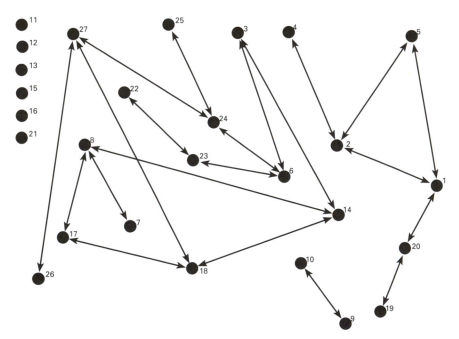

Figure 5.1 Digraph: Partridge wing

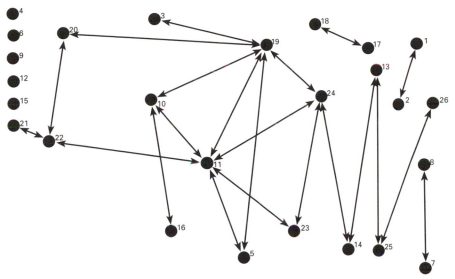

Figure 5.2 Digraph: Osprey wing

comprised the following individuals: group 1 (participants 11, 23 and 24), group 2 (participants 10, 11 and 19), group 3 (participants 5, 11 and 19) and group 4 (participants 11, 19 and 24). Participants 11, 19 and 24 belonged to more than one clique. Participant 11 belonged to all four, and both 19 and 24 belonged to three. Different background variables may help explain how these groups formed. For example, participants 5 and 11 both had jobs on the wing, and this increased their opportunity for interaction. Yet, there appeared to be no other obvious pattern: the groups were generally mixed ethnically and were from different geographical locations. Participants 11, 23 and 24 were not from London, and this may have been one factor that brought them together. Participants 11 and 23 also knew each other from a previous time in prison; the remaining individuals met during their current term. There were also a number of dyadic relationships, some of which were isolated and others that were in a more central position within the network. Others had no reciprocal ties at all (participants 4, 6, 9, 12 and 15).

Peer popularity on two wings

A social network analysis enables us to identify an individual's position on a unit. Some individuals were more isolated and others were more integrated and central to the network. In order to assess the extent to which an individual was isolated or central to the wing, I measured the number of in-degrees of each individual and the number of out-degrees. These values are presented in Figures 5.3 and 5.4 for Partridge and Osprey respectively. As can been seen in Figure 5.3, three of the 27 participants from Partridge had a large in-degree (participants 4, 6 and 14). They were nominated the most out of all the prisoners and received 7, 13 and 6 nominations respectively. These individuals did not nominate one another, however. This pattern differs from my findings in my pilot study at Brinsford of sentenced prisoners, where three received high in-degrees but also nominated one another. On Partridge, one prisoner received no in-degrees (participant 15), but certain factors may explain that: he could not speak English, was on a self-harm monitoring form, and was sharing a cell with another individual who was also very isolated.

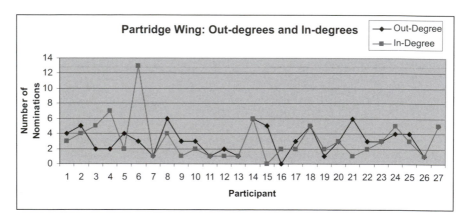

Figure 5.3 Partridge wing: out-degrees and in-degrees

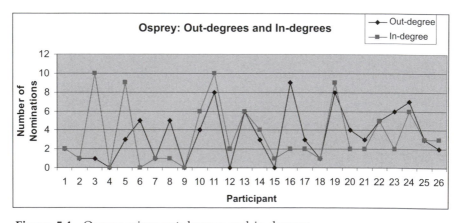

Figure 5.4 Osprey wing: out-degrees and in-degrees

As can be seen in Figure 5.4, four of the 26 participants on Osprey had a large in-degree (participants 3, 5, 11 and 19). They were nominated the most out of all the prisoners, with 10, 9, 10 and 9 nominations respectively, and some of them reciprocally nominated each other (11 and 19, 5 and 11, and 3 and 19). There was therefore a higher connection between the popular individuals on Osprey than there was on Partridge. On Osprey, three prisoners were socially isolated; receiving no in-degrees (participants 4, 6 and 9). It is interesting that one of these individuals was from Kosovo and was completely isolated on Osprey. If he had been located on Partridge, however, he might have been more integrated, as all of the individuals of this nationality interacted with one another.

So there were differences between the popularity of some individuals and the isolation of others. What factors contribute to these differences? To find out, I examined some mean differences in dichotomous out-degree and in-degree ratings. Due to the small number of vulnerable individuals in this sample (i.e. those who had harmed themselves, felt suicidal, had a problem with drug misuse or had a history of psychiatric treatment), I was not able to consider group differences according to these measures. The group differences are presented in Table 5.3.

Statistical tests of inference could not be carried out, as each individual rated more than one tie; therefore, the data comprise multiple entries per person. Nevertheless, this provides some information on possible differences. Table 5.3 shows that individual who had recently entered prison, within a month, nominated fewer people and received

Table 5.3 Group differences in out-degree and in-degree scores

Variable	Level	N	Mean out-degree	Mean in-degree
Time in prison	Less than one month	19	3.26	2.37
	More than one month	30	3.77	4.17
Custodial history	First time	28	3.18	2.89
	Been in before	21	4.09	4.24
Attends association	Yes	33	3.82	3.58
	No	26	3.01	3.25
Activity	Education	21	2.85	3.00
	Job	17	4.00	4.47
	Unemployed	15	3.33	2.40
Receives visits	Yes	29	3.76	3.90
	No	20	3.30	2.85

fewer nominations, on average, than those who had been in prison for more than a month. This finding is consistent with the interviews with individuals who had been in prison for one month, whose social adaptation occurred over time. Individuals who had never been in prison before nominated fewer people and received fewer nominations, on average, than those who had been in prison before. Prior custodial experience may therefore help individuals adapt socially. Unsurprisingly, those who attended association or had a job had higher out-degree and in-degree scores than others.

Individuals who received visits had higher out-degree and in-degree scores than those who did not receive visits. It thus appears that the more contact prisoners had with people outside prison, the more likely it would be that they would form attachments within the prison. This finding is contrary to the finding of Clemmer (1940), who suggested a trade-off between support from inside and support from outside. He argued that the individual who was more prisonised was less likely to have contacts outside and more likely to be affiliated with a 'primary' or 'semi-primary' group.[3] The association between outside support and inside support is complex and will be returned to in later chapters.

Finally, I correlated the in-degree and the out-degree scores (both dichotomous and valued) with the measure of psychological distress. One correlation reached statistical significance: there was a small negative correlation between out-degree dichotomous scores and psychological distress ($r = -.35$, $p < .05$). Individuals who were more distressed nominated fewer people (or individuals who nominated fewer people were more distressed, as the causal direction of the relationship cannot be known). It could be suggested that individuals who were more distressed were more socially withdrawn and felt less able to initiate interactions in prison. However, there was no statistically significant correlation between psychological distress and in-degree scores: an individual's level of distress did not appear to affect his being nominated by others.

From social interaction to social relationship

From the observations and social network analyses, it was clear that social connections among prisoners were complex. Social life consisted of a number of dyadic interactions and some limited group formation. Some individuals were more integrated socially than others; others remained isolated. These interactions were atomised and fragile. What is apparent is that individuals had different roles to play in prison and were involved within the prison community at different levels.

This variation will have a profound impact not only on the flow of information through the prison community but also on the flow of social support. In other words, the availability and distribution of social support were highly controlled.

Yet, to what extent can these social interactions be described as social relationships or friendships? It is important first to make a distinction between social interactions and social relationships: a social interaction occurs when two or more individuals talk to one another or engage in an activity together within a specific place and time; a social relationship, by contrast, involves trust, mutual support and a sense of connection. Individuals do not have to be physically present to have a relationship, whereas to interact they do. Relationships include the further expectation, though, that future interaction will occur, and so they contain a higher degree of certainty.

Interactions and relationships differed in the type of support they entailed. From interviews with prisoners, I identified four modes of support that they potentially could provide one another. The four modes of support were as follows:

Informational support	(provided information about the prison)
Material support	(shared their belongings with them)
Emotional support	(helped them with a personal problem)
Physical support	(helped them, or would help them, in a fight)

Informational and material support could be provided within an interaction. However, emotional and physical support constituted part of what distinguished a relationship from an interaction.

In order to understand which ties could be considered relationships, I asked prisoners to rate each tie they nominated on a scale from 1 to 5 ('strongly agree' to 'strongly disagree'). I asked each man the extent to which he perceived the individual to be his 'mate' and the extent to which he trusted him. I also asked him to rate on a scale whether the individual provided him with informational, material, emotional and physical support. Table 5.4 shows the means and standard deviations of the ties nominated from the two social networks (Partridge and Osprey). The data were recoded so that a higher value denoted stronger support. The mean scores calculated are based on all the ties nominated from both wings. Table 5.5 shows the percentage of statements about their ties with which the prisoners would strongly agree or agree. The prisoners described a total of 64.6 per cent of the ties as ties with mates or friends. Yet, there were limits to this friendship. When asked whether they would consider these people to be the same as mates

Table 5.4 Mean scores for different ties

Variable	Mean	SD
Friendship	3.71	.92
Trust	3.68	.93
Informational support	2.66	1.31
Material support	3.69	1.22
Emotional support	2.33	1.24
Physical support	3.35	1.19

outside prison, most said that that they would not; these ties were to 'prison mates' or 'associates'. With these limited terms, it was difficult to gauge the extent to which these ties were friendships.

For which of these four types of support were these ties most effective? The ties were most supportive materially. Table 5.5 shows that participants strongly agreed or agreed that in 75.8 per cent of ties the friend had shared some of his belongings. Sykes (1958) identified the deprivation of goods and services as one of the pains of imprisonment, but material support from peers may help reduce this pain somewhat. As we will see later in the chapter, material support often started relationships off in the first place. Physical support was also rated relatively highly. Participants agreed or strongly agreed that in 48.4 per cent of ties the individual had helped, or would help, them in a fight. This form of support may have an impact on an individual's level of perceived safety within the prison: the knowledge that someone may come to your assistance if need be, was beneficial. By contrast, informational support was rated less strongly. Participants agreed or strongly agreed that in 35.4 per cent of ties the individual had helped them by providing information about the prison and its workings. Although this was a smaller percentage than material and physical support, many individuals nevertheless reported that they benefited from this form of peer support, which could help them to adapt practically to the prison and the regime. Finally, though, emotional support was rated the lowest of all forms. Participants agreed or strongly agreed that only 22.2 per cent of people named in ties had helped them with a personal problem. Although this form of support did exist, it existed only in specific contexts, as among cellmates (who are discussed below). There were many barriers in prison that prevented individuals from disclosing personal problems to fellow prisoners. I will explore these later in the chapter.

Table 5.5 Percentage of prisoners who strongly agreed or agreed with items relating to different ties

Variable	%	N
Perceived friendship	64.6	115
Perceived trust	62.4	111
Informational support	35.4	63
Material support	75.8	135
Emotional support	22.4	40
Physical support	48.4	86

I also asked about levels of trust. As can be seen in Table 5.5, 62.4 per cent of the ties were considered to be trustworthy. There was a moderate correlation between rating someone as a mate and trusting him ($r = .33$, $p < .001$); it could be argued that these ties were indeed relationships. When one considers the low level of emotional support, however, this finding suggests that there are limits to the level of trust and support that prisoners provided one another. If many of these ties were relationships, they took on a specific form in prison, reflected in the assertions that these people met in prison were only 'prison mates'. These ties had their breaking points, and few prisoners reported that they would remain in these ties after release.

Nevertheless, friendships did exist at some level within the prison. I would now like to consider, more positively, what factors encouraged interactions to develop into social relationships. The first factor is time. Stratton (1963) found that those who had just entered indicated a lower preference to socialise with others, and the current research also found that. When prisoners entered, or re-entered prison, their interactions over the first few days were rather defensive and reactive. Many prisoners found it difficult to interact with other prisoners and would speak only if they were spoken to. I asked a prisoner about this:

[Interviewer: When you are out on association, do you feel lonely at all?]
Yeah, you do, 'cause you don't know no one. You don't know them to speak to, so you would go up to them and speak to them. If they want to speak to you, you let them come and speak to you. [Prisoner]
[Interviewer: So did you wait?]
Yeah. [Prisoner]
[Interviewer: Did anyone come and speak to you?]

Yeah, I spoke to about three or four people. [Prisoner]
[Interviewer: For how long?]
Not long, for a few seconds, ten seconds. [Prisoner]

If prisoners did not know one another from outside prison or from previous stays in prison, some asked a number of questions to initiate an interaction. These questions generally concerned where people came from, what they were in prison for, and how long their sentence was. As time passed, these initial interactions became slightly more relaxed, and prisoners began to interact with the others on the wing more easily:

I am still keeping to myself, but I am gradually beginning to break down the walls. I've started to kind of slowly get into the association, the interaction with other prisoners. [Prisoner]

You can make good mates in here, but it would take time to get to know them, a good few months. [Prisoner]

There was a limit to these growing friendships. These young adults did not usually elicit psychological support by explaining their personal problems openly; they relied more on encouragement, reassurance, and being a sounding board for the prisoner's complaints.

A second factor that enabled individuals to form social relationships was the type of tie that existed between them. Of the 178 ties, 77.9 per cent had met each other during the current term, 4.7 per cent had met each other on a previous term, and 17.4 per cent had known each other outside prison. Although the social network analyses did not reveal a high proportion of 'mates from the out' or 'from prison before', it must be kept in mind that the network analysis was just for that side of the wing. Prisoners had friends on the other side of the unit and indeed on other units. For individuals who knew each other from outside, the process of forming friendships was different. Walking through the corridors, I frequently observed prisoners seeing friends from outside prison while they were being escorted to work, education or visits. They also met them in reception having just entered the prison or having returned from court. Indeed, attendance at education classes, workshops, and the chapel was often motivated by the desire to meet people from outside prison. Knowing prisoners from outside prison was important and could aid practical adaptation, as the following statements highlight:

[Interviewer: How long does it take to get settled?]
In my case, because I was moved onto a wing where I knew people already from road, it didn't take me that long 'cause I was with them, and they showed me everything. [Prisoner]

If you've met someone in prison before and you come back, you get closer. You start to have a laugh, get on more. [Prisoner]

I know people from the past, both the out and in prison. If anything kicked off, I've got people behind me. [Prisoner]

Conversations last longer with people you know from the out. You trust them 'cause you know them longer. It does help to talk about your problems. [Prisoner]

Prisoners from London especially often referred to people they knew 'from road'. If they did not know people first hand from outside prison, often connections were made with other people's 'boys' who came from the same area or who belonged to the same criminal network. It became apparent from the qualitative data that, within geographical locations in London, networks were linked to specific housing estates. This local affiliation had important consequences for developing affiliations within prison, so long as prospective contacts were not opposing gang members, or someone they had 'beef' with. Representing someone from one's own area is part of what Anderson (2000) called the 'street code';[4] it was extremely important in order for the code to be perpetuated. This representation was alluded to in relation to physical support, 'backing' them in a fight, and defending their position. It was difficult, however, to establish the extent to which this code was actually endorsed in practice. Sykes (1958) referred to the difference between verbally adhering to the inmate code and actually enacting it.

Another type of tie that was often supportive was based upon shared nationality. As it is a large prison serving London, the population of Feltham includes many different nationalities, often new immigrants. Many foreign nationals felt that they could be friends only with others from their own country, as they would empathise with one another:

[Interviewer: Do you tend to want to speak to people from your own country?]
Yeah, they understand us and we understand them. We can trust each other. It is hard to trust someone you don't really know from a different country. It is very hard. [Prisoner]

This solidarity was particularly strong for individuals from Eastern Europe on Partridge, as shown in the social network analysis. The Irish Traveller community also showed strong solidarity on other wings. It appeared that national identity was a more important factor in facilitating friendship formation than race. Although many black prisoners were more demonstratively supportive of one another than white prisoners were, individuals readily interacted with individuals from different ethnic backgrounds. This readiness would be expected, given that many prisoners had grown up in multicultural neighbourhoods in London. Interview data revealed, however, that Caucasian prisoners who were not from London noticed black prisoners more and found them more intimidating. These individuals did not interact as readily with individuals from different ethnic backgrounds.

However, if some ties were based on imported factors, ties also formed within the prison. Data from the network analysis revealed that material support was the primary mode of support between prisoners and the most embryonic form. The practicalities of sharing belongings began as social interactions but served as a catalyst in developing social relationships. Many items were exchanged, including food and drink, toiletries, tapes, and magazines and newspapers; one of the main items of exchange was tobacco or, as it was termed, 'burn'. This type of social exchange differed from the economic exchange, in which goods were sold for profit. A typical example of economic exchange was selling a quarter-ounce of burn to a prisoner and expecting a half-ounce back once he got his 'canteen'. This deal was termed 'double-bubble', and officers strictly discouraged prisoners from buying tobacco in this way, as it could lead them into debt and being bullied to repay. Social exchange, on the other hand, did not bring an economic cost: the tobacco here was a gift, but in the complex, entailed sense described by anthropologists. Marcel Mauss' (1954) ethnographic study of the Trobriand Islanders described the gift as a form of social exchange, and Goffman (1961) distinguished between social exchange and economic exchange: in the former, the exchange occurs in order to stabilise the relationship rather than to make a profit. Goffman found that within the hospital, another form of total institution, many 'ritual supplies', such as cigarettes, were exchanged. He argued both that bonds between patients provided the basis of social exchange and that social exchange provided the basis for these bonds to develop in the first place. Sykes (1958) also distinguished between economic and social exchange and argued that 'giving, as opposed to selling for profit expresses the solidarity of the group and may, indeed, strengthen the social bonds among group members as contractual barter never can' (p. 93). The gift could entail, for example, a prisoner asking another to 'twos me on that', that is, asking a prisoner for a couple of 'drags' on his roll-up while playing pool on association. There was a sentiment among prisoners that 'what goes around comes around'. This principle is similar to the generalised reciprocity described in Putnam's (2000) work on social capital. One prisoner said:

> If I share, there is more chances they will share with me the next time. It is not a definite thing for it to happen, but it is a more likely thing to happen. 'Cause if God knows I have shared with someone, he might make them feel it in their heart to make them share with me kind of thing. That's how it works. [Prisoner]

A prisoner might also ask his neighbour for some tobacco and papers, or offer the tobacco in the first place. This form of exchange thus had important consequences for the subsequent formation of friendships.

Burn exchange was also a vehicle for communicating with other prisoners and formed a foundation of trust, albeit a fragile one. The manner in which a prisoner asked for 'burn', or the manner in which he responded to being asked, was used to form a judgement by the other party. One prisoner described how he asked for tobacco from his neighbour along the wing:

> I asked my other next door for something, and he didn't have it, so I asked my other next door. I asked him and he sounded like an all right dude, a down-to-earth type of guy. [Prisoner]

It was the manner in which his 'next door' responded to his request that led the prisoner to view him as 'all right' or 'safe'. If prisoners responded to requests in a negative tone, as they often did, they were not respected:

> [Interviewer: If you ask someone for something, can you tell what they are like by how they answer?]
> Yeah, man. Like when you bang on the wall, a certain fool, he will come off of it with a different tone. Like try and make him sound a bit deeper and aggressive or something. Then I just think, fuck it, I'm not even going to bother with him. [Prisoner]

Prisoners were aware when others were engaged in impression management: if they felt that an individual was exaggerating his status, instead of facilitating friendship, they would be hostile. Some prisoners would not borrow or lend, because it did not fit with their self-presentation or because they claimed to be too proud to do so:

[Interviewer: Have you been helped out by any prisoners since you've been here?]
I wouldn't say so. Like I said, I keep to myself. [Prisoner]

I am not the sharing type. [Prisoner]

[Interviewer: Do you take anything?]
No, I am too proud for that. [Prisoner]

The need for autonomy was also important here and had an impact on how relationships were formed. Similarly, if prisoners answered in a tone that revealed that they were afraid, their manner suggested a weakness that could lead to their exploitation. It was therefore important not just that a prisoner responded but how he responded when asked for 'burn'. A balance was needed, as was evidenced in much of prison life, for survival.

Practicalities and forced social interaction also nurtured the most important social relationship formed within the prison, that is, the tie between cellmates. If an inmate code existed in Feltham, this code differed slightly within the cell. The code might have held true for interactions and relationships in the public realm of an association area or workshop room. When prisoners interacted with one another here, they often 'played it cool', a maxim of the inmate code that resonated in Feltham. In order to be accepted by others, prisoners had to be composed even if feeling distressed; they had to regulate their emotional responses and behaviour. Prisoners could never relax fully in the public sphere of prison life, because they constantly had to manage their own behaviour and observe the behaviour of others. Within the cell, however, the mask of self-presentation could be dropped to a greater degree, and a different depth of relationship could be developed. The cell was the most private of places within the prison, albeit one which was still relatively public in comparison with the home outside prison. It could be thought of as what Goffman (1959) called the 'back-stage', where individuals were less likely to engage in impression management.

The relationships with cellmates often provided a vital source of social support for prisoners. Generally, these relationships in Feltham were supportive, although they varied by degree.[5] Cellmates were often a central source of support for prisoners in their first few days in the prison, and helped them get used to the practicalities:

My cellmate told me, take your cup with you, so I took my cup with me, got hot water and then, eh, you go back, you got your breakfast, bread and jam and tea pack. I didn't know about the

tea pack, but he grabbed one and we shared that. [Prisoner]
[Interviewer: How does that affect how you feel?]
It is better. It makes you feel like not as worried about 'What am I going to do now?' If I forget something, I'd end up going without no cup or something. I come with water in a cup and I thought it was cold, but it was hot, and I didn't have a tea pack, but he had one there anyway for me. [Prisoner]

As time passed in their first month, prisoners often mentioned that they got to know their cellmates more, if they were fortunate enough to have retained the same cellmate. Again, time here served as a facilitator:

[Interviewer: So when you say, 'get to know them better', what do you mean by that?]
Like, understand what he is on about, just speak and talk about stuff, what he is in here for, what I am in here for, what's on TV, what are we watching. [Prisoner]

'Cause you are closer to him the whole time and you know him more. You chat about things that you'd never chat about with other people and all that. [Prisoner]

One interesting finding was that this relationship often appeared like teamwork, with cellmates mutually assisting one another to reduce the pains of imprisonment. As prisoners stated:

Being with him, the time has gone fast. We chat so much. What we normally do is take it in turns in getting up in the morning to get the breakfast packs. [Prisoner]

A single cell is hard. When you are in a double cell, you can take your mind off things. I still think about everything upstairs like, but it takes your mind off it a small, little bit. [Prisoner]

As in the wider social sphere, cellmates also frequently shared their belongings with one another. Many stated that they could not sit and eat a packet of biscuits or smoke a cigarette while their cellmate sat there with nothing. Although this comment sounded altruistic, sharing did benefit both individuals in the cell, as between them they would have a supply of different goods throughout the week. Prisoners had to be cautious in this sharing, however, as they were aware that either of them could be moved to another cell, or prison, at any time. The transitional life of the prison had an impact on the degree of friendship formation, even among cellmates.

Moreover, the cellmate was an important source of emotional support. Cellmates were able to talk about personal problems, and this communication often helped decrease their levels of distress.

[Interviewer: Could you be open with him?]
Yeah, 'cause he came from a similar type of situation. It's his first time. He is only here for a short while. We kind of related. [Prisoner]

[Interviewer: Do you feel you can talk to your cellmate?]
Yeah, that's something I can feel good about. I can release things that are on my chest. I could have dealt with them in time, but releasing them early while the burden was still there just felt good, and he told me things as well and they kind of interrelated. [Prisoner]

If you and your cellmate are close, you can talk about close things. You've got someone to talk about your worries, and that's the main thing, and that's the main thing here, your worries. If you've got someone, then you don't have that much stress in your mind and worries. You talk it over. You talk through it, through it with them. You have jokes and this and that. Communicating basically. [Prisoner]

Just having someone there nurtured a feeling of not being alone in a cold world:

You know, you find that someone is really having the same reaction as you. You know that it is something that happens to everyone. [Prisoner]

[Interviewer: So it is not just you thinking these things?]
It is not something that is happening to me alone; it is happening to someone else. It is a regular routine that happens to everyone. It is not something to worry about. It just has to go through everyone's head. [Prisoner]

Cellmates provided each other with mutual reassurance. Being able to cope with imprisonment included developing the knowledge of what it felt like to be coping through self-reflection or meta-cognition, a reflection upon one's own ability to cope, which seemed to be learned through interaction with others: 'you find that someone is really having the same reaction as you'. Thus, through the relationship with a cellmate, prisoners had a gauge on how they were coping, a base from which to anchor themselves psychologically, as a check on or barometer of their own psychological well-being. Often prisoners were uncertain about whether they were coping. and a source of their distress was not being furnished with this knowledge.

The limits on forming friendships

Some good social relationships did exist, and there were some factors that encouraged them, and these relationships aided psychological adaptation. However, the social network data revealed an overall low density of ties within both wings (.13 and .14 for Partridge and Osprey respectively). In the interviews, many prisoners also insisted that friendships could not be formed in prison. As one prisoner commented:

> I wouldn't call them mates, just people I know more than others. You can't call people mates unless you know them from the out. [Prisoner]

What factors encouraged such a response? The first factor was transience. Despite the fact that prisoners began to interact more over the course of the first month, and especially after that, the transient nature of the community in Feltham made it very difficult for prisoners to form lasting, meaningful relationships with one another. Prisoners frequently commented that people moved in and out of the prison at a very fast pace and were permanently in transition. The prisoners noted this:

> People move. Every time I start talking to people, they move like. Everyone keeps moving. There is someone that I know who lives in my area, he came in today, no, he came in last night, and now he has gone today to a different wing already. [Prisoner]

> One down the block, next one, I don't know where he went; he just disappeared. That's what it's like here. You don't know what's going to happen. There is a few people who come in and out 'cause it's remand. [Prisoner]

Like this man, other prisoners were aware that relationships in a remand centre differed from an establishment where most people were sentenced. This mobility was often seen as a deterrent to getting to know others, as they would not be there long enough to form enduring friendships:

> It is a remand centre so I don't want to bother getting to know people 'cause you ain't gonna be with them during your sentence. It is when you get to a convicted jail you get to know people. [Prisoner]

> Remember, like I said before, you can't get to know people too much because I won't be here that long. I didn't even think I was going to come back to Feltham when I was at court; I didn't know where I was going to be sent to. [Prisoner]

Again the need for a balanced approach towards imprisonment aided adaptation and survival: becoming too close to someone was not seen as a wise decision.

Another barrier to friendship formation was the prevalence of bullying on the wing. Ireland (2002) argued that bullying behaviour is highly prevalent in young offender establishments.[6] However, at Feltham, many prisoners reported that the level of bullying had decreased in recent years and that the staff were able to detect the bullies:

> I mean there isn't bullying going on. These days you can't get bullying. Whoever bullies someone will either bully out his window or his door, or he won't bully someone at association. It'd be a fight thing. So whoever bullies will get known by the govs. [Prisoner]

> [Interviewer: But why don't they bully on association?]
> How can they bully? The govs have got eyes. Before there used to be bullies years ago, but now it's all changed. They're working harder on bullies now, you get me? [Prisoner]

Although the level of bullying was not particularly high at Feltham, it did exist, as would be expected. As the first quotation from the prisoner states, one of the main forms of bullying at Feltham was intimidation from windows by people whom the other prisoners called the 'window warriors': they hurled comments from one cell window to another, especially at night. One of the most disrespectful comments to be made among these young prisoners was about their mothers, as stated by a prisoner who was telling me about other prisoners intimidating him at the windows:

Yeah, there are guys who tell you about your mother. They tell all kind of nasty things that get you really pissed off. [Prisoner] [Interviewer: What do they say?] They say they'll fuck your mother, suck your mother, nasty things like that. That'll get to you. [Prisoner] [Interviewer: Why does it make you feel angry?] Because the love you have for your mother. You want no one to disrespect your mother. [Prisoner] [Interviewer: Can you let it go over your head?] Sometimes, sometimes, but it depends on the mood you are in. This place is very depressing. So if you are thinking about your mum at that time and someone says that, if he is near you at that time, you will hurt them. It is not all time; they will get away with that. If they keep saying, you are going to get fed up and do something about it. 'Cause sometimes you just laugh, but not all times it is going to happen. It will explode one day. [Prisoner]

Although this prisoner felt able to confront these individuals, some of the other prisoners could not, and this heightened their levels of distress and decreased their perceived levels of safety.

Another form of bullying that occurred at Feltham was ostracism. Clemmer (1940) found that some men did not interact with others because they were excluded by others. These men 'may have lacked personableness, or may have behaved in annoying ways so that the group which partially accepted them thereafter excluded them' (Clemmer 1940: 131). At Feltham, some prisoners did not interact with others because they were 'annoying' or 'muppets'. Those who had committed sexual offences tended to be excluded. It could be argued that these individuals who are ostracised in prison suffer the psychological impact of such exclusion. It could be argued that, when ostracised, those individuals may be deprived of four fundamental needs: belongingness, self-esteem, control and meaningful existence (Williams 1997, 2001). This lack of relationships with fellow inmates is not through choice but due to an inability to be accepted.

Another reason why friendships in prison existed only at a very limited level was the low level of trust that was markedly evident, as discussed in Chapter 5. Anderson (2000) argued that trust among those who adhere to the 'street code' is 'severely lacking, even for those they are close to' (p. 37). He believed this stemmed from their alienation from society: 'an adaptation to a lost sense of security' (p. 323). (As we shall see later in Chapter 6, individuals who self-harmed were often those who felt most alienated and detached from society.) Generally, prisoners described trusting another prisoner as being able to confide in them; being able to tell them something and being certain that they would not repeat this information to anyone. (This distrust was also found in Chapter 5 in relation to trusting staff.) I asked:

[Interviewer: Do you feel you can trust prisoners?]
They talk to you but I couldn't trust them. I couldn't trust them, you know. I don't know really. I just wouldn't trust them. They've got mates coming in there and could turn on you like that. [Prisoner]

[Interviewer: Have you managed to get to know different people on the unit? How many do you speak to?]
I speak to a couple. I don't trust all of them. I've learned you can't trust some of these boys. They'll change on you. You'll think they are with you, but they're not. After you see how they are acting. They are not with you. [Prisoner]

Those who did not trust in prison acknowledged that they were living in a social world that was often volatile and unpredictable. They were wary that prisoners might turn against them. These prisoners perceived the behaviour of their peers to be erratic. Within prison, to trust another prisoner was to give knowledge about oneself, and such knowledge was perceived as power for other prisoners. Prisoners were often worried that trusting someone could be used against them. To trust was to put oneself in a vulnerable position within prison.

However, this profound lack of trust was not only related to the environment of the prison, but it also seemed to be imported into prison from the detached social networks outside. As mentioned in the first section of this chapter, Clemmer (1940) discussed the impersonalisation in general society, whereby relationships had become 'touch and go'. This impersonalisation is similar to Beck and Beck-Gernsheim's (2001) process of excessive individualisation, which certainly seemed prevalent in Feltham, and the prisoners themselves commented on the wider trend:

[Interviewer: What would a person have to be like for you to trust them?]
I don't know, because I've had a lot of experience. Even outside friends, I don't trust them anymore. We are in a different world these days. It is difficult to explain how to trust. People can use it if you tell them secret things or whatever. Like, basically, if I tell you something, when we've got an argument you could turn

round and tell someone else. It is not trustable. The only person I can trust is me. [Prisoner]

I don't owe no one nothing. I drive my car. I got my chicks in my car, and I don't care about anyone else. It's just me and my best friend. He'll be in front of me in his car. It's just me and him making money, going about our business. […] I ain't got no one else to worry about, and that's the way I like it. [Prisoner]

This individualisation had an impact on the way prisoners 'do time'. Many prisoners stated that they wanted to keep themselves to themselves: 'I ain't got no one else to worry about, and that's the way I like it.' This perceived self-reliance was pursued by first-time prisoners as well as those who had been in before. For the first-time prisoner this approach might have been induced more by fear of the unknown; for recidivists, it was often the fear of the known that was the antecedent to their decision. They feared that through interacting with others they would begin to become involved in trouble, and that this trouble, in turn, would lead to their being punished. These figures are at their most extreme in the person Clemmer (1940) called the 'stranger': the prisoner who is socially cold and who is not culturalised, 'in the prison, but not of it' (p. 132).

In summary, interacting with others and developing relationships was an important aspect of social adaptation. Ties tended to be formed on a dyadic, rather than clique, basis, and those who had been in prison longer, who had been in prison before, who had a job, and who received visits tended to be more integrated within the network. Individuals differed in their level of interaction; those who were more distressed nominated fewer people. There is thus some limited evidence to suggest that an individual's level of distress and his ability to adapt socially were related. Some of the ties formed did develop from interactions into relationships. Material support was the foundation from which friendships could develop. Other factors included shared nationality or shared district within London. For those individuals who had met only in prison, the most important tie was that with the cellmate. Often individuals who shared a cell moved towards building a relationship, and when they could do so, this reduced the pains of imprisonment. There were other factors, however, that prevented interactions from developing into relationships: the transient world of Feltham; individuals' fear of victimisation; the low level of trust. Perhaps most important was the perceived necessity of self-reliance. These factors kept solidarity at bay and prevented individuals from readily entering into supportive relationships.

Notes

1 Density formula is total number of edges divided by maximum possible number of edges. The maximum number of edges for a digraph is calculated as n(n–1).

2 The mean out-degree and in-degree scores should be equal, but, as one case is missing, this was not so for Partridge. The data set contains this individual's in-degree nominations and therefore does not allow for the means to be equal. For definition of in-degree and out-degree, see Chapter 2.

3 He termed prisonisation, 'the taking on in greater or less degree of the folkways, mores, customs, and general culture of the penitentiary' (Clemmer 1940: 299).

4 Anderson (2000) carried out an ethnographic study in Philadelphia among inner-city African-Americans. He provides a detailed account of the 'street code' and violence among these individuals.

5 Cellmates who did not get along were usually relocated to different cells, despite the fact that prison staff were working with a tight number of spaces. Their heightened vigilance may have been due to the murder of Zahid Mubarek, mentioned in Chapters 1 and 2. This brought about the introduction of a 'cell-sharing risk assessment' where prisoners who were identified as being at risk of violence, racism or homophobic abuse were allowed to be located only in a single cell. That fewer individuals at Feltham were located in double cells may have reduced the amount of support received from cellmates.

6 Ireland (2002) defined bullying as follows: 'An individual is being bullied when they are the victim of direct and/or indirect aggression happening on a weekly basis, by the same or different perpetrator(s). Single incidents of aggression can be viewed as bullying, particularly when they are severe and when the individual either believes or fears that they are at risk of future victimisation by the same perpetrator or others. An incident can be considered as bullying when the imbalance of power between the bully and his/her victim is implied and not immediately evident' (p. 26).

Chapter 6

Self-harm among young men in prison

This chapter sets out to examine the experiences of individuals who found it especially difficult to adapt to life in prison and who harmed themselves. It explores the experiences of this highly distressed group in relation to the different concepts detailed in previous chapters: locus of control, safety, prison social support and outside social support. It examines the incidence of self-harm and the reasons people give for such behaviour. It then explores the differences between the individuals who self-harmed and those who did not.

Suicide and self-harm among young people continues to be a problem in the general community. In 2002, the suicide rate in the UK among 15–24-year-old males was 11.0 per 100,000 (the rate was 3.0 per 100,000 for females). The total rate for males generally was 14.0 per 100,000 (the Samaritans 2004). It has been documented that the suicide rate among young males increased dramatically during the 1980s to the mid-1990s by some 81.1 per cent (Houston *et al.* 2001). The suicide rate for this age group has now begun to decline, although it is still substantially higher than in previous decades. It is difficult to compare these rates with the rates of young adults in prison; to do so, we would need a matched sample.

Research among young people in the general community has focused on identifying rates and risk factors associated with suicide (Hawton *et al.* 1993, 1999a; Houston *et al.* 2001) and self-harm (Hawton *et al.* 1997, 1999b, 2002, 2003; Haw *et al.* 2001; Hultén *et al.* 2001; Rodham *et al.* 2004). Houston *et al.* (2001) carried out the first psychological autopsy study of suicides (including open verdicts) in young people aged 15–24. Of the 27 individuals who died, 70.4 per cent had a psychiatric disorder, 29.6 per cent had a problem with alcohol use, 25.9 per cent had a problem with drugs, 63 per cent had made a previous suicide attempt, 37 per cent had received psychiatric treatment, 48.1 per cent had seen a doctor within six months of their death, 52 per cent had been in trouble with the police, and 25.9 per cent had a family history of deliberate self-harm. Considering problems encountered, 66.7 per cent of respondents felt that the deceased had a mental health problem, that 63 per cent of them had occupational problems, that 51.9 per cent had problems with their partner, and that 48.1 per cent had problems with relatives.

A significant number of individuals who complete suicide have harmed themselves in the past (Hawton and Fagg 1988; Hawton *et al.* 1993). Indeed, the best predictor of completed suicide is a previous suicide attempt (Greer and Bagley 1971). Hawton *et al.* (1998) found that the association between suicide and deliberate self-harm was stronger for males aged 15-24 than other groups. A correlation of .65 was found between deliberate self-harm and suicide among young males. Hawton *et al.* (1998) argued that although those who attempt suicide differ from those who complete it in terms of characteristics and motives, the two behaviours nevertheless overlap. Studies of self-harm are therefore also of importance when attempting to understand completed suicide.

Although there is no official record of self-harm data available in the UK, self-harm data are being gathered as part of the WHO: EURO Multi-centre Study of Suicidal Behaviour. For most of the countries in this study, the highest rates of deliberate self-harm are for females aged 15–24; but the figures for males have been increasing steadily (Hawton *et al.* 1998, 2000). Hawton *et al.* (2000) reported that the rate of deliberate self-harm among those 13–19 years of age had increased by 27.7 per cent between 1985/6 and 1995/6. Hawton *et al.* (1997) reported that the rate of deliberate self-harm among those 15–24 years of age was 400 per 100,000. Hawton *et al.* (2002) conducted a self-report survey of deliberate self-harm by adolescents in schools in England. Of the sample, 90 per cent were 15–16 years of age. Results from their survey found that 13.2 per cent had a lifetime history of deliberate self-harm, 8.6 per cent of the sample having harmed themselves within one year. Meltzer *et al.* (1999) found a lower lifetime rate of 6.6 per cent. Of those who had not harmed themselves, 15 per cent reported suicidal ideation. Females were three times more likely than males to have thought about suicide. Factors found to be associated with deliberate self-harm included smoking and the consumption of alcohol, drug taking, bullying, physical and sexual abuse, depression, anxiety, impulsivity and low self-esteem. For males, significant predictors of self-harm one year later included deliberate self-harm among peers or among family members, drug misuse and low self-esteem. Haw *et al.*

(2001) conducted a follow-up study of 118 people of 15 years of age and over who had deliberately self-harmed. They found that 92 per cent were diagnosed with at least one psychiatric disorder and 45.9 per cent with a personality disorder. They concluded that these rates are higher than found in other studies in the UK but are similar to those reported in studies of completed suicides.

Studies in the UK have primarily focused on identifying risk factors associated with self-harm among young people. In the USA, several studies have aimed to develop models of suicidal behaviour among adolescents (see Rudd 1990). Although model testing allows several independent variables to be examined simultaneously, a purely quantitative approach does restrict the analysis to only the variables that have been systematically asked and does not allow the participants to provide their own explanations.

Within prison research, it was Liebling (1992) who first highlighted the significant role that coping and the prison experience had on the manifestation of suicidal behaviours. Her model of vulnerability arose from research that departed from previous prison suicide studies in that it involved interviewing both male and female young and adult prisoners who had attempted suicide, and comparing them with those who had not. Previous studies had focused primarily on completed suicides, seeking to identify predictive risk factors and attempting to construct a suicidal inmate profile from official documents and case records (Danto 1973; Burtch and Ericson 1979; Topp 1979; Dooley 1990). The greatest differences to emerge from Liebling's research concerned how both groups experienced prison life. An exploration of interpersonal social relationships inside prison found that suicide attempters were less likely to describe their fellow inmates as friends, were more likely to have met them inside prison than outside, had more difficulties with other inmates, and had less contact with the probation service. Moreover, what contact they did have, they perceived as less useful. In terms of interpersonal social relationships outside prison, those who had attempted suicide were less likely to receive visits, wrote fewer letters, kept in touch with people less, and missed specific people more. Those who had attempted suicide spent more time doing nothing in their cells, were more likely to be averse to physical education, were more bored, daydreamed more, had greater problems sleeping at night, had more complaints about the disciplinary system, and found the experience of imprisonment more difficult. Suicide in prison seemed to be 'to a large extent a problem of coping' (Liebling 1992: 236).

Inch et al. (1995) also carried out semi-structured interviews with 25 male young prisoners in the UK (16–21 years of age) who had self-harmed and 25 controls. They defined self-harm as any attempt at inflicting self-injury, with incidents taking place usually within a week. No significant differences were found in relation to employment history, time spent in local authority care or education qualifications. Groups differed, however, in terms of history of self-harm (70 per cent versus 12 per cent for the self-harm and the control groups respectively), and family history of self-harm (24 per cent versus 18 per cent of responses respectively). In interviews, they found that the most common reasons given for self-harming were bullying and difficulties with family or relationships (44 per cent and 20 per cent of responses respectively). Difficulties with family and relationships included 'loss of contact, being disowned, relationships ending and worries about the family's feelings and response to imprisonment' (Inch *et al.* 1995: 167). Moreover, 32 per cent reported difficulties in coping, feeling overwhelmed by being 'locked in' and 'banged up'. Inch *et al.* concluded that 'the common thread linking almost all the acts of self-harm in our study was a desperate desire to escape from a situation which had become intolerable and which had overwhelmed the coping mechanisms of the individual concerned' (ibid.: 168).

Further quantitative studies have examined the roles of coping strategies of young men in prison. Biggam and Power (1999a) conducted a study in Scotland, comparing the problem-solving abilities and psychological distress of male suicidal prisoners (those on strict suicidal supervision), the bullied, those protected for their own safety and a comparison group. They conclude that there was 'a hierarchy of distress', the strictly supervised inmates 'displaying the most elevated level of distress (often at a level that would merit clinical intervention), followed by victims of bullying and then inmates placed on protection. The lowest levels of distress were found in the comparison group' (Biggam and Power 1999a: 211). They found a correlation between increased psychological distress and a deficit in problem-solving ability, considering the group as a whole. As this study was cross-sectional and correlational in nature, directionality could not be determined. But they note that it is 'plausible that both of these constructs may predate assignment to the distress groups examined in this study, although the situational influences of the inmate's status is likely to enhance distress' (Biggam and Power 1999a: 212).[1] The role of problem-solving deficits has figured largely in suicide research in the general community (Schotte and Clum 1982, 1987, 1990) and more recently within penal settings (Ivanoff *et al.* 1992; Biggam and Power 1999a, 1999b). There is a debate as to whether problem-solving deficits are to be construed as a trait or state phenomenon. Biggam and Power (1999b) carried out a study looking at the state–trait debate on problem-solving deficits with 61 young male offenders, aged 16–21 years, in Scotland. Their study was similar to an earlier study carried out by Ivanoff *et al.* (1992) on 93 male prison inmates in the USA. Biggam and Power's (1999b) results suggested that 'although problem-solving is not a trait phenomenon, it may be a state corollary to suicidality' and 'psychological distress is both a trait and state indicator of parasuicidal behaviour' (Biggam and Power, 1999b: 37).

Methods of self-harm and reasons for self-harm

In exploring the experiences of young men in prison at Feltham, I examined the role of perceptions of safety, locus of control and support in relation to self-harming behaviour. I interviewed a total of 25 individuals who had recently self-harmed (within three days of the interview) and compared them with a matched control group of 25 individuals who had not self-harmed. This latter group were matched to the self-harming individuals on the variables of length of time in prison (in the current term), prior custodial history (first time in prison or not), custodial status (remanded, convicted but not sentenced and sentenced) and ethnicity. (The demographic and background information on this sample is detailed in Chapter 1.) Table 6.1 shows data on the self-harm incidents within the sample. A total of 56 per cent of incidents occurred on normal location, 40 per cent occurred in health care, and 4 per cent occurred in the segregation unit. Of the 14 individuals who harmed themselves on a normal wing, 10 were moved to the health-care centre (71 per cent). A total of 32 per cent were on medication prior to self-harming, and 68 per cent were on an open F2052SH form. One individual who overdosed had to be transferred to hospital.

In research on this topic, it is important to decide what to include as an incident of self-harm. I decided to interview anybody who carried out an act that harmed himself regardless of whether or not he intended to die.[2] The issue is complex, and it was difficult to separate a suicide attempt, with an intention to die, from an incident of self-harm, without that intention. Some individuals were ambivalent as to their intent in this respect. Furthermore, lethality of method is not a reliable gauge. An individual may have used a less lethal method, thinking that it would kill him, or a highly lethal method, but not thinking that it would (see Dear *et al.* 2000). I therefore refer to all of these incidents as self-harm, although some may be more appropriately termed suicide attempts. The people in the sample employed a range of different methods to harm themselves. These included cutting, hanging, head banging, wall punching and swallowing objects. I also included four individuals who made a noose and who were in the process of attaching it to a ligature point when staff intervened. These individuals might not have harmed themselves if they had not been found, but there was the possibility that they might. The most frequent method of self-harm was cutting (32 per cent). Individuals differed in the part of their body they cut, what they used to cut, and how severely they cut. They used any object that was sharp: they broke plastic spoons and cups and used the sharp ends; they 'stashed' razor blades in their cells for later use (see Chapter 2), and smashed toilet seats and used them as cutting devices. The next most frequent method in the sample was hanging (a total of 28 per cent of the sample). People found ligature points in their cells (more often than not, the bars on their window), and would tie bed sheets or other material to make nooses. Two prisoners swallowed objects to harm themselves. One prisoner swallowed pieces of razor blades wrapped in bread and the other tried to swallow a ping-pong ball.

But why did these individuals harm themselves in the first place? Previous studies of people who have self-harmed have identified a number of different reasons. Snow (2002) conducted a study of the motivations of individuals who had self-injured and those who attempted suicide.[3] She carried out a total of 124 interviews across ten prisons and included young and adults prisoners, male and female. She found that there were five major motivations for these behaviours: offence-related,

Table 6.1 Details of incidents of self-harm

Variable		%	N
Location	Normal	56.0	14
	Health care	40.0	10
	Segregation	4.0	1
Cell type	Normal	88.0	22
	Safer cell	12.0	3
Method	Hanging	28.0	7
	Cutting	32.0	8
	Overdosing	4.0	1
	Head banging/wall punching	12.0	3
	Swallowing objects	8.0	2
	Noose making	16.0	4
On medication	Yes	32.0	8
Admitted to health care	Yes	40.0	10
	No	20.0	5
Already in healthcare		40.0	10
Outside hospital	Yes	4.0	1
On an F2052SH at time	Yes	68.0	17

Table 6.2 Reported reasons for self-harm

General category	Specific concern
Internal prison event/circumstance	Conflict with other prisoners Conflict with staff Placement in cell, wing, prison
Consequence of crime/imprisonment	Missing family and partners Worry about impact on family Guilt over crime Self-disgust Desire to escape Unable to cope with being in prison Fast re-entry into prison cycle Lack of control over life Being told what to do Concerned about life after release

Aspect of wider criminal justice system	Uncertainty over when next
	   back at court
	Uncertainty over bail
	Uncertainty over length of sentence
	In order for judge to give a
	   more lenient sentence

Outside problems	Problem with relationship partner Ostracism by family Lack of family visits Not knowing where family are Death of family member Birth of child Lack of accommodation
Psychological symptoms	Traumatic memories Drug withdrawal Depression Hallucinations (auditory or visual) Self-harm for stress relief Self-anger Cognitive and emotional flooding

interpersonal, symptom relief, instrumental and situational. Dear *et al.* (2001b) found five main categories of precipitating factors: internal prison event/circumstance, consequence of crime/imprisonment, aspect of wider criminal justice system, outside problems and psychological symptoms. I have used the categories and subcategories put forward by Dear *et al.* (2001b) and have subsequently added a number of other subcategories. These can be seen in Table 6.2. As can be seen, there were a vast array of concerns and events that led people to harm themselves while in prison. These concerns included problems inside prison as well as problems outside prison. Many of these problems were similar to those reported by other young men within their first month: the difference was that these problems were more psychologically painful for those who went on to self-harm. What was also apparent was that these prisoners gave multiple reasons for their self-harm.

Dear *et al.*'s (2001b) classifications were a useful way of examining the different reasons for self-harm among young men at Feltham. However, rather than solely relying on their classifications, I identified four groups, but these groups overlapped considerably; they were not discrete. These groups were as follows: young men who repetitively self-harmed for relief of tension; young men who had psychological health difficulties; young men who experienced extreme entry shock, many of whom also suffered from drug withdrawal; and, finally, young men who responded to a particular triggering event. However, although they overlap, it is easier to understand each separately.

Repetitive self-harm

There were some individuals who self-harmed on a regular basis. Although they might have done so in a response to a particular trigger, sometimes they reported no triggers. I obtained data on each individual I had interviewed (over time) to see if he subsequently self-harmed while I remained at Feltham. Table 6.3 shows that 52 per cent of participants in the sample self-harmed more than once, with 24 per cent self-harming more than four times.

One such prisoner cut his arms after five days but proceeded to harm himself a total of nine times before being transferred to another establishment. He had never been in prison before, felt unsafe, and missed his family and girlfriend in particular. I asked him:

> [Interviewer: So what was going through your head at the time?] I just did it. I don't normally think about it. It's just one of them problems. Sometimes I don't even realise I'm doing it till it's done and I'm bleeding everywhere. [...] I've been doing it for about a year and a half. It's my way of dealing with my depression, I think. It relieves my anger. [Prisoner]

Self-harm for him was a method of relieving stress and anger. Snow (2002) found in her study that young male prisoners and women were more likely than other groups to harm themselves in order to relieve

Table 6.3 Frequency of repetitive self-harm

Total number of times self-harmed	%	N
1	48	12
2	28	7
3	0	0
4	4	1
5	4	1
6	4	1
7	0	0
8	0	0
9	8	2
10	4	1
Total	100	25

negative feelings or emotions. She also reported a difference between individuals who had self-injured without suicidal intent and those who intended suicide: those who self-injured were more likely to be motivated by the desire to relieve stress, tension or anger; those who attempted suicide were more likely to report concrete problems, such as those with relationships. I interviewed several individuals who said that cutting themselves made them feel calmer and more in control.

> Everyone has a way of releasing anger. Usually when I am outside, I would get into a fight or smash something up, but in here I've been trying to keep my head down, and I took it out on myself. [Prisoner]

> It is like my head is blowing up. When I lost the blood, I felt nice. […] I reckon that is what makes people do it. If someone has done that before. they will do it again 'cause of what they felt afterwards. [Prisoner]

They would use this method to relieve pressure whenever they felt that it was necessary.

Those who repeatedly harmed themselves present a particular problem. The Howard League (2003b) highlighted repetitive self-harm among female prisoners in their report *Suicide and Self-Harm Prevention: Repetitive Self-Harm among Women and Girls in Prison,* and some research has examined repetitive suicidal behaviour in the general community.

Sakinofsky (2002) concluded that those who habitually harm themselves were 'notoriously resistant to treatment' (p. 398). (How individuals respond to offers of support will be discussed later in this chapter.) Hawton *et al.* (1999b) found that adolescents 13–18 years of age who had a history of self-harm, or who self-harmed throughout the subsequent year of their study, differed from those who did not do so repeatedly. They scored higher on depression, hopelessness and anger, and had lower self-esteem and impaired problem-solving abilities, compared with those who had not self-harmed repeatedly. Hawton *et al.* (2000) also found an increase of 56.9 per cent in the number of males who self-harmed repeatedly between 1985/86 and 1994/95. Finally, Hultén *et al.* (2001) carried out a longitudinal follow-up study of 1,264 individuals 15–19 years of age who had made suicide attempts in 1989–95. They found that a previous suicide attempt was associated with repetition: 24 per cent of individuals who had made an attempt did so again within one year.

Psychological health difficulties

Over half of the individuals I interviewed had received psychiatric treatment in the past (58 per cent). Psychological health problems have been associated with self-harm in the general community (Haw *et al.* 2001) and in prison (Liebling 1992; Meltzer *et al.* 1999; Lader *et al.* 2000). Meltzer *et al.* (1999) also found that personality disorders were common among individuals who harmed themselves (46 per cent of male remands), and that neurotic disorders and alcohol abuse were more common among those who had attempted suicide in the last year. Often, in the interviews at Feltham, it seemed evident that the prisoners who had self-harmed suffered from psychological problems. (However, I had no training in mental health at the time and was not able, nor in a position, to assess their problems fully.) The prisoners who had self-harmed suffered from depression, borderline personality disorder and psychosis. These people felt that their priority was to receive the correct medication, particularly for those who experienced visual or auditory hallucinations, which were often cited as the motive for self-harm:

> It's the stupid voices in my head that make me do it. Hopefully, they'll be gone soon and I won't be bothering myself about this madness. [Prisoner]

Another prisoner, who had a towel wrapped around his head and ears, explained that:

I am trying to block my ears as I am hearing strange sounds in my ears, and the doctors are telling me different stories every day. It is helping 'cause I can't really hear them as much. At night-time it is worse, saying scary things in my ears. When I am alone in my cell, I can hear them saying, 'Kill yourself, do this, do that'. I can't sleep, man. [Prisoner]

Some people also experienced traumatic memories. Two, who had moved to the UK when they were younger, after wars in their home countries of Rwanda and the former Yugoslavia, recalled traumatic events from this early stage of their life. Another person was traumatised over the death of his girlfriend: he was a heroin addict and had supplied her with the drugs on which she overdosed. He felt that his life was no longer worth living and had made several suicide attempts. Some might also have been suffering from post-traumatic stress disorder, but I did not obtain data on this problem. Unfortunately for these young men, there was no opportunity for one-to-one psychotherapy.

The experience of extreme entry shock

There was a group of prisoners who self-harmed as they were experiencing entry shock. They had self-harmed within three days of arriving in custody. Table 6.4 shows the timing of the self-harm incidents, measuring from reception. As can be seen 60 per cent of the incidents occurred within seven days of entering prison and 72 per cent within the first month in custody. As detailed in Chapter 2, many individuals found the first three days in prison especially distressing, but those who self-harmed felt this distress with greater intensity. Similarly, separation and loss were felt by many within the prison (particularly at the early arrival stage), but those who self-harmed found these feelings more painful and intolerable, as other studies have found (Dear *et al.* 1998).

Table 6.4 Length of time in prison

Variable		%	N
Length of time in prison	< 3 days	28	7
	> 3 days to 7 days	32	8
	> 7 days to 1 month	12	3
	> 1 month to 3 months	12	3
	> 3 months to 1 year	16	4

Of the seven prisoners who self-harmed at the early stage, six had a problem with drugs before entering custody and were suffering some psychological symptoms of withdrawal, which exacerbated their distress further, quite apart from the physical pains of withdrawal. One prisoner who had attempted to hang himself was withdrawing from drugs. He explained the physical symptoms of his withdrawal, but said that what he found most difficult was the emotional torture:

> You don't sleep and you start thinking properly again. When you take heroin, you don't feel nothing for anyone, but then when you're coming off it you start thinking about all the things you've done and the way you treated people and your family. [...] When you're coming off drugs, things come back to you really hard. Your emotions come back really hard. [Prisoner]

Another stated:

> I just felt like I didn't – like I didn't want to be here anymore. Where my head was feeling and my body was feeling – horrible – I'd rather have not been there. [Prisoner]

They were unable to control their thoughts and emotions about this rupture and felt more anxious than others that their relationships would disintegrate. Some were afraid that their relationships would not remain when they eventually returned to the community:

> No. Since I've been in prison I've been really stressed out 'cause I don't know what is going to happen to me when I come out of jail. I don't know where my parents are. I don't know where to go when I come out of jail. I am thinking of it all over and over again, and thought it was better for me to kill myself than have nowhere else to go. [Prisoner]

Young men who harmed themselves at this entry stage found it exceptionally difficult to be removed from their families and loved ones. Nor were those who had been in prison before immune to this distress, nor to harming themselves. Prisoners who had self-harmed felt they could not cope with the lack of freedom and being locked up.

Responding to a specific trigger

Over half of them harmed themselves in a response to a particular event, such as a conflict with staff, a conflict with other prisoners, not receiving help when they had asked for it, not receiving a visit, not receiving bail at court, the death of a family member, or the birth of a child. These events made prisoners feel powerless and out of control. Some prisoners cited an incident with a member of staff as the event which precipitated the self-harm incident. Sometimes an argument had occurred or a member of staff had failed to respond to what the prisoner felt was a reasonable request.

> It was 9 o'clock and I asked for a light, and she said I couldn't have one. She came over, and I started getting angry and started hitting the walls and all that. [...] You get treated unfairly here, in that you are not allowed to have matches, like, and that winds me up. I am a big boy. I am old enough to buy matches. [Prisoner]

Prisoners who felt that staff did not treat them well harmed themselves to make a statement. One prisoner self-harmed after an argument with a prison officer, and said:

> I was just thinking of myself. I was just showing them they have to care for you while you are in here. I wanted to show them that I'll do something they'll regret. [Prisoner]

Among other events, some people who harmed themselves mentioned physical bullying as a precipitating event, but seldom readily. However, psychological abuse was reported: one prisoner was remanded for rape and had been tormented by the other prisoners about his crime:

> I tell no one why I am in prison, but someone know why I am in prison and my head went mad. [...] Everyone told me on Mallard I was horrible. I told them it not true, and the governor changed my unit and I go to Partridge. I stayed there my first night, and my head had gone mad and I cut myself. The governors tried to help me, and I told the governor I don't need no help. I don't need nothing to help me. [Prisoner]

This teasing was one factor which precipitated his self-harm.

However, triggering events occurred beyond the prison walls; these events often concerned family members. Snow (2002) found that among young men, more than among other demographic groups, self-harm was prompted by factors pertaining to interpersonal relationships. Interpersonal relationships often prompted self-harm in Feltham. One prisoner suffered when he could not attend his mother's funeral:

It has been crazy. In a way it hasn't hit me completely yet 'cause I haven't been to my mum's funeral or anything, so it hasn't sunk in. It has and it hasn't; and having my girlfriend just given birth two weeks after my mum died: it is mad. I try not to think about it. I try to block it out 'cause there is nothing I can do while I am in here. [...] I've been stressed out. I wasn't trying to kill myself, but I cut myself because I was stressed out. I just did it for the stress to come out. I don't know. [...] I've never done it before. It's just been since my mum died. It is nothing to do with the prison. It is just I feel bad that I never got to the funeral, and I blame myself. I am blaming myself for not being at my mum's funeral. I am blaming myself that I weren't there when my little girl was born. I am stressed out and I took it out on myself. [Prisoner]

A second prisoner's girlfriend had also recently given birth to his child. This event was traumatic for him, as he felt guilt and sadness that he was not there for the birth. This distress was compounded by the fact that his fellow prisoners started to tease him about it:

Some boys started saying, 'You ain't gonna see your kid, ra ra ra'. Instead of hitting them, I tried to ignore them. But when I went back to my cell at night, it just – all everything that they were saying came back into my head somehow. [...] It just upset me 'cause I wasn't there for the birth or anything. All the idiots on the wing starting winding me up, and it just got too much for me. [Prisoner]

When these events triggered self-harm, the individual often did not consider the consequences of his actions. For example, the need to survive and be with one's family was clouded by this heightened level of distress:

[Interviewer: When staff found you, what did they say to you?] They said, 'That's been selfish. That's the easy way out, trying to end your life. You've got to think about your baby, your fiancée, your family.' [Prisoner]
[Interviewer: And what did you think about what they were saying?]
It made, sense but when I am going to do silly things like that, that don't cross my mind one bit. It never does. [Prisoner]

Family contact was one of the most cited reasons for self-harming behaviour among young men in prison. The importance of family contact will be discussed more fully in this chapter and in the chapter to follow.

Differences between the groups

I now turn to some quantitative differences that emerged between individuals who had self-harmed and those who had not, in order to understand their different experiences of prison. Firstly, it is important to recognise that individuals who harmed themselves entered prison with more vulnerability than individuals who did not harm themselves. Table 6.5 shows the different measures of imported vulnerability used. Of the self-harming participants, 56 per cent had received psychiatric treatment compared with 8 per cent of the matched group. A total of 16 per cent had self-harmed on a prior custodial term and 48 per cent had self-harmed outside prison. By contrast, only 4 per cent (one participant) from the matched group had self-harmed in the past, and this was outside prison. The percentage of prisoners with a drug problem prior to entering prison was high. A total of 60 per cent of the self-harm sample self-reported a problem with drugs, compared with 15 per cent of the matched sample. Although vulnerability did not predict mean levels of psychological distress with prisoners interviewed at three days (in Chapter 2), it seemed to be the case that individuals who had self-harmed had accumulated considerable vulnerability that affected their prison experience.

Table 6.5 Chi-squared differences on vulnerability measures

Variable	Self-harm		Matched		chi-square	Sign
	%	N	%	N		
Received psychiatric treatment	56.0	14	8.0	2	13.24	.001
Self-harmed inside prison before (before this term)	16.0	4	0.0	0	4.35	.110
Self-harmed outside prison	48.0	12	4.0	1	12.58	.001
Drug problem prior to custody	60.0	15	16.0	4	10.27	.003

Table 6.6 Differences between individuals who had self-harmed and those who had not on quantitative dimensions

	Self-harm		Matched control		T	Sign
	M	SD	M	SD		
Psychological distress	4.18	.63	2.99	.74	6.12	.001
Social support outside	3.57	1.10	3.69	.81	−.439	.660
Prison social support	3.08	.74	2.88	.62	1.04	.304
Locus of control	2.76	.61	3.18	.50	−2.69	.01
Safety	2.72	.78	3.39	.69	−3.20	.002
Perceived adaptability	2.64	.72	3.26	.60	−3.30	.002

In order to explore further differences, I carried out t-tests and looked at group mean differences on the following dimensions (reported in Chapter 2): locus of control, prison social support, psychological distress, perceived ability to adapt and outside social support. Table 6.6 shows the results of these analyses. The mean scores on psychological distress for individuals who had self-harmed were significantly higher (indicating higher distress) than the mean scores on distress for those who had not self-harmed, M = 4.18 and 2.99 respectively, $t(48)$ = 6.12, p = .001. As expected, individuals who self-harmed experienced higher levels of distress. Moreover, 88.0 per cent (22 participants) of the self-harm group had suicidal thoughts; only one participant from the matched control group had these thoughts. A total of 36 per cent of the self-harm group had self-harmed before during this current prison term, all of them were on an open F2052SH form, and 20.0 per cent (five participants) had been on a form before.

How did those who self-harmed score on other dimensions discussed previously? Individuals who self-harmed reported a lower perceived ability to adapt than those who had not self-harmed (M = 2.64 and 3.26 respectively, $t(48)$ = 6.12, p = .002, where a high score indicates a higher perceived ability to adapt). How did individuals perceive the safety of the prison? They also reported lower levels of safety than those who had not self-harmed (M = 2.72 and 3.39 respectively, $t(48)$ = −3.20, p = .002, where a high score indicates a higher perceived level of safety). Again this is in line with results reported in Chapter 2, individuals who were highly distressed reporting lower levels of perceived safety. Was there a difference on locus of control scores between the groups? The mean score on locus of control for individuals who had self-harmed was significantly lower, indicating a more external locus of control, than the mean scores on locus of control for those who had not self-harmed

(M = 2.76 and 3.18 respectively, t(48) = –2.69, p =.01). Individuals who self-harmed were more external in their locus of control. This result is congruent with the regression analysis presented in Chapter 2 that found that individuals who were more distressed were also more external in their locus of control. With social support, however, there were no statistically significant differences. Now I examine these results in more detail.

The role of perceived safety and locus of control

Many of the prisoners who self-harmed commented that they felt physically unsafe, despite the fact that few had been physically bullied. One prisoner reported bullying as the prompt for harming himself:

> I just had some troubles with some lads and tried to commit suicide and was brought down here. I just want to get out of jail, but I've got to do the rest of my licence now. That is one thing I hate about being on remand is, you don't know what time you are getting at all. [Prisoner]
> [Interviewer: So when you were on Teal you said you had some trouble with some lads?]
> Yeah, I was getting in trouble with some lads. They are starting on me, saying they were going to get me, picking on me, innit? [Prisoner]
> [Interviewer: Where was this?]
> Through my door. One of them said, my friend is gonna get you, and I couldn't take that shit. [Prisoner]
> [Interviewer: What did you do then?]
> I made a noose. I can't take it no more. They kept coming to my window saying they were going to kill me when I get out on 'sosh, get me in the showers, beat me up. [Prisoner]
> [Interviewer: Did you know any of them?]
> No, I didn't know none of them. All the old people I knew on Teal were gone. They all got shipped out, sent to next prisons, got discharged, everything. [Prisoner]

Other prisoners, although they had not experienced direct victimisation or intimidation themselves, feared that they could be attacked:

> No one has bullied me yet, but that is what I still feel like 'cause I see people fighting and I think that could be me, innit? [Prisoner]

Some prisoners who self-harmed felt unsafe when they had to make a transition to another wing or even cell. They perceived their environment to be unpredictable, and they felt unsettled. One individual self-harmed when he was moved to a different cell in the health-care centre:

> I didn't feel safe for some reason, and then they brought me back down to cell number 20. [Prisoner]
> [Interviewer: What was going through your head when you moved?]
> I was all right about moving. It was just when I got there, I didn't like it. [Prisoner]
> [Interviewer: Did the cell look different?]
> Yeah, the cell I'm in now has got a bed and little wall unit with a shelf and that on it. The other cell just had a bed with a toilet and sink and that. I just didn't like it. I didn't feel comfortable in it. I didn't feel as safe up there for some reason. [Prisoner]
> [Interviewer: Safe from what?]
> I don't know. It's just one of them things. But where I am now, I feel all right. [Prisoner]

Individuals who did not feel safe related this to not being able to place trust in individuals in the environment.

Safety related to feelings of security more generally in these prisoners' lives. One prisoner stated that he was 'scared of living'. I asked him what he wanted to happen when he harmed himself:

> I wanted to go to heaven with God, innit? So I could be safe. I am scared, I am scared to live. I am scared of living. [Prisoner]

The concept of safety was complex, and did not pertain solely to fear of physical attack. It took on a broader conceptualisation and encompassed feelings of psychological security, attachment and trust. Related to the perceived lack of safety was an external locus of control (as discussed in Chapter 2). Individuals who had self-harmed felt that they had less control over their immediate environment and over their lives more generally. In fact, 80 per cent of individuals who had self-harmed (20 participants) strongly agreed or agreed with the statement that 'most of what happens to me in prison is out of my hands'. This percentage was 56 per cent (14 participants) for those who had not harmed themselves. A total of 56 per cent (14 participants) who had self-harmed strongly agreed or agreed with the statement that 'Prison is so negative that I can't help but be influenced in a negative way', compared with 24 per cent (six participants) of those who had not self-harmed. This perceived lack of control sometimes triggered incidents of self-harm:

'Cause I was a cleaner, everyone was sending me to go and get them a couple of roll-ups off someone else, and I didn't have nothing for myself. [...] I just couldn't handle the surroundings after that sort of thing. What everybody was saying was going through one ear and out the other sort of thing. I just couldn't hack it. It was like people all that day were telling me to do things for them. I was fucked off with people telling me what to do sort of thing. I can't say fuck all. No one is giving me the chance to say nothing. So, I just done that out of stupidity. [Prisoner]

This individual, who subsequently swallowed razor blades, felt out of control, and he could not cope with this feeling.

People who had re-entered prison quickly, and who had self-harmed, also felt that they had little control when they rapidly returned to prison. They told me that they had tried not to come back but somehow felt that they had no control over their fate. Although many prisoners experienced the control-limiting nature of the environment, individuals who self-harmed experienced this limitation more severely:

When you are in the prison, it is all in their hands. They tell you what to do. [Prisoner]

I tried to commit suicide down there [in the court cells]. I had enough of prison. You keep coming back, and you can see it ending up in front of you, and you can't do nothing about it, you can't do nothing about it. [Prisoner]

I can see someone controlling my life, playing with my life in their hands. There is too much suffering and too much pain. I've got too much problems. My head was about to explode. [Prisoner]

These individuals were more external in their locus of control and perceived others to be controlling their lives. The act of self-harm might have seemed an extreme means to assert some control over themselves and their world.

Some people, though, did not want to harm themselves and saw their self-harm too as something beyond the control of their own impulses:

> I'm not going to do that [attempt suicide], but I can't make a promise 'cause I'm not in control of what happens to me. When it happens, I'm not in control of myself. [Prisoner]

These individuals felt they were at the mercy of their own feelings. They asked staff to help them to control these urges by the removal of their belongings when they felt like self-harming:

> They took my stuff out my cell. Everything sharp so that I could hurt myself with and gave me it back the next day. [...] I asked them 'cause I said I don't feel I can control myself. [Prisoner]

Individuals who self-harmed felt less able to control their thoughts, emotions and behaviour, and felt that the world around them was more unpredictable. They perceived less control than those who had not self-harmed, felt that they could not influence outcomes in their lives, and were more concerned with the deprivation of autonomy than individuals who had not harmed themselves.

The role of social support within prison

An important protective factor to consider when examining self-harming behaviour is social support. Westefeld *et al.* (2000) concluded, from their review of the literature, that the 'absence of social support is especially relevant in terms of predicting suicidality. Increased social support for the suicidal person reduces the likelihood of suicide and increases the likelihood of obtaining social support after an attempted suicide' (Westefeld *et al.* 2000: 452). Over the past decade, research into suicidal behaviour and social support has proliferated, with studies of a diverse range of topics and populations.[4] Research examining social support has been carried out with adolescents and college students in the general community and has developed some useful aetiological models of suicidal ideation and behaviour (Rudd 1990; Clum and Febbraro 1994; Yang and Clum 1994). Windle and Windle (1997) examined data from a survey of 975 adolescents and found that adolescents who had attempted suicide reported lower levels of social support than those who had not. DeWilde *et al.* (1994) examined the relationship between social support, life events, and various behavioural characteristics of adolescents who were at high risk of suicidal behaviour. The group which was deemed to be of the highest risk differed from the group deemed to be of the lowest risk in that the former reported less social support and understanding from relationships outside the family and siblings within the family.

Moreover, although suicidal individuals are less likely to have social support resources available to begin with, they may also be less likely to use any existing sources they do have. Being suicidal may have an impact on whether help is sought and then received in the first place. Carlton and Deane (2000) examined the impact of suicidal ideation on the intentions of New Zealand high school students 12–18 years of age to seek professional help. They hypothesised that suicidal ideation would function as an approach factor, like psychological distress, encouraging these individuals to seek help; but, in fact, they found that a higher level of suicidal ideation resulted in people seeking help less; it acted as an avoidance factor. This result is in line with the findings of Rudd *et al.* (1995), who found help negation in psychiatric patients who were suicidal. Help negation is defined as 'the refusal to accept or access available helping resources as a likely function of the manifestation of hopelessness, pessimism and cynicism' (Rudd *et al.* 1995, quoted in Carlton and Deane 2000: 36). Moreover, Deane *et al.* (1999) found that prisoners' intentions to seek professional help for suicidal thoughts were less than for other personal or emotional problems (cited in Carlton and Deane 2000). Some evidence thus exists to suggest that being suicidal may have an impact on the extent to which help is sought.

Research has thus assessed the impact of perceived social support on psychological and suicidal behaviour and has usually found that social support does protect an individual from engaging in such behaviours. Yet, findings also show that being suicidal may prevent individuals from seeking support in the first place. It is therefore necessary to look at the help-seeking behaviour of those who are suicidal, and those who are not, in order to uncover the complex role of social support. Moreover, unlike the studies of social support more generally, studies of social support in relation to suicidal behaviour have failed to locate its role within the context of social relationships. They have not yet examined the complex processes of giving and receiving social support, and whether this relates to suicidal behaviour.

So what role did social support within the prison play for individuals who had self-harmed? Although significant differences were found between those who self-harmed and those who did not in relation to psychological distress, perceived ability to adapt, locus of control and safety, fewer differences were found between the groups in how much support they perceived both inside and outside the prison. The relationship between psychological distress and social support, inside and outside the prison, was complex. Individuals who self-harmed did not differ significantly from others in the level of support they perceived from staff within the prison. The quantitative data suggest that individuals who self-harmed were in fact reporting slightly higher levels of perceived support than those who did not self-harm. The problem with interpreting the data is that after they had self-harmed, the institution responded and provided them with considerable support. The data are thus contaminated in this respect. It is difficult, then, to determine whether the prisoners who self-harmed perceived less support before the incident occurred. It could even be suggested that there was a *deficit* in perceived support, given that these individuals had *actually* received more support by the time I came to interview them. Although the figures suggest higher perceptions of support, these perceptions are not in proportion to the amount of support offered by the prison to them after they had self-harmed. Most prisoners who had self-harmed agreed that staff had interacted with them after the incident and had done so in the past, but they varied in how they perceived and responded to this interaction.

Those who did perceive support generally reported one or two specific members of staff who had helped them, rather than reporting support from the staff as a whole. This perception has possible implications for including specific questions about the source of support. One individual, who had been suffering from depression and had cut himself, felt that the staff members who had helped him were more caring and less aggressive than the others. Prisoners made a distinction between staff who 'really cared' for them and those who were there 'just to do their job'. Staff members whom they identified as caring were also identified as more truthful and more genuine in their concern:

[Interviewer: Why do you find him helpful?]
Because he is caring. He cares about my welfare. He cares whether I hurt myself or not, and he does his best to help me with whatever I need doing. If he can't do it for some reason, he'll tell me the truth, not make up some excuse. [Prisoner]

They felt that some staff had provided them with emotional support and had been comforting. Again the *manner* of support was important:

[Interviewer: The officer you get on with, what's different about him?]
It is how he approaches me when I am in a bad way, yeah. [Prisoner]

[Interviewer: So when you are feeling in a bad way, how do you need to be approached?]
Softly like, softly approach. Like asking me to come and speak to them and not twisting me up. [Prisoner]

The source of support was important in determining how effective the support was felt to be. Many of those who felt supported commented in particular upon the approach of the outreach team, as in the following case:

[Interviewer: How was the outreach guy?]
He was all right. He said, 'You swear, you give me your word, you are not going to do yourself in'. I said 'I give you my word'. He said, 'You need me, I'll come. I won't be there at the click of my fingers, but sit tight and I will come.' That was good. [Prisoner]

They also cited members of the health-care staff, and the chaplaincy, while officers were cited but with less frequency:

I'd talk to the nurses 'cause at the end of the day an officer is an officer. He is a screw at the end of the day. A nurse, nurses are the same as any nurse that works in a hospital. They are there to help us. Fair enough, the officers are as well, but I don't know. It is just easier talking to a nurse. [Prisoner]

These findings are consistent with the survey results that found that the chaplain was the primary preferred source of support for emotional problems. Those with mental health problems were more willing to talk to the doctors and psychiatrists. On the whole, those who perceived that they had benefited from support still sharply distinguished between the various staff: they really appreciated particular individuals and would not interact with others. Individuals who had self-harmed made even sharper distinctions between different members of staff than did those who had not self-harmed.

There was a second group of individuals who *did* perceive support to be available but, unfortunately, could not *respond* to this support or benefit from it. So, while they agreed that they had been helped, they also reported that they felt the same even after the supportive interaction. These individuals' level of distress was high, and they could not progress across the threshold in order to benefit from support. Moreover, they simply did not want to be helped, and they were least willing to seek support. They were not even likely to seek help immediately after harming themselves. Members of staff had usually been alerted to their plight by a cellmate pressing a cell bell or by their observations. These individuals were the most hopeless of all: many felt that nothing could help and that their problems were insoluble:

> I don't want help. I've been like this for a year, and I ain't gonna change. [Prisoner]

This individual (who was mentioned above) could not come to terms with the death of his girlfriend through an overdose of heroin. He felt that support from staff would not be able to solve this problem nor how he felt about it. Another example came from the prisoner whose mother had recently died (also mentioned above):

> [Interviewer: How willing are you to talk to someone when you feel stressed out?]
> No, man, I don't like talking to people. I am just talking to you to help you out with your thing. There ain't nothing they can do. No one is going to solve your problems. The fact is, I never got to go to the funeral and nothing is going to help change that. [Prisoner]
> [Interviewer: What does it feel like when you are stressed out?]
> It is like something is bothering you and you can't do nothing about it. That is the killer. Usually you can do something about it. It is like a problem that you can't do nothing about. No matter what you do, there is nothing to solve it. My mum is not going to be alive again. Nothing can change that, so it is difficult to know what to do. There is nothing to do. [Prisoner]

This quotation aptly captures the helplessness and powerlessness experienced by some prisoners who self-harm. His situation certainly could not be reversed, but nor did he see any means of managing the emotional distress that it had caused. Seeking social support was not a coping strategy he thought would benefit him.

There was a further group of individuals who did not perceive support to be available to them, despite the fact that it was highly probable that staff had attempted to provide some form of support. This final group can be further subdivided into those who took a defensive stance against the institution, and those who demanded very specific forms of help. The first subgroup, the defensive subgroup, felt that the staff had total control and that accepting support from them would further decrease their self-control. These individuals thought of themselves as self-reliant and independent and of the staff as agents of interference:

[Interviewer: Since you've been here, would you say you've been helped out by the staff?]
I don't know you know. I guess I could say yes, but I guess I could say no. If someone want to die, yeah, what the point in bugging them, yeah? Just leave them and let them do what they got to do. But no, they come and interfere. 'Let me stop this. I'll be the hero.' You get me? They are just nosy. [Prisoner]

Another prisoner had the following comment:

[Interviewer: Have you been helped out by staff since you've been here?]
Staff are wankers: standard! [Prisoner]
[Interviewer: Why do you say that?]
I hate them all. Trust. I hate them all. You need to, you ask them to do something for you, 'cause you're in your cell, and they completely ignore you. They will be standing up there, yeah, like a second from your door, yeah, and they'll completely ignore you like you don't even exist, and that is wrong. You get all these mad feeling, and you don't know what to do with them. [Prisoner]

These prisoners held negative attitudes towards the staff and overtly rejected any help that had been offered. They were often suspicious of staff and felt that staff only pretended to help them, in order to meet bureaucratic demands for care. They did not trust the staff, nor did they trust the world more generally. This group of prisoners also presented staff with disciplinary problems from time to time. These individuals were perhaps more external in their locus of control.

Secondly, there was the subgroup of individuals who did not perceive support because they only wanted help on their *own terms* and demanded a rather specific form of assistance. One prisoner stated:

I want them to leave me alone unless I have to talk to them. Be there when I need to talk. [Prisoner]

One prisoner told me that he did not want to interact with staff on a daily basis; he would do so only when he needed something. He then explained how frustrated he became when staff did not answer his requests immediately:

When I am pressing the buzzer to talk to someone and when no one listens to me, I just go mad, man. [Prisoner]

Others within this group demanded perhaps too much support from staff and would constantly ask them for help. These demands caused difficulties for both the prisoner and the member of staff. Often unrealistic demands would be placed on staff, asking for help a lot, but then not being satisfied with what had been provided:

> [Interviewer: So have you been helped by staff since you've been here?]
> No, man. They don't help you, man. [Prisoner]
> [Interviewer: For them to help you, what would you like them to do?]
> They can't help you to your own satisfaction. They can help you but not to your own satisfaction. What you need, what you really want, they can't give you. [Prisoner]
> [Interviewer: What do you really want?]
> Sometimes when you ask them, you ask them for something, they said they can't do that in prison. [Prisoner]
> [Interviewer: What do you ask for?]
> One day I said I need a shower 'cause I was feeling really stressed, 'cause if I could shower I will calm down myself, and they said, 'You are in prison. You have to wait your turn.' That is taking the piss. [Prisoner]

It was difficult for these prisoners to accept the limitations of their situation. Whereas prisoners who were less distressed and more internal in their locus of control were able to mould their environment to suit their needs, those who had self-harmed and who sought support without considering the particular environment would elicit inconsistent responses from staff. These individuals would also be more likely to demand help at the most inappropriate times. For example, a prisoner might want to have a shower or make a telephone call but instead of choosing a convenient time would make this request during prisoner movements or when the staff member was dealing with another request. This one chance to receive support was minimised due to the time and manner in which the help was sought. Having social skills and the ability to recognise others' emotions (i.e. the officer's) was an important aspect of adapting to life in prison.

For these individuals, self-harm sometimes acted as a means of communicating this constant need for, and perceived deficit of, support. If help did not come their way as and when they felt that they needed it, self-harm served as a means of mobilising or communicating their distress. Feeling unsupported furthered their sense of isolation and desperation and pushed them over the threshold to self-harm. One prisoner who attempted to hang himself explained that he was upset coming back from court because he had expected to be bailed. He had no opportunity to discuss his court case with his solicitor and wanted the staff to help him. Although his request was valid, another more resilient prisoner might have waited for a suitable time to solve the problem; with less resilience, he sought an instant solution:

> I came back from court and tried to talk to an officer, but they don't care. They didn't give me the chance to phone my solicitor. I didn't have the number to phone him. [Prisoner]

When he attempted to hang himself, the officers prevented him from doing so. The outreach team were then contacted, the number of his solicitor was found, and a telephone call was made. Another prisoner told me that he cut himself so that the staff realised how annoyed he was with them for not coming with his medication on time.

> 'Cause every time I ask him to do something for me, he does it. But when I ask everyone else and they say, 'Yeah', and then when you ask them if they've done it, they say, 'Shit, I forgot, or I didn't have time, or someone was kicking off,' and they weren't really. It was just an excuse that they made 'cause they couldn't be bothered to do it. [Prisoner]

Self-harm acted as a mobilising device for help in these cases. As a separate but related issue, some individuals self-harmed for reasons that they admitted were strategic:

> I am getting sentenced next month, but with all the problems I've got the judge might not give me the sentence I deserve. He might cut it down a lot. [...] I was talking to a boy the other day, saying I was going back for sentencing, and he said, 'Why don't you act like you are mad, and you'll be sent to hospital.' [Prisoner]

Some prisoners wanted to be placed on a self-harm monitoring form, as they felt staff would be kinder, or not transfer them to another prison, if it was thought they were suicidal.

When we examine support inside prison and its relationship to distress, it is important to look at its availability, its perception and the individual's ability to respond to it when it is offered. It was clear that many individuals in the sample had not sought help themselves before self-harming and were unable to perceive support in proportion to the amount that had been given to them. Many were in an even more difficult state, where they were unable to respond to help that was offered; these individuals were the most hopeless in the sample. Although social support had the potential to protect individuals against distress, if their level of distress was initially too high, the impact of the support would not be recognised or they were unable to respond to it.

The role of social support outside prison

I will now consider the role of social support from family and friends beyond the prison world. Research carried out in the general community has found that those adolescents who had made previous attempts or were currently at risk of suicide perceived that they had low family support (Eskin 1995). Morano (1993) conducted a cross-sectional study of the relationship between suicidal behaviour, depression, hopelessness and social support among psychiatric inpatients (20 suicide attempters and 20 non-suicide attempters matched on levels of depression). Findings indicated that low levels of family support and loss were most predictive of suicide attempts among adolescents. Similarly, within prisons, research has found that individuals who had self-harmed had less contact with family and friends outside prison and perceived less support to be available to them (Liebling 1992; Wichmann 2000; Dear et al. 2001a).

What was the role of outside support for individuals who had self-harmed at Feltham? As with the results examining inside support, the t-test results indicated no significant differences between individuals who had self-harmed and those who had not in their level of perceived support from outside the prison. Again the role of support from outside prison requires further quantitative and qualitative enquiry. Support from outside prison was also of central importance when examining self-harm. Indeed, as stated earlier in this chapter, relationships were a key concern for individuals who had self-harmed. Separation from their loved ones was painful, and the breakdown in ties was cited as a reason for self-harm. But what were these ties like? Did individuals who had self-harmed differ in their social networks from those who had not harmed themselves? Table 6.7 shows these networks. The main point to notice is that individuals who self-harmed were more likely to have no fixed abode: some of these individuals were living with friends temporarily, and others were living rough on the streets. By contrast, none of the matched individuals who had not self-harmed was homeless.

Table 6.7 Differences in social networks between individuals who had self-harmed and those who had not

Variable		Self-harm		Matched control	
		%	N	%	N
Lived with	Mum (and siblings)	21	5	24.0	6
(within last 7 days	Dad	0	0	8.0	2
of coming to prison)	Parents (and siblings)	12.5	3	24.0	6
	Alone	12.5	3	28.0	7
	Partner	16.7	4	12.0	3
	No fixed abode	25.0	6	0	0
	Siblings or extended family	8.3	2	0	0
	Friends	4.2	1	4.0	1
Who do you feel	Mum (and siblings)	27.3	6	36.4	8
closest to?	Dad	0	0	9.0	2
	Parents (and siblings)	4.5	1	0	0
	Partner	22.7	5	22.7	5
	Extended family and siblings	27.3	6	22.7	5
	Friends	9.0	2	4.5	1
	No one	9.0	2	4.5	1
How many close friends?		3.57		3.69	

When I asked prisoners to describe their families and social networks outside prison, those who had self-harmed talked more about abandonment:

I was kicked out when I was 13, 'cause that's when I picked up my drug problem, and I stopped getting along with my mum and dad. I came back when I was 14. I was only back for a little while and then I was on bail for a crime I done. I think it was aggravated TDA [taking and driving away], dangerous driving, 'cause I stole a car. I went back home. My mum and dad were going on holiday a week later, and we had a big argument and that. They said I stole holiday money, which was a load of lies. They just didn't want me around. They just didn't want me around the house when they were on holiday, sort of thing. So they ended up dropping my bail conditions, and I went into care. [Prisoner]

[Interviewer: So how long did you stay in care?]
I went back home a couple of times, but it never worked out. My mum and dad were always drinking, so I couldn't stand being there. I had a drug problem that needed sorting out. It was just getting worse. I'd come off the drugs and relapsed 'cause of my family, if you know what I mean? 'Cause I couldn't handle the surroundings around me. I ended up getting my own flat through the council when I was 17 and then ended up losing it when I did a six-month sentence. [Prisoner]

Another prisoner recalled an experience when a car ran over his hand when he was a child, and he had nobody to look after him. This neglect was typical of the lack of care that many of these individuals experienced in early childhood:

I was put in a children's home from when I was three. [...] I was left out on the streets when I was aged four, and see that finger is bent? All my fingers got broken. I was on the road playing and a car went over me. No one was even there, and I just carried on. I spent most of my life in some day-care centre. [Prisoner]

Many reported continuing problems in their relationships with their families. Some prisoners not only had their own problem with drugs before entering prison, but also had mothers who were addicts:

See, my mum takes drugs as well. That's why it is hard for me to get off it, because the only address I've got is my mum's address, and there is my mum there and my mum's boyfriend, and they both take heroin, so it is hard. [Prisoner]

Their childhoods were more likely to be reported as turbulent, and many who self-harmed had absent fathers. Some expressed resentment towards their fathers:

I hope he's dead. There's nothing else, you get me? I know for one, yeah, that if I've got any kid, yeah, there is no way, yeah, that I'm not gonna want to see my kid in nine years. That is just totally wrong, you get me? It don't matter how many kids you've got, yeah, you should always make the time to see them no matter what it costs, you get me? [Prisoner]

Although the group who had self-harmed and the group of matched controls did not differ significantly in the number of close friendships outside prison, the quality of these friendships was weaker among those who self-harmed. Many in this group commented that they did not have any true friends, due to their involvement in drugs:

> I don't have no good friends to be quite honest. They are all riff-raff, if you know what I mean. They are all either junkies or they are involved in crimes. They are either being my friends to try and get something out of me, or just associate to do crime with. [Prisoner]

Generally, the friendships of individuals who self-harmed were fragile and unstable. As we saw in the social network analysis earlier, there was some relationship between the ability to form ties within prison and the amount of contact with family and friends outside the prison; in particular, the people with less contact outside prison received fewer nominations and nominated fewer other people too. (Table 6.8 recaps this part of those data.) A study by Slosar (1978) found that prisoners who were more integrated in the prison had more contacts outside prison, and concluded that 'rather than intra- and extra-institutional ties being interchangeable, or one serving as a substitute for the other, it appears that the characteristics or conditions that promote one also promote the other' (p. 67). These findings counteract the older study by Clemmer (1940). Data from my social network analysis may also suggest some link between an ability to maintain relationships outside prison and forming ties within it. Incidentally, individuals who received visits also reported that they felt that the staff had been more helpful than did individuals who had not received visits. When we turn back to the interviews with individuals who had self-harmed, I found something similar. Table 6.9 shows the percentage of prisoners who were supported. A total of 32.0 per cent of individuals who had self-harmed agreed that they had been helped out in the last week by someone outside prison; this figure was 72.0 per cent for individuals who had not self-harmed. Moreover, only 32 per cent of individuals who had self-harmed received visits compared with 64.0 per cent of individuals who had not harmed themselves. Finally, 56 per cent of individuals who had self-harmed were in contact (through any mode) compared with 84.0 per cent of those who had not self-harmed. Individuals who self-harmed were less supported by people outside prison than those who had not self-harmed.

However, the results are not as simple as first made out. While the individuals who had self-harmed clearly reported lower levels of support, as measured by discrete items in Table 6.9, there were no statistically significant differences in the measure of *perceived* support from outside

Table 6.8 Group differences in out-degree and in-degree scores

Variable	Level	N	Mean out-degree	Mean in-degree
Receives visits	Yes	29	3.76	3.90
	No	20	3.30	2.85

Table 6.9 Further measures of social support: differences between individuals who had self-harmed and those who had not

Item	Self-harm %	N	Matched %	N	Chi-square	Sign
Been helped out in past week	32.0	8	72.0	18	8.01	.01
Received visits	32.0	8	64.0	16	5.13	.05
In contact by letter, telephone, visits	56.0	14	84.0	21	4.67	.06

the prison. Table 6.10 shows the percentage of individuals who strongly agreed or agreed with the items measuring outside support. Generally, high levels of support were reported by both those who had self-harmed and the matched controls. How can the discrepancy in results of different measures be explained? How can individuals, on the one hand, explain that they have not received much tangible support from people outside prison and, on the other hand, *claim to feel* supported? Within the interviews, there were similar apparent contradictions but also clues to their explanation. Often prisoners would describe their family relationships, and the practical levels of support they provided, as poor; but they would then state that their families 'do care for them really'. Even if they were not receiving support at present, they often insisted that their families still loved them:

> I know my mum and dad love me to bits like. I know parents will always love their kids no matter what they do, no matter what they are like sort of thing, but I love my parents to bits as well, but to be honest we just don't get along, if you know what I mean? It is like I can never please them. [Prisoner]

One explanation, apparent in many interviews, was that the prisoners felt guilt and responsibility for their negative relationships with their families. This guilt was especially apparent in those with addictions to

Table 6.10 Percentage of prisoners who strongly agreed or agreed with items relating to outside support: differences between individuals who had self-harmed and those who had not

	Self-harm		Matched	
Item	%	N	%	N
There are people I know outside who do things to make me happy	60.0	15	52.0	13
There are people I know outside who make me feel cared for	60.0	15	64.0	16
There are people I know outside who can be relied on no matter what happens	68.0	17	64.0	16
There are people I know outside who accept me as I am	68.0	17	72.0	18
There are people I know outside who make me feel an important part of their lives	68.0	17	52.0	13
There are people I know outside who give me support and encouragement	56.0	14	60.0	15

drugs. These people may have been able to recognise that their families did love them and did care for them, but could no longer support them, given the situations they had caused; they took partial responsibility for the breakdown in familial relationships. Perhaps it was also too painful to admit on a quantitative measure that family members did not care. Thus, measuring and understanding outside social support was complex.

However, from their claims, it became apparent that family support was central to individuals' concerns. Moreover, I found that support also appeared to influence prisoners' willingness to seek support. The general survey of seeking support revealed that those who received visits reported a higher mean score on willingness to seek support for an emotional problem from officers than those who did not receive visits (M = 3.1, SD = 2.2 for visits; M = 2.1, SD = 1.8, for no visits, t(47) = 2.44, p = .02). Receiving support outside prison had implications for how support was perceived within it. Those who were in contact with their families were also more willing to seek support in prison. That may be because having a secure family outside enabled prisoners to feel more comfortable in their day-to-day lives inside; or that may be because being able to maintain family ties outside prison enabled prisoners to develop ties inside prison. Not only were the individuals who self-harmed more external in their locus of control, but they also had more difficulties in forming and maintaining relationships with others, whether among the staff or outside. They most needed to rely on others and were least able to do so.

Notes

1 One of the main problems with this study is that suicidality was not measured. Those included in the suicide group were the first 25 cases brought to the surgery under strict suicide supervision. It is possible that those individuals in the other three groups also displayed suicidal thoughts or behaviours, either in the past or present, or both. Again, therefore, it is possible that these groups are not mutually exclusive.

2 Incidents of self-harm at Feltham were recorded on the F213 form, devised by the Safer Custody Group to collate statistics on self-harm across the prison estate, and by consulting this record on a daily basis, I obtained the sample.

3 The term 'attempted suicide' included all incidents of self-inflicted injury with the sole intent of ending one's life. The term 'self-injury' includes all incidents that involved the purposeful infliction of injury that were undertaken for something other than cessation of life (Snow 2002).

4 Research has been carried out on social support and suicidal ideation and attempts among adults (Vilhjalmsson *et al.* 1998; Bille-Brahe *et al.* 1999), suicide risk in patients with post-traumatic stress disorder (Kotler *et al.* 1993), suicidal behaviour among African-American women (Nisbett 1996 Gibbs 1997; Kaslow *et al.* 2000), suicidal ideation and depression among African-American college students (Kimbrough *et al.* 1996; Harris and Molock 2000), suicidal ideation and behaviour among those with HIV-AIDS (Kalichman *et al.* 2000), suicidal ideation and behaviour among the elderly (Alexopoulos *et al.* 1999), suicidal ideation and behaviour among the homeless (Schutt *et al.* 1994), suicidal ideation and behaviour among recent immigrants (Hovey 1999, 2000; Ponizovsky and Ritsner 1999) and suicide attempts among alcoholics (Hewitt *et al.* 1998).

Chapter 7

Transition, adaptation and attachment

Men who are vulnerable often assert an independence they do not feel, and defy those whose goodwill they need. (Toch 1992: 104)

I went in with an armoury of concepts, theoretical ideas and categories. On the other hand, I did not initially regard these as sacrosanct – early on they were regarded as provisional in the sense that they could be modified, abandoned, confirmed or retained as required by the unfolding of new data or changing theoretical priorities and relevancies. (Layder 1998: 58)

This book set out to understand how young men survived and adapted to life within one remand centre in the UK. It examined a number of different constructs that were thought to contribute to prisoners' level of psychological distress, including locus of control, safety, prison support and trust, and outside support. In this chapter, I will conclude by reflecting upon the results presented in this book and will discuss the value of attachment theory in understanding the psychosocial experiences of young men in prison.

The experience of transition and adaptation

The transition into prison was a difficult experience for prisoners. As Toch (1992) stated, 'rapid forceful changes in environmental conditions test one's capacity to cope. If the individual does not possess or acquire the emergency resources to assist him in maintaining balance when facing such abruptly changing situations, he may ultimately break down' (p. 185). Although there were common experiences at this early entry phase (preoccupation with safety, uncertainty, losing control and freedom, and separation and loss), individuals differed in the level of psychological distress these experiences caused. At three days, prisoners' locus of control, their perceived ability to adapt and their perceived safety were related to their levels of psychological distress. Those with an internal locus of control, who felt that they could adapt and who felt safer, experienced lower levels of psychological distress than those with an external locus of control. The prisoners needed a number of psychological resources in order to cope with this transitional experience.

Prisoners also adapted differentially to their first month in prison. Indeed, 'the same prison offers different opportunities and different threats to different inmates exposed to it' (Toch 1977: 182). I found there were three types of adaptation (practical, social and psychological) and three stages through which people might progress within the first month (liminality, acceptance and equilibrium). Generally, people who had moved towards equilibrium had a less distressing early and intermediate experience of custody. They quickly demonstrated a capacity to regulate their thoughts and emotions, and were more quickly able to become involved in the regime. It appears that the capacity to regulate their emotions, albeit at a moderate level at first, enabled them to begin to adapt. They were more able to exert more control over their environment, meeting the environment half way, moulding themselves to fit it, but also moulding the environment and its various social relationships. They were more able to seek support and accept support that was offered to them.

Not all prisoners, though, managed to adapt themselves and their environment in this way. Some found it difficult to move beyond the liminal stage of imprisonment, even after 30 days. They were the most distressed on initial entry and found it difficult to regulate their thoughts and emotions. Some had thoughts of suicide and some were withdrawing from drugs. Rumination and inability to regulate thoughts and emotions prevented this small group from adapting. There appeared to be a crucial hurdle of distress that prisoners had to jump. If they could not regulate their thoughts and emotions when they encountered the difficulties of entering prison, they would find it difficult to understand the practical aspects of prison and would be more likely to withdraw socially and turn inward. These prisoners tended to stay longer on induction, and if they experienced transitions within their first month, they found them difficult for they added uncertainty and fed feelings of helplessness and lack of control. These individuals were more determined by their environment than determining it; they made little attempt to master their world and lacked agency. For example, they were likely still to be unemployed within the prison. Although support was available to the distressed in Feltham, this support did not alleviate psychological pain for many of them. The institution had attempted to meet their needs, but they had to be willing and able to accept what was offered. Responding to support and benefiting from it were skills that some young men had not developed.

Adaptation was a dynamic, and not a strictly linear, process, however. Although those who entered prison with lower levels of distress found it easier to adapt, some also moved backwards during the first month in prison. Adaptation was not predictable, and different life events and circumstances continued to play an important role in influencing it. Yet, those who showed resilience were less often thrown off balance by such events and more often had personal and social resources to help them survive; for the more vulnerable, the unpredictable events had the potential to have a devastating psychological impact.

The importance of locus of control, social support, trust and safety

One important concept that emerged was locus of control. I found that individuals who had an internal locus of control were less distressed on entering prison. Moreover, individuals who had harmed themselves were more likely to have an external locus of control than those who had not. Individuals who were less distressed managed to interact with their environment in a more positive manner. Rather than being passive members of the prison regime, they adapted it to suit their needs. One manner in which they did so was through creating niches. Seymour (1977) defined 'niche' as a 'functional sub-setting containing desired objects, space, resources, people, and relationships with people' (Seymour 1977: 237). One prime example of a niche was the cell and the cellmate relationship (described in Chapter 5). Toch (1977) argued that 'even when environmental conditions appear most hostile people create, seemingly from rock like or diaphanous material, a fabric of life' (Toch 1977: 236). It could be suggested that individuals who entered prison with an internal locus of control brought about a higher degree of control over their surroundings in a manner which was acceptable to the prison staff. It could be suggested that individuals who were more internal in their locus of control were readier to seek and accept support, without resenting it as reducing their autonomy. Being able to receive support made people able to exert a higher degree of control over their own lives.

On the other hand, individuals who were more external in their locus of control were less able to seek support, as they acted with a perceived independence. For these individuals, accepting help symbolised relinquishing control. Indeed, as Toch (1977) noted, 'if one seeks support, one reduces the range of one's independence and freedom of choice' (p. 156). Toch and Adams (2002) identified pursuing autonomy as one behavioural pattern in their study of individuals who had 'acted out'. It could be argued that individuals who had concerns over autonomy versus dependence were in fact more external in their locus of control; they perceived that they had less control over their world. Toch and Adams (2002) argued that the prison setting 'invites autonomy–dependence concerns' (p. 202). These were dependence (expecting and relying on others), conditional dependence (alternating between being dependent on others and being rebellious), defying authority (being anti-authority) and, finally, rejecting constraints (individuals believe that others have 'no right' to tell them what to do). It could be argued that individuals in Feltham who were more external in their locus of control asserted more autonomy and independence, but in fact were the most dependent; they were certainly the most distressed. They were 'protesting self-sufficiency while feeling completely un-self-sufficient' (Toch 1992: 107).

Concerns with autonomy would have an impact on how individuals sought and responded to the help that was on offer. The manner in which the prison's staff interacted with prisoners was crucial in ensuring that prisoners perceived support to be available to them. Four types of support were identified (informational, material, emotional and physical), and different sources were available to provide this help. Prisoners differed in the extent to which they sought support from different members of staff or peers and for different types of problems. Social support from staff did aid individuals' practical and psychological adaptation. However, those individuals who were most distressed and in most need of this support were less willing to seek it and less able to respond to offers of support. This unwillingness and inability were common among individuals who had self-harmed. When we examine the role of support, it is important to consider the initial level of distress and the response to the support at particular points in time. The role of support was complex, and it was important to disentangle actual supportive transactions from perceived support and the ability of the individual to respond and benefit from the support provided.

Support and trust were also closely interconnected. Liebling (2004) argued that 'relationships require certain degrees of support, and respect, and perhaps, finally trust, in order to be established and to function'

(p. 258). Liebling (2004) examined trust as part of her study of 'moral performance'. She defined trust as 'reliance on the honest, reliable and good sense of a person; the level of responsibility or confidence invested in and experienced by individuals' (p. 254). She found that the five prisons in her study were 'low trust environments'. I have found that, without trust, supportive transactions were extremely limited, whereas trusting people were able to benefit from supportive interactions. The level of trust was low among prisoners, and this restricted the extent to which social interactions developed into social relationships with staff. As Liebling (2004) argued, 'supportive relationships are constituted despite, rather than through, low levels of trust' (pp. 251–2).

Trust has been examined extensively within the general community (Seligman 1997; Sztompka 1999; Uslaner 2002). Uslaner (2002) found that those who could not trust saw the world as a threatening and unsafe place. A sense of safety may therefore be underpinned by how trusting an individual is in his environment. Safety entails psychological as well as physical security. Indeed, Liebling (2004) defined safety as 'a feeling of security or protection from harm, threat, or danger, and of physical and psychological trust in the environment' (p. 302). Toch (1977) also found that the individual who was concerned with the environmental need for safety lived in a world of 'low trust, high vigilance, uncertainty and discomfort' (p. 56). Safety was an important concept in this current research and was related to levels of psychological distress at the early entry phase of imprisonment. Liebling *et al.* (2005) also found that low levels of perceived safety predicted psychological distress. Moreover, I found that people who self-harmed felt less safe than those who had not self-harmed.

Although I did not find a significant statistical correlation between prison support (which included trust) and safety, I did find significant correlations between locus of control and safety, and also locus of control and support found in prison. Uslaner (2002) argued that what 'drives' generalised trust are optimism and the belief that 'most of what happens to them is in their own hands' (Uslaner 2002: 35). He stated that this sense of optimism and the ability to trust are learned early in life and that the children who had the 'warmest' parents were those who were most able to trust. (I will discuss below the importance of early-life experiences.) Uslaner (2002) found that those who did not trust perceived that others controlled their lives and were pessimistic about the future. He also found that they were younger, were less educated, were loners, feared more for their personal safety, and did not have social support networks. These characteristics match characteristics of the population of prisoners, particularly those who had self-harmed (Liebling 1992). An internal locus of control may have enabled individuals to place trust in others. Furthermore, placing trust in the environment enabled prisoners to seek support from it. Support (and placing trust in others) made the world a more predictable place and actually provided individuals with more control over their lives. As Johnson (2002) stated, 'one can achieve autonomy and security, that is control over one's life, through relatedness to others' (p. 93). The support that was provided need not decrease an individual's sense of autonomy. Indeed, as Toch (1992) stated, 'a person must be supported when he needs support, but he must also have the chance, when he is able, to play a more responsible role' (p. 400). The problem lies in the fact that those who are more external in their locus of control and who perceive the least control find it most difficult to set this cycle in motion initially and are the least able to benefit from the support that may be available to them.

Finally, outside social support networks also played an important role in the psychosocial experiences of young men in prison. I found that individuals who self-harmed had significantly less contact with friends and family outside prison and had received less support from them. For example, they received fewer visits and were less likely to have been helped by someone outside prison within the last week. However, most prisoners were nevertheless concerned that they should stay in contact with the people whom they had left on the other side of the boundary and found it painful being apart from them. Indeed, as Adams (1992) concluded: 'separation from and loss of contact with family, relatives and friends is one of the most difficult features of prison life to endure' (p. 286). These outside ties served as both a source of distress and as a desired source of comfort. Individuals who self-harmed found this separation the most painful of all, despite the fact they had more fragile social networks. Toch (1992) found that one of the most common crises in jails, for individuals who self-harmed, was 'self-linking', involving 'a person's protest against intolerable separation from significant others, against perceived abandonment by them, or against the inability to function as a constructive member of a group' (Toch 1992: 65). Similar findings emerged in this research. Perhaps because these individuals also had an external locus of control and felt more insecure within the prison, any ties that they had outside prison were even more important to their psychological survival; but because these ties were more fragile, the likelihood of their disintegrating was also higher.

The level of outside contact also affected how support was received inside prison. I found that those who received visits, and therefore had more outside contact, were more willing to seek support inside the prison and were more able to accept support from staff. Outside contact was important not only in alleviating a prisoner's distress but also in contributing to his actively seeking support for that distress. Those who had more contact outside prison were also in a better position to seek support inside it, and in a better position to receive it, an important element in a supportive interaction. They therefore benefited more from the different sources of support that were available within the prison. Toch (1977) stated that 'in total institutions the immediate environment may not only be a perceived source of emotional feedback; but also a mediator of feedback from the "outside"' (p. 70). It is necessary for the environment to be a mediator of outside emotional feedback first, before it can itself become an effective source of perceived emotional feedback. Therefore, access to those loved ones on the outside world contributed to prisoners' successful adaptation to life in prison.

The applicability of attachment theory

However, I will not end my analysis here but will now take a broader perspective to include the role of attachments. I will argue that an individual's ability to form and maintain social attachments is central to understanding the findings in this book. Attachment theory, put forward by Bowlby (1969, 1973, 1980) in his three-volume work on attachment and loss, is a theory about making and breaking relationships. It is interesting to note that Bowlby first developed his ideas when working at a home for maladjusted boys, an experience that led to the publication of his paper 'Forty-four Juvenile Thieves: Their Characteristics and Home Life' (Bowlby, 1944). Attachment theory, which he started to develop then, may be applicable to young men imprisoned at Feltham.

Bowlby (1979) stated that 'many of the most intense of all human emotions arise during the formation, the maintenance, the disruption and renewal of affectional bonds' (quoted in Holmes 1999). Holmes (2002) stated that attachment theory begins with the premise that individuals have a fundamental 'need for psychological security' (p. 1). Holmes (2002) identified four hypotheses put forward by Van Ijzendoorn and Sagi (1999) that pertain to attachment theory: firstly, the 'universality hypothesis' (infants are attached to one or more caregivers); secondly, the 'normality hypothesis' (a total of 70 per cent of infants become securely attached); thirdly, the 'sensitivity hypothesis' (to become securely attached, infants need a sensitive caregiver); and, fourthly, the 'competence hypothesis' (individuals who become securely attached are more socially competent than those who do not). He also added two additional hypotheses: the continuity hypothesis and the mentalisation hypothesis. The continuity hypothesis posits that 'attachment patterns in childhood have far-reaching effects on relationship skills and their mental representations in adult life' (ibid.: 7). The mentalisation hypothesis argues that 'secure attachment is based on, and leads to, the capacity for reflection on the states of mind of self and others' (ibid.: 7). Individuals who have a secure attachment are more able to regulate their own emotions. Indeed, it is argued that the 'capacity to experience one's own distress and to manage it effectively are acquired and are clearly related to effective secure attachments' (Ross and Pfafflin 2004: 260–1).

One of the most central concepts within attachment theory is the 'secure base' (Bowlby 1998). This 'originally referred to the care-giver to whom the child turns when distressed' and 'as a representation of security within the individual psyche' (Holmes 2002: 7). For psychological survival, it is argued that individuals need a secure base: 'to feel attached is to feel safe and secure' (Holmes 1999: 67). It is argued that people's early experiences are crucial in the development of an internal working model, that guides how they interact with others, including how they elicit care from others. Early experiences of being cared for (or not being cared for) 'confirm and maintain intuitive expectations about others and oneself' (Thompson 1999: 267), in particular, how responsive and accessible others will be, and lead to beliefs about how much care people feel they deserve. It is argued that these representations are self-perpetuating in that they guide attachment-related behaviours and give rise to responses. The internal working model thus allows for continuity from infancy to adulthood but can also be modified as new experiences come to light (Crowell *et al.* 1999).

Individuals who are securely attached are able to seek support from others and indeed recognise that relationships can be supportive in nature. Moreover, Crowell *et al.* (1999) reviewed the studies that had used the Inventory of Parent and Peer Attachment (IPPA) (Armsden and Greenberg 1987) and concluded that adolescents who were more securely attached to their parents and peers reported higher levels of self-esteem, increased use of problem-solving strategies, lower levels of loneliness and lower levels of psychological distress.

On the other hand, individuals who are insecurely attached (with an avoidant, ambivalent or disorganised attachment style) do not achieve a full base of security. The avoidant (or dismissing) individual does not form close relationships with others for fear of rejection. The ambivalent (or preoccupied) individual 'has been subjected to inconsistent responses when distressed, and so clings to the care-giver even when no danger is present: hyperactivation of attachment responses and exploration of autonomy are jettisoned in return for security' (Holmes 2002: 3). Those with disorganised attachment have experienced traumatic caregiving and oscillate between approach and avoidance. Adolescents who are insecurely attached (preoccupied and dismissing) have been found to have problems with psychosocial functioning (Armsden and Greenberg 1987). Internalising problems (e.g. depression) have been associated with preoccupied attachment, and externalising problems (e.g. substance misuse and aggression) have been associated with preoccupied and dismissing attachment styles (Allen and Land 1999).

Associations have therefore been made between attachment and psychosocial difficulties. But how might attachment theory throw light on my findings from Feltham? In what ways can attachment theory serve as a useful device for understanding the psychosocial experience of young men in prison? Attachment theory provides a framework for understanding adaptation. The concept of the secure base helps us to understand what is important when supporting prisoners, highlights the importance of family relationships when examining adaptation, and illuminates why some young men find it difficult to seek and respond to offers of support in prison. It must be noted that I did not measure attachment and therefore cannot conclude which prisoners had which attachment styles. (To have measured an individual's attachment style, I would have needed to have been trained in using the Adult Attachment Interview (AAI) (George *et al.* 1984) or to have used one of the self-report measures. See Crowell *et al.* (1999) for a review of these measures.) However, although I did not measure attachment styles, it became clear that they were relevant and could help us to understand the findings of this book.

The secure base and prisoner adaptation

Prisoners differ in their early-life experiences and may differ in the degree to which they enter prison with a secure base. Depending on their early experiences of care, young men develop an internal working model of how they see themselves and how they relate to others around them. Prisoners who entered prison with a secure base might have had an internal locus of control; might have felt safer in their surroundings, both physically and psychologically; might have known when to trust others and when not to; and might have dealt more easily with uncertainty. According to the mentalisation hypothesis, these young men might have been able to regulate their thoughts and emotions; subsequently, they might have felt less extreme forms of psychological distress. Moreover, these young men might have been more willing to seek support inside and outside prison, and, indeed, have relationships outside that they could turn to. Of course, separation from these loved ones would be psychologically painful, but if these relationships were secure, the individual would know that he would not be ostracised and would be able to rely on his family to help deal with his life inside.

The constructs thus discussed throughout this book can be linked together by attachment theory. Young men who enter with a number of internal social and psychological resources may be more equipped to deal with the pains of imprisonment. These young men have resilience in the face of adversity. Although distress may be experienced, it may be kept at a manageable level, and these individuals may be more able to survive psychologically. However, there are others who do not enter prison with a secure base. Previous research has found that people with secure attachment styles are underrepresented among people who have committed criminal offences (Adshead 2004). Adshead (2004) found that only 19 per cent of males and 22 per cent of females in forensic settings had a secure attachment representation. More generally, research has found that young people in prison had disruptive upbringings, with a high proportion being in local authority care (Liebling 1992; Social Exclusion Unit 2002). Shelton (2004) carried out research at Feltham and compared individuals residing in the health-care centre, with mental health problems, to those on ordinary locations within the prison. He found that those in the health-care centre consistently reported receiving less care from both maternal and paternal figures and reported their families to be more dysfunctional.

Indeed, many young men at Feltham had difficulties with their families and their attachments to them. Although these difficulties were more apparent among individuals who had self-harmed, they were also apparent among prisoners who had not. This trend was recognised by the staff at Feltham. As an outreach worker stated:

> Many prisoners have similar circumstances, broken families, to coin a phrase, whatever that means, but you know what I mean, like, you know, lack of contact with parents, or one particular parent out of the picture. Often the common theme has been abuse from relatives, either father or mother, or uncle or aunt. [Outreach worker]

The staff also recognised that it was important to ask sensitively about the prisoners' lives outside, particularly in relation to their loved ones. The link worker said:

It is important for us to know what is going on in their heads, not just in prison but what's going on in their lives outside. We talk to them about if they have any problems with their families, you know, have they got a girlfriend, is everything going OK, how do people in their lives on the outside feel about them being in prison. [Link worker]

The staff recognised that many young men coming through the prison gates brought with them a number of negative life experiences and that these experiences might have contributed to their plight. I hypothesise that some of these arrivals had an insecure attachment style and could not develop an internal secure base. These individuals were more external in their locus of control, had difficulties trusting others around them and felt less safe psychologically and physically. They found it most difficult to seek help and to recognise when help was being offered to them. Regulation of emotions might have been more difficult for young men who had not developed a secure base, and therefore they might have been the most distressed. Finally, these young men might have been less likely to have developed secure relationships outside prison. Although they might have still been in contact with a loved one, this relationship might have been fragile, exacerbating the fear of a complete relationship breakdown. Moreover, it was perhaps for these individuals that the relationship with a partner was most important, but, again, this was a relationship susceptible to collapse. Many of these prisoners were still learning how to form attachments with others, and an acute disruption of these ties elicited fear and uncertainty (as described in Chapter 2).

The concept of the secure base and attachment theory help to explain different adaptation patterns among young men in prison and link together the different constructs examined within this book. However, it must be said that I am not taking a deterministic standpoint, nor am I suggesting that a secure base will bring success in life, nor that an insecure base will bring difficulties. The relationship between the individual and the environment is complex: a similar developmental origin can lead to different outcomes (the concept of multifinality), and different development origins can come together and have the same outcome (the concept of equifinality) (Yates et al. 2003). However, if an individual has a secure base, it is reasonable to suggest that his likelihood of interacting with the prison environment in a successful way will be increased. Having a secure base may enable him to keep distress at a manageable level on entering prison and to adapt practically, socially and psychologically.

The secure base and supporting prisoners

Although attachment theory elucidates what young men import with them into the prison, it can also elucidate the manner in which staff interact with prisoners in order to support them inside. Adshead (2004) argued that attachment theory can be used to help think about how to create a secure base for those residing in secure settings, such as 'forensic institutions, where staff and residents are involved in long-term dependency relationships that involve care and control' (p. 147). I do not want to imply here that prisoners are like infants and staff are the sole attachment figures, or their parents, but there are analogies between the two types of interactions. Chapter 4 showed how manner was crucial in determining whether a prisoner perceived support to be available from staff in the prison. The manner in which staff interacted with prisoners covered many of the qualities of a caregiver's response and contributed to prisoners feeling supported. Attachment theory posits that the actions of the caregiver will encourage secure attachment in the individual receiving that care. Holmes (2002) identified a number of key factors for such an interaction: sensitivity, consistency, reliability, attunement, the capacity to absorb protest and mind-mindedness.

Interacting in a pro-social manner with prisoners is analogous to creating a secure base for these young men, albeit a limited base. Aiyegbusi (2004) argued that the 'milieu' or social context of the forensic setting requires thought and planning in relation to creating a secure base for individuals. In order for prisoners to feel supported, and safe, a secure base must be developed, and prisoners need to be able to form limited attachments with staff. Of course, these attachments would be different from those formed with loved ones outside prison. As Liebling (2004) stated, 'relationships between staff and prisoners can hardly be expected to be the companionable interactions described by Bowlby, Holmes and others' (p. 251), nor should they be, within the custodial setting. In prison, boundaries must be set in place between staff and prisoners for both ethical and operational reasons. Furthermore, the staff members, too, are transient, and it would be unwise for a young man to attach too closely to any particular one. These limitations must all be borne in mind in thinking about these attachments.

Interestingly, however, some staff at Feltham commented that some prisoners saw them in a role similar to that of a father or mother. One prison officer said:

> It depends on who they relate to. Some lads relate to a father figure sometimes, which tends to be myself and Mr X, probably because of our age, whereas other lads would relate to a mother

figure, or sister, and that tends to be the link worker or a female member of staff. [Prison officer]

Note that he said that prisoners 'relate to' staff, and not the other way round. The officers of course leave the prison each day and have their own relationships outside. Another said:

I might not look like their friend, but I do come across as someone that they can trust and someone they can talk to. Some of the other staff call me Uncle X because some of the boys out there will only talk to me. [Senior officer]

It is interesting that the staff sometimes address one another, albeit jokingly, in terms which suggest their familial relationships with the prisoners. With the reputation of Feltham (noted in Chapter 1), it might surprise some people to hear such admissions of the need to allow prisoners to form attachments to the staff.

Staff also recognised the importance of consistency, reliability, approachability and listening skills in order for prisoners to feel supported by them. At an even more fundamental level, staff commented that it was important to interact with prisoners; interaction is more limited in the busy and supposedly punitive environment of the prison. Nevertheless, many staff at Feltham saw their role as much more than locking up prisoners, and they stressed that interacting with, and relating to, prisoners was the fundamental part of their job. One prison officer said:

Staff on here play table tennis with them; they'll play pool; they'll play these new machines on here. Staff will walk about and will talk to them – interact as best you can throughout the association period. You need to interact. And it's, 'Hang on, he's human, perhaps I'll talk to him later on 'cause I've got a problem. I'm not going to talk to that one over there because he never says nothing. He doesn't get involved.' They very well may have not spoken to anyone for a week staff-wise because they feel intimidated or pressured, and suddenly find this one's playing table tennis: 'He is talking while I am playing pool. Perhaps I'll see him later on. Perhaps he can deal with a problem I have.' It may be nothing to do with self-harm, but it lowers his stress levels. [Prison officer]

This officer did not describe attachments to favourites, which would be unethical and detrimental to management; he described being on the wing during association and attending to whoever seemed to need interaction that day, or whoever had not talked to someone for a while – the opposite of encouraging particular attachments in fact. Furthermore, the officer commented on the initial need for any interaction at all: he imagined a prisoner who 'may not have spoken to anyone for a week staff-wise'. Perhaps such a prisoner, he imagined, would feel 'intimidated' by interacting, and so it would be better to break the ice by playing table tennis with him. The staff member needed to attune himself to the prisoner's wavelength, in order to create a secure base for the prisoner.

Staff also recognised that if the prisoners were to form attachments within which they could seek help, they needed to be recognised as an individual:

> When all is said and done, they are individuals and if you lose sight of the individual, then you've lost the plot. It's no use in saying two lads from Kosovo are exactly the same 'cause they're not. Neither are two lads from Islington. [Prison officer]

Of course, social and ethnic diversity needs to be considered by staff working in prisons. Moreover, within each social and ethnic group, each person must be recognised as having individual needs, as it is on a one-to-one level that they can feel supported and form a limited attachment to individual members of staff.

Although many officers on the wings encouraged prisoners to seek support, other sources of support were available (as discussed in Chapter 4), including fellow prisoners. It could be argued that other sources of support (e.g. the chaplain, the outreach team) would be in a better position to provide these young men with something akin to a secure base. One important group that helped to create a secure base for prisoners was the outreach team. This team was originally set up by an officer eight years before the involvement of NHS trusts. The officer concerned told me:

> The team aimed to marry a support network for the lads and the staff, to build a fluid link between inpatient setting and ordinary location. The idea at the time, and I hope it has come to fruition, was that individuals would feel more able to cope if they felt more supported by the unit staff and a separate body of people whose primary aim was to keep people safe. [Suicide prevention co-ordinator]

This team developed over the years and consisted of outreach workers and community psychiatry nurses. The outreach team responded to prisoners who were on an open F2052SH form, it responded to referrals made by any other members of staff if they had any concerns about the prisoner, and it carried out mental health assessments. The team responded in a timely, approachable and reliable manner; this had the potential to encourage these young men to form a secure base. Moreover, the outreach team also liaised with other supportive agencies within the prison on the prisoners' behalf, thus increasing the span of the secure base. Finally, the team provided support for wing staff, in that the staff felt supported and less overwhelmed when supporting a prisoner. If staff were to be expected to provide a secure base for prisoners, the staff, too, needed to feel supported in the process.

In considering the idea of developing a secure base for prisoners, it is important to stress that this is not synonymous with creating dependence. Prisoners with a secure base felt more in control and would have the self-efficacy to make choices for themselves, albeit choices that were limited by the prison regime. Prisons are control-limited environments, but there are choices that prisoners can make for themselves. Indeed, as an outreach worker commented:

Trying to take away their feelings of powerlessness and making them feel they are in charge of themselves tends to help. [Outreach worker]

A link worker said:

I think you need to give them a bit of credit and say, what do you think? What do you want us to do? How do you want us to look at this situation? Talk to them like adults. They've got their own minds and can make their own decisions. I'm not saying I do that all the time, but all I am saying, that is just another option available, appealing to their sensibilities about themselves. Just trying to say, you've got a brain, use it. You tell me and put the ball back in their court. [Link worker]

Providing a secure base might help the prisoners to survive in prison and to feel more autonomous. Moreover, it might help them to adapt their internal working model of how they relate to the world.

Staff therefore had a role to play in helping prisoners adapt to life inside. But, of course, the staff also played a vital role in ensuring that prisoners maintained, or even developed, their attachments with their families outside prison. Indeed, prisons in Scotland, and a handful of prisons in England and Wales, have appointed Family Contact Development Officers, whose role is to 'develop policies to support family contact, hearing complaints from families about visits and other matters, and involving families in many aspects of the prison regime' (Loucks 2005: 3). As mentioned previously, outside contact was an extremely important need for the young men at Feltham. Staff facilitated family contact through enabling visits, but they could also help in their general one-to-one interaction with young men on the wing. One officer said that he thought it was important to help prisoners to contact their families and to give them advice about how to do so. He would ask them, he said:

> What do your family think about this? How does your mum feel? You get some who say, 'Oh, mum is used to it,' and you get others who burst into tears. You say, 'The best thing you can do, and if you have trouble doing it, someone will help you, or I will, is to write a letter to your mum and put it all down that way.' [Senior officer]

Aside from these informal means of facilitating family contact, other formal practices were in place which might have developed or maintained a secure base. Outside the prison gates, the visitor centre played a central role in supporting family and friends who were visiting Feltham (see Loucks (2002) for a review of the role of visitor centres). Inside the prison, one of the main roles of the link workers was to 'try to reinforce the connection between family and friends and encourage these young men to keep in contact with their family and friends' (Link worker). At the time I carried out my fieldwork, the link worker not only interviewed each young man on his first night, but contacted a family member or partner on his behalf. The link worker thought that this contact was beneficial, because it ensured that the practicalities of visiting were taken care of:

> A lad comes in and we make a phone call for him, and it enables us to make sure the family gets the right information because we know it all. We've got lads who can't read or write. They can't understand it. We've got lads who it is their first time in and they don't know what the hell is going on. The first three or four minutes they'll spend telling them the arrangements. We can do that for them. We can deal with what property they can bring in and the times of the visits. [Link worker]

She also thought that important information could be better obtained from families, when carrying out an assessment of the young man's needs:

They say things like, 'Has he told you his best friend just died in a car crash? Has he told you that me and his dad are splitting up and he is really upset? Has he told you he tried to kill himself two weeks ago, took an overdose?' Yeah, well sometimes he has, sometimes he hasn't. Even things like getting the lads on medication, getting numbers from the doctor, which speeds up time for health-care. (Link worker)

Facilitating contact with family members thus enabled the staff at Feltham to provide appropriate support. Contacting a significant other outside prison also provided reassurance to the family or partner and provided an opportunity for them to vent any frustrations that they might have. The link worker said:

One of the very important things we do is act as a buffer between him and his family. We take all the anger, the upset, the tears, the fury from the family relations and dissipate it. So the time he gets on the phone himself, you know, that person has vented on us and then sees things a bit clearer, plus the family do like talking to someone who isn't a social worker, psychologist. Families like it. They say, 'Are you a screw?' I say, 'No, I am just a mum. I am a civilian here. Just a mum like you.' And they talk to me on a mum level. [Link worker]

It was important to recognise that families also experienced the separation adversely, and in order for them to be a secure base for their son, they needed the prison to communicate with them. Indeed, previous research has highlighted the impact imprisonment has on families, that they are often left without information and are the hidden victims within the criminal justice system (Murray 2005). It is also interesting to notice from this quotation the importance of relating to someone 'on a mum level'. There was a need for a caring response from the prison and for family members to see that there are caring people working within the prison system. This process of contacting family members also gave the link worker a unique insight into the response of the family or partners:

If I had a pound for every time some mum or girlfriend said, 'I hate him. I don't want him darkening my door step again. He is no son of mine. He has really let me down. Tell him I'm not going to let him see his kid anymore. I'm dumping him.' [Link worker]

Being sent to prison could rupture attachments with the young man's family, partner or the mother of his own children. The potential for loss is great, especially given the fact that some of these relationships may be fragile in the first place. It was important for staff to recognise that relationships outside prison might have been fragile and that this fragility might have affected the young man's day-to-day interactions within the prison.

Another formal practice that was developed at Feltham was family work and work with partners carried out by the clinical psychologist. This service involved setting up family therapy sessions within the prison. For example, one session was set up before a prisoner was transferred to a secure unit and one session was set up to help improve family relations before a prisoner was released back into the community. Other work included arranging interviews with the family members of young men who had been admitted to the health-care centre and for this information to be assimilated into the assessment and formulation of these prisoner's difficulties. A family-awareness group was also developed for prisoners admitted to health-care, who found it difficult to receive visits. These prisoners were encouraged to write to their families about what they had done in the group.

These examples show the value of such work and the importance of helping prisoners to maintain, or restore, attachments with loved ones outside. Family contact was important, and it was essential that relationships that they had did not break down. Indeed, part of surviving and adapting to life inside is ensuring that there is a life outside to go back to. Adaptation extends beyond the prison walls and into their future lives. Although this book has focused on the early entry period of imprisonment and the first month, it is, of course, important not to forget the different resettlement issues that these people have to face upon their release (Farrant 2006). Concerns over their longer-term future were evident even on entering prison, and it was vital that young men were given as much opportunity as possible to maintain, or develop, a secure base outside ready for their return there.

The secure base and seeking support

But, of course, the prison can only do so much to help prisoners feel supported. Prisoners must also have the ability to seek support or respond to offers of help. Not only is attachment theory useful in understanding what constitutes a supportive interaction, and what the prison can do to facilitate this, but it can also help in understanding prisoners' willingness to elicit support from staff. Attachment theory posits that an individual's attachment style will affect his care-eliciting behaviour: 'a securely attached individual can draw on the support of others (via the "secure base") when needed and can talk coherently and with appropriate affect about psychological pain and difficulty' (Holmes 2002: 1). As stated earlier, these individuals may be more willing to seek support and respond to support that is on offer. Individuals with insecure attachment patterns, on the other hand, are argued to be less likely to draw on support from others. It could also be argued that individuals who have insecure attachment patterns are less able to trust, as Uslaner (2002) and Erikson (1963) postulated. Individuals with insecure attachments have different expectations about the amount of concern and understanding they think staff should show them. Indeed, 'when consistent, responsive, early care giving has been absent, later confidence in other people meeting one's emotional needs will be undermined' (Aiyegbusi 2004: 177). In interviews, prisoners expressed reluctance to form attachments or to seek support from others generally in their lives, and they expressed themselves with excessive individualism. For those with an insecure attachment style, seeking and accepting support would symbolise losing control. There were others (as detailed in Chapter 6) who sought support to an excessive level and who tried to depend too closely on staff. The individuals sometimes then received a negative response from staff, given the pressures that staff members were under and given the excessively high expectations of their capacity to provide support.

Staff recognised that some prisoners would not be willing to seek help from them and were explicit about this reluctance. Although the prisoner had to meet the prison's staff halfway, in seeking and receiving support, the prison's staff had the added responsibility of recognising that young men found this seeking and receiving difficult; the prison's staff had to be proactive in encouraging prisoners to seek help from them. The link worker, among others, encouraged attachments to be formed with staff within the prison:

> Some of the guys have real problems telling someone in authority and the uniform and everything else. And we do say, 'These guys [staff] are human beings. They are people like you. They've got feelings, emotions like you, and they have good and bad days. They are prison officers, but they are not just here to lock you away. They are someone you can talk to and have a relationship with. Talk to them about your problems because when we leave here, you know, it's the officers who are taking over.' [Link worker]

Furthermore, it was important for staff to recognise the tension between seeking support and reinforcing feelings of powerlessness. The staff could help to overcome this by reinforcing that they were available and thus normalising help-seeking behaviour. As the link worker stated:

> It is just letting them know that we don't think they are silly and stupid, or it's weak to ask for help. They've got some egos, some bigger than others, and it's just letting them know it is OK. It is OK to ask for help. It is stronger to ask for help. It is not a sign of weakness. It is a strength to admit, 'I do need help with something'. And actually sitting there with them and saying to them, that's a good thing to do. People don't tell them that; they say, if you need any help, just ask us. And? You need to say to these guys, it is OK for you to do that. It is good to do that. [Link worker]

Staff at Feltham recognised that prisoners found it difficult to talk to them about particular issues. It was important that staff understood that when they offered help to prisoners, their offers might be rejected.

Individuals with insecure attachment patterns might have been less able to elicit consistent support from staff and less able to respond to it. Individuals with an avoidant attachment style, in particular, might have been less willing to seek support. Those less willing and able to seek support also appeared to be the ones who found it difficult to regulate their thoughts and emotions. They were more controlled by their world than controlling of it. There is perhaps a link between a sense of will and the willingness to seek help. Individuals who had the will to determine their environment could see accepting help as a means towards self-improvement through interacting with others, rather than seeing it as a relinquishing of self-control. However, those least able to adapt, even to the extent of harming themselves, had never learned how to profit from a supportive interaction with others. Interviews revealed that they were more socially withdrawn inside the prison, received fewer visits and, by their own accounts, already had histories of fragile connections with, and even rejection by, friends and family outside. In such backgrounds, they have been forced to learn a sense of independence and individualism which prevented them from accessing and accepting help from others. As some prisoners said, 'Like I said, I keep myself to myself'; 'I am not the sharing type'; ' No, I am too proud for that'.

By the time I arrived at Feltham, the staff at the prison had begun to offer help to the most vulnerable individuals – although there is, of course, still more work to be done. However, these efforts are only half the solution. The other half lies beyond the prison, in the lack of control individuals perceived over their lives and in the inability to connect with others, that these young adults had acquired from the wider society and brought with them into the prison. Schoon (2006), in her developmental-contextual model for resilience, recognised the family as an important context to include when analysing adjustment across the lifespan. She also recognised the importance of understanding earlier life experiences when attempting to understand how an individual adapts at any one moment. Indeed, 'any point in the lifespan has to be understood as the consequence of past experiences' (Schoon 2006: 26). Applying attachment theory to my findings reveals the importance of earlier life experiences in moulding individuals' current ability to adapt. If an individual, for whatever reasons, lacks a sense of agency, his levels of psychological distress will remain high, despite efforts made by others to help him. On the other hand, if a sense of agency is developed within him, this sense will enhance his ability to adapt to the difficult world of the prison.

References

Adams, K. (1992) 'Adjusting to prison life', in M. Tonry (ed.) *Crime and Justice: A Review of Research,* 16 (pp. 275–361). Chicago: University of Chicago Press.

Adshead, G. (2004) 'Three degrees of security: attachment and forensic institutions', in F. Pfafflin and G. Adshead (eds) *A Matter of Security: The Application of Attachment Theory to Forensic Psychiatry and Psychotherapy.* Forensic Focus 25 (pp. 147–66). London: Jessica Kingsley.

Aiyegbusi, A. (2004) 'Forensic mental health nursing: care and security in mind', in F. Pfafflin and G. Adshead (eds) *A Matter of Security: The Application of Attachment Theory to Forensic Psychiatry and Psychotherapy.* Forensic Focus 25. (pp. 167–92). London: Jessica Kingsley.

Albrecht, T.L. and Adelman, M.B. (1987) 'Communicating social support: a theoretical persecptive', in T.L. Albrecht and M.B. Adelman (eds) *Communicating Social Support* (pp. 18–39). London: Sage.

Alexopoulos, G., Bruce, M., Hull, J., Sirey, J. and Kakuma, T. (1999) 'Clinical determinants of suicidal ideation and behavior in geriatric depression', *Archives of Geriatric Depression,* 56 (11): 1048–53.

Allen, J.P. and Land, D. (1999) 'Attachment in adolescence', in J. Cassidy and P.R. Shaver (eds) *Handbook of Attachment: Theory, Research and Clinical Applications* (pp. 319–35). London: Guilford Press.

Anderson, E. (2000) *Code of the Street. Decency, Violence and the Moral Life of the Inner City.* London: W. H. Norton.

Antonucci, T.C. and Jackson, J.S. (1990) 'The Role of Reciprocity in Social Support', in B.R. Sarason, I.G. Sarason and G.R. Pierce (eds) *Social Support: An Interactional View* (pp. 173–198). New York: John Wiley.

Armsden, G.C. and Greenberg, M.T. (1987) 'The inventory of parent and peer attachment: individual differences and their relationship to psychological well-being in adolescence', *Journal of Youth and Adolescence,* 69: 1406–19.

Bartollis, C. (1982) 'Survival problems of adolescent prisoners', in R. Johnson and H. Toch (eds) *The Pains of Imprisonment* (pp. 165–80). London: Sage.

Beck, G. (1995) 'Bullying among young offenders in custody', *Issues in Criminological and Legal Psychology*, 22: 54–70.

Beck, U. and Beck-Gernsheim, E. (2001) *Individualization: Institutionalized Individualism and Its Social and Political Consequences*. London: Sage.

Beigel, A. and Russell, H.E (1973) 'Suicidal behaviour in jail: prognostic considerations', in B.L. Danto (ed) *Jail House Blues: Studies of Suicidal Behavior in Jail and Prison* (pp. 107–18). Orchard Lake, MI: Epic Publications.

Benezech, M. (1999) 'Suicide and its prevention in French prisons', *Annales Medico-Psychologiques*, 157 (8): 561–6.

Biggam, F.H. and Power, K.G. (1997) 'Social support and psychological distress in a group of incarcerated young offenders', *International Journal of Offender Therapy and Comparative Criminology*, 41 (3): 213–30.

Biggam, F.H. and Power, K.G. (1999a) 'A comparison of the problem-solving abilities and psychological distress of suicidal, bullied, and protected prisoners', *Criminal Justice and Behavior*, 26: 196–216.

Biggam, F.H. and Power, K.G. (1999b) 'Suicidality and the state-trait debate on problem solving deficits: a re-examination with incarcerated young offenders', *Archives of Suicidal Research*, 5: 27–42.

Bille-Brahe, U., Egebo, H., Crepet, D., DeLeo, D., Hjelmeland, H., Kerkhof, A., Lonnqvist, J., Michel, K., Renberg, E.S., Schmidtke, A., and Wassermann, D. (1999) 'Social support among European suicide attempters', *Archives of Suicide Research*, 5 (3): 215–31.

Blatier, C. (2000) 'Locus of control, causal attribution, and self-esteem: a comparison between prisoners', *International Journal of Offender Therapy and Comparative Criminology*, 44 (1): 97–110.

Bogue, J. and Power, K. (1995) 'Suicide in Scottish prisons 1976–93', *Journal of Forensic Psychiatry*, 6 (3): 527–40.

Bonner, R.L. (1992) 'Isolation, seclusion, and psychosocial vulnerability as risk factors for suicide behind bars', in R.W. Maris, A.L. Berman, J.T. Maltsberger, and R. I. Yufit (eds) *Assessment and Prediction of Suicide* (pp. 398–419). New York: Guilford.

Bonner, R.L. and Rich, A.R. (1990) 'Psychosocial vulnerability, life stress, and suicidal ideation in a jail population: a cross-validation study', *Suicide and Life-Threatening Behavior*, 20 (3): 213–24.

Borrill, J. (2002) 'Self-inflicted deaths of prisoners serving life sentences 1998–2001', *British Journal of Forensic Practice*, 4 (4): 30–8.

Borrill, J., Burnett, R., Atkins, R., Miller, S., Briggs, D., Weaver, T. and Maden, A. (2003) 'Patterns of self-harm and attempted suicide among white and black/mixed race female offenders', *Criminal Behaviour and Mental Health*, 13 (4): 229–40.

Borrill, J., Snow, L., Medlicott, D., Teers, R. and Paton, J. (2005) 'Learning from "near misses": interviews with women who survived an incident of severe self-harm in prison', *Howard Journal of Criminal Justice*, 44 (1): 57–69.

Bottoms, A. (2003) 'Theoretical reflections on the evaluation of a penal policy initiative', in L. Zedner and A. Ashworth (eds) *The Criminological Foundations of Penal Policy: Essays in Honour of Roger Hood* (pp. 107–96). Oxford: Oxford University Press.

Bottoms, A. and Dignan, J. (2004) 'Youth justice in Great Britain', in M. Tonry and A.N. Doob (eds) *Youth Crime and Youth Justice: Comparative and Cross-National Perspectives. Crime and Justice: A Review of the Literature*, vol. 31 (pp. 21–183). Chicago: University of Chicago Press.

Bowlby, J. (1944) 'Forty-four juvenile thieves: their characters and home life', *International Journal of Psychoanalysis*, 25: 19–52.

Bowlby, J. (1969) *Attachment and Loss. Vol. 1: Attachment.* London: Hogarth Press.

Bowlby, J. (1973) *Attachment and Loss. Vol. 2: Separation: Anxiety and Anger.* London: Hogarth Press.

Bowlby, J. (1980) *Attachment and Loss. Vol. 3: Loss: Sadness and Depression.* London: Hogarth Press.

Bowlby, J. (1988) *A Secure Base: Clinical Applications of Attachment Theory.* London: Routledge.

Brace, N., Kemp, R. and Snelgar, R. (2003) *SPSS for Psychologists: A Guide to Data Analysis Using SPSS for Windows.* (2nd edn). Hampshire: Palgrave Macmillan.

Bronfenbrenner, U. (1979) *The Ecology of Human Development: Experiments by Nature and Design.* Cambridge, MA: Harvard University Press.

Brookes, M. (1994) 'At the beginning: meeting prisoners' needs at the commencement of their sentence', *Issues in Criminological and Legal Psychology*, 21: 41–7.

Burtch, B.E. and Ericson, R.V. (1979) *The Silent System: An Inquiry into Prisoners Who Suicide and Annotated Bibliography.* Centre of Criminology: University of Toronto.

Carlton, P.A. and Deane, F.P. (2000) 'Impact of attitudes and suicidal ideation on adolescents' intentions to seek professional psychological help', *Journal of Adolescence*, 23: 35–45.

Carter, P. (2003) *Managing Offenders, Reducing Crime: A New Approach.* London: Home Office.

Clemmer, D. (1940) *The Prison Community.* New York: Holt, Rinehart & Winston.

Cloward, R.A. (1960) 'Social control in the prison', in *Theoretical Studies in Social Organization of the Prison* (pp. 20–48). New York: Social Science Research Council.

Clum, G.A. and Febbraro, G.A.R. (1994) 'Stress, social support, and problem-solving appraisal/skills: prediction of suicide severity within a college sample', *Journal of Psychopathology and Behavioral Assessment*, 16 (1): 69–83.

Cohen, S. and Taylor, L. (1972) *Psychological Survival.* Harmondsworth: Penguin.

Cohen, S. and Wills, T.A. (1985) 'Stress, social support, and the buffering hypothesis', *Psychological Bulletin*, 98: 310–57.

Cohen, S. Gottlieb, B.H. and Underwood, L.G. (2000) 'Social relationships and health', in S. Cohen, L.G. Underwood and B.H. Gottlieb (eds) *Social Support Measurement and Intervention: A Guide for Health and Social Scientists* (pp. 3–25). Oxford: Oxford University Press.

Crighton, D. and Towl, G. (1997) 'Self-inflicted deaths in prisons in England and Wales: an analysis of the data for 1998–90 and 1994–95', in G. Towl (ed.) *Suicide and Self-Injury in Prisons. Issues in Criminological and Legal Psychology,* 28: 12–20.

Crowell, J.A., Fraley, R.C. and Shaver, P.R. (1999) 'Measurement of individual differences in adolescent and adult attachment', in J. Cassidy and P.R. Shaver (eds) *Handbook of Attachment: Theory, Research and Clinical Applications* (pp. 434–65). London: Guilford Press.

Curtona, C.E. and Russell, D.W. (1990) 'Type of social support and specific stress: towards a theory of optimal matching', in B.R. Sarason, I.G. Sarason and G.R. Pierce (eds) *Social Support: An Interactional View* (pp. 319–66). New York: Wiley.

Dalton, V. (1999) 'Suicide in prison 1980 to 1988: an overview', *Trends and Issues in Crime and Criminal Justice.* www.aic.gov.au.

Danto, B. (1973) *Jail House Blues: Studies of Suicidal Behavior in Jail and Prison.* Orchard Lane, MI: Epic.

Deane, F.P., Skogstad, P. and Williams, H. (1999) 'Effects of attitudes, ethnicity, and quality of prior therapy on New Zealand male prison inmates' intentions to seek professional psychological help', *International Journal for the Advancement of Counselling,* 21: 55–67.

Dear, G.E. (2000) 'Functional and dysfunctional impulsivity, depression and suicidal ideation in a prison population', *Journal of Psychology,* 134 (7): 77–80.

Dear, G.E., Thomson, D.M., Hall, G.J., and Howells, K. (1998) 'Self-inflicted injury and coping behaviours in prison', in R.J. Kosky, H.S. Eshkevari, R. Hassan, and R. Goldney (eds) *Suicide Prevention: The Global Context* (pp. 189–99). New York: Plenum Press.

Dear, G.E., Thomson, D.M. and Hills, A.M. (2000) 'Self-harm in prison. Manipulators can also be suicide attempters', *Criminal Justice and Behavior,* 27: 160–75.

Dear, G.E., Thomson, D.M., Howells, K. and Hall, G.J. (2001a) 'Self-harm in western Australian prisons: differences between prisoners who have self-harmed and those who have not', *Australian and New Zealand Journal of Criminology,* 34: 277–92.

Dear, G.E., Thomson, D.M., Howells, K. and Hall, G.J. (2001b) 'Non-fatal self-harm in western Australian prisons: who, where, when and why?', *Australian and New Zealand Journal of Criminology,* 34 (1): 47–66.

DeWilde, E.J., Kienhorst, C.W.M., Diekstra, R.F.W. and Wolters, W.H.G. (1994) 'Social support, life events, and behavioral characteristics of psychologically distressed adolescents at high risk of attempting suicide', *Adolescence,* 29 (113): 49–60.

Dooley, E. (1990) 'Prison suicide in England and Wales, 1972–87', *British Journal of Psychiatry,* 156: 40–5.

Drake, D. (2006) *A Comparison of Quality of Life, Legitimacy and Order in Two Maximum Security Prisons.* Unpublished doctoral dissertation, University of Cambridge.

Dunlop, A.B. and McCabe, S. (1965) *Young Men in Detention Centres*. London: Routledge and Kegan Paul.

DuRand, C.J., Burtka, G.J., Federman, E.J., Haycox, J.A. and Smith, J.W. (1995) 'A quarter century of suicide in a major urban jail: implications for community psychiatry', *American Journal of Psychiatry*, 152: 1077–80.

Dyson, G. (2005) 'Examining bullying among institutionalized young offenders: triangulation of questionnaires and focus groups', in J. Ireland (ed.) *Bullying Among Prisoners: Innovations in Theory and Research* (pp. 84–108). Cullompton: Willan Publishing.

Eckenrode, J. and Wethington, E. (1990) 'The process and outcome of mobilizing social support', in S. Duck (ed.) *Personal Relationships and Social Support* (pp. 83–103). London: Sage.

Edgar, K., O'Donnell, I. and Martin, C. (2003) *Prison Violence. The Dynamics of Conflict, Fear and Power*. Cullompton: Willan Publishing.

Elder, G.H. (1998) 'The life course as developmental theory', *Child Development*, 69: 1–12.

Ericson, R. (1975) *Young Offenders and Their Social Work*. Farnborough: Lexington Books.

Erikson, E. (1963) *Childhood and Society*. New York: W. W. Norton.

Eskin, M. (1995) 'Suicidal behaviour as related to social support and assertiveness among Swedish and Turkish high school students: a cross-cultural investigation', *Journal of Clinical Psychology*, 51 (2): 158–72.

Esparza, R. (1973) 'Attempted and committed suicide in county jails', in B.L. Danto (ed.) *Jail House Blues: Studies of Suicidal Behavior in Jail and Prison* (pp. 27–46). Orchard Lake, MI: Epic Publications.

Farrant, F. (2005a) *A Sobering Thought: Young Men in Prison. Out for Good Research Briefing: 1*. London: Howard League for Penal Reform.

Farrant, F. (2005b) *Young, Neglected and Back: Young Men in Prison. Out for Good Research Briefing: 2*. London: Howard League for Penal Reform.

Farrant, F. (2005c) *The Keys to the Future? The Housing Needs of Young Adults in Prison. Out for Good Housing Briefing*. London: Howard League for Penal Reform.

Farrant, F. (2006) *Out for Good: Meeting the Resettlement Needs of Young Men*. London: Howard League for Penal Reform.

Fawcett, J. and Marrs, B. (1973) 'Suicide at the county jail', in B.L. Danto (ed.) *Jail House Blues: Studies of Suicidal Behavior in Jail and Prison* (pp. 83–106). Orchard Lake, MI: Epic Publications.

Field, A. (2000) *Discovering Statistics: Using SPSS for Windows*. London: Sage.

Fotiadou, M., Livaditis, M., Manou, I., Kaniotou, E. and Xenitidis, K. (2006) 'Prevalence of mental disorders and deliberate self-harm in Greek male prisoners', *International Journal of Law and Psychiatry*, 29 (1): 68–73.

Fruhwald, S., Frottier, P., Eher, R., Aigner, M., Gutierrez, K. and Ritter, K. (2000) 'Assessment of custodial suicide risk: jail and prison suicides in Austria 1975–1996', *Psychiatrische Praxis*, 27 (4): 195–200.

Fulwiler, C., Forbes, C., Santangelo, S.L. and Folstein, M. (1997) 'Self-mutilation and suicide attempt: distinguishing features of prisoners', *Journal of the American Academy of Psychiatry and Law*, 25: 69–77.

Gallo, E. and Ruggiero, V. (1991) 'The "immaterial" prison: custody as a factory for the manufacture of handicaps', *International Journal of the Sociology of Law*, 19(3): 273–91.

George, C., Kaplan, N. and Main, M. (1984) *Adult Attachment Interview Protocol.* Unpublished manuscript, University of California, Berkeley.

Gibbs, J. (1982a) 'Disruption and distress: going from the street to jail', in N. Parisi (ed) *Coping with Imprisonment* (pp. 29–44). London: Sage.

Gibbs, J. (1982b) 'The first cut is the deepest: psychological breakdown and survival in the detention centre', in R. Johnson and H. Toch (eds) *The Pains of Imprisonment* (pp. 97–114). London: Sage.

Gibbs, J.T. (1997) 'African American suicide: a cultural paradox', *Suicide and Life-Threatening Behavior*, 27 (1): 68–79.

Gillespie, W. (2002) *Prisonization: Individual and Institutional Factors Affecting Inmate Conduct.* New York: LFB Scholarly Publishing.

Goffman, E. (1959/1990) *The Presentation of Self in Everyday Life.* London: Penguin.

Goffman, E. (1961/1991) *Asylums. Essays on the Social Situation of Mental Patients and Other Inmates.* London: Penguin.

Goldson, B. (2002) *The New Youth Justice.* Lyme Regis, Dorset: Russell.

Goodstein, L. and Wright, K.N. (1989) 'Inmate adjustment to prison', in L. Goodstein and D.L. MacKenzie (eds) *The American Prison: Issues in Research and Policy* (pp. 229–51). London: Plenum Press.

Goodstein, L., MacKenzie, D. and Shotland, R. (1984) 'Personal control and inmate adjustment to prison', *Criminology*, 22 (8): 343–69.

Gover, A.R., MacKenzie, D.L. and Armstrong, G.S. (2000) 'Importation and deprivation explanations of juveniles' adjustment to correctional facilities', *International Journal of Offender Therapy and Comparative Criminology*, 44 (4): 450–67.

Green, C., Kendal, K., Andre, G., Looman, T. and Polvi, N. (1993) 'A study of 133 suicides among Canadian federal prisoners', *Medicine, Science, and the Law*, 33 (2): 121–7.

Greer, S. and Bagley, C. (1971) 'Effect of psychiatric intervention in attempted suicide: a controlled study', *British Medical Journal*, 1 (5744): 310–12.

Greve, W., Enzmann, D. and Hosser, D. (2001) 'The stabilization of self-esteem among incarcerated adolescents: accommodative and immunizing processes', *International Journal of Offender Therapy and Comparative Criminology*, 45 (6): 749–68.

Hamilton, N.A. and Ingram, R.E. (2001) 'Self-focused attention and coping: attending to the right things', in C.R. Snyder (ed.) *Coping with Stress: Effective People and Processes* (pp. 178–95). Oxford: Oxford University Press.

Hammersley, M. and Atkinson, P. (1997) *Ethnography: Principles and Practice.* London: Routledge.

Harris, T.L. and Molock, S.D. (2000) 'Cultural orientation, family cohesion, and family support in suicide ideation and depression among African American college students', *Suicide and Life Threatening Behavior*, 30 (4): 341–53.

Harvey, J. (2007) 'An embedded multi-method approach to prison research', in R. King and E. Wincup (eds) *Doing Research on Crime and Justice* (2nd edn). Oxford: Oxford University Press.

Haw, C., Hawton, K., Houston, K. and Townsend, E. (2001) 'Psychiatric and personality disorders in deliberate self-harm patients', *British Journal of Psychiatry*, 178: 48–54.

Hawton, K. and Fagg, J. (1988) 'Suicide, and other causes of death following attempted suicide', *British Journal of Psychiatry*, 152: 359–66.

Hawton, K., Fagg, J., Platt, S. and Hawkins, M. (1993) 'Factors associated with suicide after parasuicide in young people', *British Medical Journal*, 306 (6893): 1641–4.

Hawton, K.. Fagg, J., Simkin, S., Bale, E. and Bond, A. (1997) 'Trends in deliberate self-harm in Oxford, 1985–1995, and their implications for clinical services and the prevention of suicide', *British Journal of Psychiatry*, 171: 556–60.

Hawton, K., Arensman, E., Wasserman, D., Hulten, A., Bille-Brahe, U., Bjerke, T., Crepet, P., Deisenhammer, E., Kerkhof, A., De Leo, D., Michel, K., Ostamo, A., Philippe, A., Querejeta, I., Salander-Renberg, E., Schmidtke, A. and Temesvary, B. (1998) 'Relationship between attempted suicide and suicide rates among young people in Europe', *Journal of Epidemiology and Community Health*, 52: 191–4.

Hawton, K., Fagg, J., Simkin, S., Bale, E. and Bond, A. (2000) 'Deliberate self-harm in adolescents in Oxford, 1985–1995', *Journal of Adolescence*, 23: 47–55.

Hawton, K., Hall, S., Simkin, S., Bale, E., Bond, A., Codd, S. and Stewart, A. (2003) 'Deliberate self-harm in adolescents: a study of characteristics and trends in Oxford, 1990–2000', *Journal of Child Psychology and Psychiatry and Allied Disciplines*, 44: 1191–8.

Hawton, K., Houston, K. and Shepperd, R. (1999a) 'Suicide in young people: a study of 174 cases, aged under 25 years, based on coroners' and medical records', *British Journal of Psychiatry*, 175: 1–6.

Hawton, K., Kingsbury, S., Steinhardt, K., James, A. and Fagg, J. (1999b) 'Repetition of deliberate self-harm by adolescents: the role of psychological factors', *Journal of Adolescence*, 22: 369–78.

Hawton, K., Rodham, K., Evans, E. and Weatherall, R. (2002) 'Deliberate self-harm in adolescents: self-report survey in schools in England', *British Medical Journal*, 325: 1207–11.

Hayes, L. (1995) *Prison Suicide: An Overview and Guide to Prevention.* Washington, DC: US Department of Justice.

Heilig, S. (1973) 'Suicide in jails', in B.L. Danto (ed.) *Jail House Blues: Studies of Suicidal Behavior in Jail and Prison* (pp. 47–56). Orchard Lake, MI: Epic Publications.

Hewitt, P.L., Norton, G.R., Flett, G.L., Callander, L. and Cowan, T. (1998) 'Dimensions of perfectionism, hopelessness, and attempted suicide in a sample of alcoholics', *Suicide and Life-Threatening Behavior*, 28 (4): 395–406.

HMCIP (1997) *Young Prisoners: A Thematic Review by HM Chief Inspector of Prisons for England and Wales*. London: Home Office.

HMCIP (1999a) *HM Young Offenders and Remand Centre Feltham. Report on an Unannounced Full Inspection: 30 November – 4 December 1998*. London: Home Office.

HMCIP (1999b) *Report on a Short Unannounced Inspection of HM YOI and RC Feltham: 28–30 September 1999*. London: Home Office.

HMCIP (1999c) *Suicide is Everyone's Concern. A Thematic Review by HM Chief Inspector of Prisons for England and Wales*. London: Home Office.

HMCIP (2001) *Report on a Short Unannounced Inspection of HM YOI and RC Feltham: 23–26 October 2000*. London: Home Office.

HMCIP (2002) *Report on a Full Announced Inspection of HM YOI Feltham: 14–23 January 2002*. London: Home Office

HMCIP (2004a) *Report on a Follow-up Inspection of HM Young Offenders Institution Feltham: 25–27 February 2004*. London: Home Office.

HMCIP (2004b) *Annual Report of HM Inspectorate of Prisons for England and Wales 2002/2003*. London: Home Office.

HMCIP (2005) *Report on a Full Announced Inspection of HM Young Offender Institution Feltham. 15–20 May 2005*. London: Home Office.

HMCIP for Scotland (1998) *Report on HM National Induction Centre*. Edinburgh: Scottish Executive.

HM Prison Service (2001) *Suicide Prevention in Prison: An Internal Review*. London: Safer Custody Group.

HM Prison Service (2004a) *Self-Inflicted Deaths in Custody: A Six-Year Overview: 1998/9 to 2003/4. Safer Custody Group Research Briefing 5*. London: Safer Custody Group.

HM Prison Service (2004b) *Recorded Self-Harm in the Prison Service. Safer Custody Group Research Briefing 2*: London: Safer Custody Group.

HMSO (1999) *Saving Lives: Our Healthier Nation*. White Paper. London: HMSO.

HMSO (2001) *Criminal Justice: The Way Ahead*. London: HMSO.

Hobbs, G.S. and Dear, G.E. (2000) 'Prisoners' perceptions of prison officers as sources of support', *Journal of Offender Rehabilitation*, 31 (1–2): 127–42.

Holmes, J. (1999) *John Bowlby and Attachment Theory*. Hove: Brunner-Routledge.

Holmes, J. (2002) *The Search for the Secure Base: Attachment Theory and Psychotherapy*. Hove: Brunner-Routledge.

Home Office (1999) *Detention in a Young Offender Institution for 18–20-Year-olds: A Consultation Paper*. London: Home Office.

Home Office (2003) The Criminal Justice Act 2003. www.homeoffice.gov.uk/justice/sentencing/criminaljusticeact2003/

Home Office (2004) *Reducing Re-offending National Action Plan*. London: Home Office.

Houston, K., Hawton, K. and Shepperd, R. (2001) 'Suicide in young people aged 15–24: a psychological autopsy study', *Journal of Affective Disorders*, 63: 159–70.

Hovey, J.D. (1999) 'Moderating influences of social support on suicidal ideation in a sample of Mexican immigrants', *Psychological Reports*, 85 (1): 78–9.

Hovey, J.D. (2000) 'Acculturative stress, depression, and suicidal ideation among Central American immigrants', *Suicide and Life-Threatening Behavior*, 30 (2): 125–39.

Howard League (2003a) *Busy Doing Nothing: Young Men on Remand*. London: Howard League for Penal Reform.

Howard League (2003b) *Suicide and Self-Harm Prevention. Repetitive Self-Harm Among Women and Girls in Prison*. London: Howard League for Penal Reform.

Hultén, A., Jiang, G.-X., Wasserman, D., Hawton, K., Hjelmeland, H., De Leo, D., Ostamo, A., Salander-Renberg, E. and Schmidtke, A. (2001) 'Repetition of attempted suicide among teenagers in Europe: frequency, timing and risk factors', *European Child and Adolescent Psychiatry*, 10: 161–9.

Inch, H., Rowlands, P. and Soliman, A. (1995) 'Deliberate self-harm in a young offenders' institution', *Journal of Forensic Psychiatry*, 6 (1): 161–71.

Ireland, C.A. (2001) *Problems in Adapting to Prison Life*. Unpublished doctoral dissertation, University of Central Lancashire.

Ireland, J. (2000) 'A descriptive analysis of self-harm reports among a sample of incarcerated adolescents', *Journal of Adolescence*, 23 (5): 605–13.

Ireland, J. (2002) *Bullying Among Prisoners: Evidence, Research and Intervention Strategies*. Hove: Brunner-Routledge.

Ireland, J.L. (2005) 'Psychological health and bullying behaviour among adolescent prisoners: a study of young and juvenile offenders', *Journal of Adolescent Health*, 36: 236–43.

Ireland, J.L., Boustead, R. and Ireland, C.A. (2005) 'Coping style and psychological health among adolescent prisoners: a study of young and juvenile offenders', *Journal of Adolescence*, 28: 411–23.

Irwin, J. (1970) *The Felon*. Englewood Cliffs, NJ: Prentice-Hall.

Irwin, J. and Cressey, D. (1962) 'Thieves, convicts and the inmate culture', *Social Problems*, 10: 142–55.

Ivanoff, A. (1992) 'Background risk factors associated with parasuicide among male prison inmates', *Criminal Justice and Behavior*, 19: 426–36.

Ivanoff, A. and Jang, S.J. (1991) 'The role of hopelessness and social desirability in predicting suicidal behavior: a study of prison inmates', *Journal of Consulting and Clinical Psychology*, 59: 394–9.

Ivanoff, A., Jang, S.J. and Smyth, N.J. (1996) 'Clinical risk factors associated with parasuicide in prison', *International Journal of Offender Therapy and Comparative Criminology*, 40: 135–46.

Ivanoff, A., Smyth, N.J., Grochowski, S., Jang, S.J. and Klein, K.E. (1992) 'Problem solving and suicidality among prison inmates: another look at state versus trait', *Journal of Consulting and Clinical Psychology*, 60: 970–3.

Johnson, R. (2002) *Hard Time: Understanding and Reforming the Prison* (3rd edn). Belmont: Wadsworth.

Jones, R.S. and Schmid, T.J. (2000) *Doing Time: Prison Experience and Identity Among First Time Inmates*. Stamford, CT: JAI Press.

Joukamma, M. (1997) 'Prison suicide in Finland, 1969–1992', *Forensic Science International*, 89 (3): 167–74.

Kalichman, S., Heckman, T., Kockman, A., Sikkema, K. and Bergholte, J. (2000) 'Depression and thoughts of suicide among middle-aged and other persons living with HIV-AIDS', *Psychiatric Services*, 51 (7): 903–7.

Kaslow, N., Thompson, M., Meadows, L., Chance, S., Puett, R., Hollins, L., Jesse, S. and Kellermann, A. (2000) 'Risk factors for suicide attempts among African American women', *Depression and Anxiety*, 12 (1): 13–20.

Kessler, R.C. (1992) 'Perceived support and adjustment to stress: methodological consideration', in H. Veiel and U. Bauman (eds) *The Meaning and Measurement of Social Support* (pp. 259–71). London: Hemisphere.

Kimbrough, R., Molock, S. and Walton, K. (1996) 'Perception of social support, acculturation, depression, and suicidal ideation among African American college students at predominantly black and predominantly white universities', *Journal of Negro Education*, 65 (3): 295–307.

Kotler, M., Finkelstein, G., Molocho, A., Botsis, A.J., Plutchik, R., Brown, S. and van Pragg, H. (1993) 'Correlates of suicide and violence risk in an inpatient population. Coping styles and social support', *Psychiatric Research*, 47: 281–90.

Labour Party (2001) Labour Party General Election Manifesto. *Ambitions for Britain*. London: Labour Party.

Lader, D., Singleton, N. and Meltzer, H. (2000) *Psychiatric Morbidity among Young Offenders in England and Wales*. London: ONS.

Laireiter, A. and Bauman, U. (1992) 'Network structures and support functions – theoretical and empirical analysis', in H. Veiel and U. Bauman (eds) *The Meaning and Measurement of Social Support* (pp. 33–55). London: Hemisphere.

Lakey, B. and Cohen, S. (2000) 'Social support theory and measurement', in S. Cohen, L.G. Underwood and B.H. Gottlieb (eds) *Social Support Measurement and Intervention: A Guide for Health and Social Scientists* (pp. 29–52). Oxford: Oxford University Press.

Layder, D. (1998) *Sociological Practice. Linking Theory and Social Research*. London: Sage.

Lazarus, R. and Folkman, S. (1984) *Stress, Appraisal, and Coping*. New York: Springer.

Lazarus, R.S. (1966) *Psychological Stress and the Coping Process*. New York: McGraw-Hill.

Lazarus, R.S. (2000) 'Evolution of a model of stress, coping and discrete emotions', in V. Hill Rice (ed.) *Handbook of Stress, Coping, and Health. Implication for Nursing Research, Theory and Practice* (pp. 195–222). London: Sage.

Leary, M.R. (2001) *Interpersonal Rejection*. Oxford: Oxford University Press.

Leathman, G. and Duck, S. (1990) 'Conversations with friends and the dynamic of social support', in S. Duck (ed.) *Personal Relationships and Social Support* (pp. 1–29). London: Sage.

Lester, D. and Danto, B. (1993) *Suicide Behind Bars. Prediction and Prevention*. Philadelphia: Charles Press.

Liebling, A. and Krarup, H. (1993) *Suicide Attempts in Male Prisons*. London: Home Office.

Liebling, A. (1992) *Suicides in Prison*. London: Routledge.

Liebling, A. (1995) 'Vulnerability and prison suicide', *British Journal of Criminology*, 35 (2): 173–87.

Liebling, A. (1999) 'Prison suicide and prisoner coping', in M. Tonry and J. Petersilia (eds) *Crime and Justice: A Review of Research*, Vol. 26 (pp. 283–360). Chicago: University of Chicago Press.

Liebling, A. (2004) *Prisons and Their Moral Performance. A Study of Values, Quality and Prison Life*. Oxford: Oxford University Press.

Liebling, A. and Arnold, H. (2002) *Measuring the Quality of Prison Life. Research Findings 174*. London: Home Office.

Liebling, A. and Price, D. (2001) 'The Prison Officer.' HMP Leyhill: *Prison Service Journal*.

Liebling, A., Tait, S., Durie, L., Stiles, A. and Harvey, J. (2005) An *Evaluation of HM Prison Service's Safer Locals Programme*. Report Submitted to HM Prison Service.

Lindquist, C. (2000) 'Social integration and mental well-being among jail inmates', *Sociological Reform*, 15 (3): 431–55.

Little, M. (1990) *Young Men in Prison: The Criminal Identity Explored Through the Rules of Behaviour*. Dartmouth: Aldershot.

Loucks, N. (2002) *Just Visiting? A Review of the Role of Prison Visitors' Centres*. London: Prison Reform Trust.

Loucks, N. (2005) *Keeping in Touch: The Case for Family Support Work in Prison*. London: Prison Reform Trust.

Lyon, J., Denison, C., and Wilson, A. (2000) *'Tell Them So They'll Listen': Messages from Young People in Custody*. London: Home Office.

MacKenzie, D.L., Goodstein, L.I. and Blouin, D.C. (1987) 'Personal control and prison adjustment: an empirical test of a proposed model', *Journal of Research in Crime and Delinquency*, 24 (1): 49–68.

Maden, A., Chamberlain, S. and Gunn, J. (2000) 'Deliberate self-harm in sentenced male prisoners in England and Wales. Some ethnic factors', *Criminal Behaviour and Mental Health*, 10 (3): 199–204.

Marcus, P. and Alcabes, P. (1993) 'Characteristics of suicides by inmates in an urban jail', *Hospital and Community Psychiatry*, 44 (3): 256–61.

Masten, A.S. and Powell, J.L. (2003) 'A resilience framework for research, policy and practice', in S.S. Luthar (ed.) *Resilience and Vulnerability: Adaptation in the Context of Childhood Adversity* (pp. 1–25). Cambridge: Cambridge University Press.

Mathiesen, T. (1965).*The Defences of the Weak: A Sociological Study of a Norwegian Correctional Institution*. London: Tavistock.

Mauss, M. (1954/2002) *The Gift: The Form and Reason for Exchange in Archaic Society*. London: Routledge.

McFarlane, A.H., Neale, K.A., Norman, G.R., Roy, R.G. and Streiner, D.L. (1981) 'Methodological issues in developing a scale to measure social support', *Schizophrenia Bulletin*, 7: 90–100.

McManus, J.J. (1994) *Mentally Disturbed Prisoners: Issues in the Identification and Management of the Mentally Disturbed within Penal Establishments*. Scottish Prison Service Occasional Papers Report No. 4. Edinburgh: Scottish Prison Service.

Meltzer, H., Jenkins, R., Singleton, N., Charlton, J. and Yar, M. (1999) *Non-fatal Suicidal Behaviour Among Prisoners*. London: HMSO.

Meltzer, H., Jenkins, R., Singleton, N., Charlton, J. and Yar, M. (2003) 'Non-fatal suicidal behaviour among prisoners', *International Review of Psychiatry*, 15 (1–2): 148–9.

Mohino, S., Kirchner, T., and Forns, M. (2004) 'Coping strategies in young male prisoners', *Journal of Youth and Adolescence*, 33 (1): 41–9.

Morano, C.D., Cisler, R.A. and Lemerond, J. (1993) 'Risk factors for adolescents suicidal behavior: loss, insufficient family support, and hopelessness', *Adolescence*, 28 (112): 851–65.

Murray, J. (2005) 'The effects of imprisonment on families and children of prisoners', in A. Liebling and S. Maruna (eds) *The Effects of Imprisonment* (pp. 442–62). Cullompton: Willan Publishing.

NACRO (2001) *Young Adult Offenders: A Period of Transition*. London: NACRO.

NOMS (National Offender Management Service) (2006) *Population in Custody: Monthly Tables January 2006*. London: NOMS.

Neustatter, A. (2002) *Locked in Locked Out. The Experience of Young Offenders Out of Society and in Prison*. London: Calouste Gulbenkian Foundation.

Nieland, M.N.S., McCluskie, C. and Tait, E. (2001) 'Prediction of psychological distress in young offenders', *Legal and Criminological Psychology*, 6: 29–47.

Nisbett, P.A. (1996) 'Protective factors for suicidal black females', *Suicide and Life-Threatening Behavior*, 261 (4): 325–41.

Palmer, E.J. and Connelly, R. (2005) 'Depression, hopelessness and suicide ideation among vulnerable prisoners', *Criminal Behaviour and Mental Health*, 15 (3): 164–70.

Papageorgiou, C. and Wells, A. (eds) (2004) *Depressive Rumination: Nature, Theory, and Treatment*. Chichester: Wiley.

Pierce, G.R., Sarason, B.R. and Sarason, I.G. (1990) 'Integrating social support perspectives: working models, personal relationships, and situational factors', in S. Duck (ed.) *Personal Relationships and Social Support* (pp. 172–89). London: Sage.

Ponizovsky, A. and Ritsner, M. (1999) 'Suicide ideation among immigrants to Israel from the former Soviet Union: an epidemiological survey of prevalence and risk factors', *Suicide and Life-Threatening Behavior*, 29 (4): 376–92.

Pugh, D.N. (1993) 'The effects of problem-solving ability and locus of control on prisoner adjustment', *International Journal of Offender Therapy and Comparative Criminology*, 37: 163–76.

Pugh, D.N. (1994) 'Revision and further assessments of the prison locus of control scale', *Psychological Reports*, 74: 979–86.

Putnam, R. (2000) *Bowling Alone: The Collapse and Revival of American Community*. London: Simon & Schuster.

Reis, H. and Collins, N. (2000) 'Measuring relationship properties and interactions relevant to social support', in S. Cohen, L.G. Underwood and B.H. Gottlieb (eds) *Social Support Measurement and Intervention: A Guide for Health and Social Scientists* (pp. 136–92). Oxford: Oxford University Press.

Reitzel, L.R. and Harju, B.L. (2000) 'Influence of locus of control and custody level on intake and prison-adjustment depression', *Criminal Justice and Behavior*, 27 (5): 625–44.

Rodham, K., Hawton, K. and Evans, E. (2004) 'Reasons for deliberate self-harm: comparison of self-poisoners and self-cutters in a community sample of adolescents', *Journal of the American Academy of Child and Adolescent Psychiatry*, 43: 80–7.

Rook, K. (1992) 'Detrimental aspects of social relationships: taking stock of an emerging literature', in H.O.F. Veiel and U. Bauman (eds) *The Meaning and Measurement of Social Support* (pp. 157–90). London: Hemisphere.

Ross, T. and Pfafflin, F. (2004) 'Violence and attachment: attachment style, self-regulation and interpersonal problems in a prison population', in F. Pfafflin and G. Adshead (eds) *A Matter of Security: The Application of Attachment Theory to Forensic Psychiatry and Psychotherapy. Forensic Focus 25* (pp. 225–49). London: Jessica Kingsley.

Rotter, J. (1966) 'Generalized expectancies for internal versus external control of reinforcement', *Psychological Monographs*, 80 (full volume).

Rudd, M.D. (1990) 'An integrative model of suicidal ideation', *Suicide and Life-Threatening Behavior*, 20 (1): 16–28.

Rudd, M.D., Joiner, T.E., Jr. and Rajab, M.H. (1995) 'Help negation after acute suicidal crisis', *Journal of Consulting and Clinical Psychology*, 63: 499–503.

Sakinofsky, I. (2002) 'Repetition of suicidal behaviour', in K. Hawton and K. van Heeringen (eds) *The International Handbook of Suicide and Attempted Suicide* (pp. 385–404). Chichester: Wiley.

Samaritans (2004) www.samaritans.org/sams.html/suiuk.html

Schaller, G., Zimmermann, C. and Raymond, L. (1996) 'Suicidal gestures (including wrist slashing) in a Swiss prison: identifying the risk factors', *Sozial-und Praventivmedizin*, 41 (4): 249–56.

Schoon, I. (2006) *Risk and Resilience. Adaptations in Changing Times*. Cambridge: Cambridge University Press.

Schotte, D.E. and Clum, G.A. (1982) 'Suicide ideation in a college population: a test of a model', *Journal of Consulting and Clinical Psychology*, 50 (5): 690–6.

Schotte, D.E. and Clum, G.A (1987) 'Problem-solving skills in suicidal psychiatric patients', *Journal of Consulting and Clinical Psychology*, 55 (1): 49–54.

Schotte, D.E. and Clum, G.A (1990) 'Problem-solving deficits in suicidal patients: trait vulnerability or state phenomenon?', *Journal of Consulting and Clinical Psychology*, 58 (5): 562–4.

Schutt, R.K., Meshede, T. and Rierdan, J. (1994) 'Distress, suicidal thoughts, and social support among homeless adults', *Journal of Health and Social Behavior*, 35 (2): 134–42.

Seligman, A.B. (1997) *The Problem of Trust*. Princeton, NJ: Princeton University Press.

Seligman, M.E.P. (1975/1992) *Helplessness: On Development, Depression, and Death*. New York: W. H. Freeman.

Seymour, J. (1977/1992) 'Niches in prison', in H. Toch (ed.) *Living in Prison: The Ecology of Survival* (pp. 235–66). Washington, DC: American Psychological Association.

Shaw, J., Appelby, L. and Baker, D. (2003) *Safer Prisons: A National Study of Prison Suicides 1999–2000 by the National Confidential Inquiry into Suicides and Homicides by People with Mental Illness*. London: Department of Health.

Shelton, D. (2004) *Mentally Disordered and Non-mentally Disordered Young Offenders: A Comparison of Family Functioning and Perceived Parenting Style*. Unpublished manuscript. Department of Systemic and Family Psychotherapy, Institute of Family Therapy, London.

Singleton, N., Meltzer, H., Gatward, R., Coid, J. and Deasy, D. (1998) *Psychiatric Morbidity Among Prisoners in England and Wales*. London: ONS.

Skegg, K. and Cox, B. (1993) 'Suicide in custody – occurrence in Maori and non-Maori New Zealanders', *New Zealand Medical Journal*, 106 (948): 1–3.

Slosar, J.A. (1978) *Prisonization, Friendship, and Leadership*. Toronto: Lexington Books.

Smith, P.K., Pendleton, E. and Mitchell, H. (2005) 'Bullying and anti-bullying policies: a young offender institution and an adult prison', in J. Ireland (ed.) *Bullying Among Prisoners: Innovations in Theory and Research* (pp. 109–25). Cullompton: Willan Publishing.

Smith, R. (2003) *Youth Justice: Ideas, Policy and Practice*. Cullompton: Willan Publishing.

Smyth, N.J., Ivanoff, A. and Jang, S.J. (1994) 'Changes in psychological maladaptation among inmate parasuicides', *Criminal Justice and Behavior*, 21: 357–65.

Snow, L. (2002) 'Prisoners' motives for self-injury and attempted suicide', *British Journal of Forensic Practice*, 4 (4): 18–29.

Snow, L., Paton, J., Oram, C. and Teers, R. (2002) 'Self-inflicted deaths during 2001: an analysis of trends', *British Journal of Forensic Practice*, 4 (4): 3–17.

Snyder, C.R. (2001) *Coping with Stress: Effective People and Processes*. Oxford: Oxford University Press.

Social Exclusion Unit (2002) *Reducing Re-offending by Ex-Prisoners*. London: Social Exclusion Unit.

Solomon, E. (2004) *A Lost Generation: The Experiences of Young People in Prison*. London: Prison Reform Trust.

Spain, A.C. (2005) 'Bullying among young offenders: findings from a qualitative study', in J. Ireland (ed.) *Bullying Among Prisoners: Innovations in Theory and Research* (pp. 62–83). Cullompton: Willan Publishing.

Stratton, J.R. (1963) *The Measurement of Inmate Change During Imprisonment.* Ph.D. dissertation, University of Illinois, Urbana.

Sykes, G. (1958) *The Society of Captives.* Princeton, NJ: Princeton University Press.

Sykes, G. and Messinger, S. (1960) 'The inmate social system', in *Theoretical Studies in Social Organisation of the Prison* (pp. 5–19). New York: Social Science Research Council.

Sztompka, P. (1999) *Trust. A Sociological Theory.* Cambridge: Cambridge University Press.

Tabachnick, B.G. and Fidell, L.S. (1996) *Using Multivariate Statistics* (3rd edn). New York: HarperCollins.

Tatarelli, R., Mancinelli, I., Taggi, F. and Polidori, G. (1999) 'Suicide in Italian prisons in 1996 and 1997. A descriptive epidemiological study', *International Journal of Offender Therapy and Comparative Criminology,* 43 (4): 438–47.

Thomas, C. (1977) 'Theoretical perspectives on prisonization: a comparison of the importation and deprivation models', *Journal of Criminal Law and Criminology,* 68: 135–45.

Thompson, R.A. (1999) 'Early attachment and later development', in J. Cassidy and P.R. Shaver (eds) *Handbook of Attachment: Theory, Research and Clinical Applications* (pp. 265–86). London: Guilford Press.

Toch, H. (1977/1992) *Living in Prison: The Ecology of Survival.* Washington, DC: American Psychological Association.

Toch, H. (1992) *Mosaic of Despair: Human Breakdowns in Prison.* Washington, DC: American Psychological Association.

Toch, H. and Adams, K. (2002) *Acting Out: Maladaptive Behavior in Confinement.* Washington, DC: American Psychological Association.

Topp, D.O. (1979) 'Suicide in prison', *British Journal of Criminology,* 143: 24–7.

Tortolero, S.R. and Roberts, R.E. (2001) 'Differences in nonfatal suicide behaviors among Mexican and European American middle school children', *Suicide and Life Threatening Behavior,* 31 (2): 214–23.

Towl, G. (1999) 'Self-inflicted deaths in prisons in England and Wales from 1988 to 1996', in G. Towl, M. McHugh and D. Jones (eds) *Suicides in Prisons. Research, Policy and Practice* (pp. 13–20). Brighton: Pavilion Publishing.

Trotter, R.T. (2000) 'Ethnography and network analysis: the study of social context in cultures and societies', in G.L. Albrecht, R. Fitzpatrick, and S.C. Scrimshaw (eds) *Handbook of Social Studies in Health and Medicine* (pp. 210–29). London: Sage.

Turner, V. (1969) *Ritual Process: Structure and Anti-structure.* London: Routledge and Kegan Paul.

Uslaner, E.M. (2002) *The Moral Foundations of Trust.* Cambridge: Cambridge University Press.

Van Gennep, A. (1960) *The Rites of Passage.* London: Routledge.

Van Ijzendoorin, M. and Sagi, A. (1999) 'Cross-cultural patterns of attachment: universal and contextual dimensions', in J. Cassidy and P.R. Shaver (eds) *Handbook of Attachment: Theory, Research and Clinical Applications* (pp. 713–34). London: Guilford Press.

Vaux, A. (1992) 'Assessment of social support', in H. Veiel and U. Bauman (eds) *The Meaning and Measurement of Social Support* (pp. 193–216). London: Hemisphere.

Vilhjalmsson, R., Kritsjandottir, G. and Sweinbjarmardottir, E. (1998) 'Factors association with suicide ideations in adults', *Social Psychiatry and Psychiatric Epidemiology*, 33 (3): 97–103.

Wasserman, S. and Faust, K. (1999) *Social Network Analysis: Methods and Applications*. Cambridge: Cambridge University Press.

Weiss, R.S. (1976) 'The provisions of social relationships', in Z. Rubin (ed) *Doing Unto Others* (pp. 17–26). Englewood Cliffs, NJ: Prentice-Hall.

Westefeld, J.S., Range, L.M., Rogers, J.R., Maples, M.R., Bromley, J.L. and Alcorn, J. (2000) 'Suicide: an overview', *The Counseling Psychologist*, 28 (4): 445–510.

Wheeler, S. (1961) 'Socialization in correctional communities', *American Sociological Review*, 26: 697–712.

White, J., Leggett, J. and Beech, A. (1999) 'The incidence of self-harming in the male population of a medium-secure psychiatric hospital', *Journal of Forensic Psychiatry*, 10 (1): 59–68.

Wichmann, C., Serin, R. and Motiuk, L. (2000) *Predicting Suicide Attempts Among Male Offenders in Federal Penitentiaries*. Research Branch Correctional Service Canada.

Williams, K.D. (1997) 'Social ostracism', in R.M. Lowalski (ed) *Aversive Interpersonal Behaviors* (pp. 133–70). New York: Plenum.

Williams, K.D. (2001) *Ostracism: The Power of Silence*. New York: Guilford Press.

Windle, R.C. and Windle, M. (1997) 'An investigation of adolescents' substance use behaviors, depressed affect, and suicidal behavior', *Journal of Child Psychology and Psychiatry and Allied Disciplines*, 38 (8): 921–9.

Wooldredge, J.D. (1999) 'Inmate experiences and psychological well-being', *Criminal Justice and Behavior*, 26 (2): 235–50.

World Health Organisation (1999) *Health in Prison Project*. Available at www. hipp-europe.org.

Wright, K.N. and Goodstein, L. (1989) 'Correctional environments', in L. Goodstein and D.L. MacKenzie (eds) *The American Prison: Issues in Research and Policy*, IV, (pp. 253–66). London: Plenum Press.

Wright, T., Holman, T., Steele, T. and Silverstein, G. (1980) 'Locus of control and mastery in a reformatory: a field study of defensive externality', *Journal of Personality and Social Psychology*, 38: 1005–13.

Yang, B. and Clum, G.A. (1994) 'Life stress, social support, and problem-solving skills predictive of depressive symptoms, hopelessness, and suicidal ideation in an Asian college student sample: a test of a model', *Suicide and Life-Threatening Behavior*, 24 (2): 127–39.

Yates, T.M., Egeland, B. and Sroufe, A. (2003) 'Rethinking resilience: a developmental process perspective', in S.S. Luthar (ed.) *Resilience and Vulnerability: Adaptation in the Context of Childhood Adversities* (pp. 243–66). Cambridge: Cambridge University Press.

Zamble, E. and Porporino, J. (1988) *Coping, Behavior and Adaptation in Prison*. New York: Springer-Verlag.

Appendix I

Interview schedule

Background information

- Is this your first time in prison?
- If no, how many times have you been in prison before?
- [If the prisoner had been in this prison before] How many times have you been in prison before? Have you been in Feltham before?
- What is your current status? (remand, convicted but not sentenced, sentenced)
- [If the prisoner had been sentenced] How long is your sentence?
- How old are you?
- Which regime level are you on?
- What is your main daytime activity?
- What is your ethnic group?
- When there is association, do you always go, sometimes go, rarely or never go?
- Have you received psychiatric treatment in the past?
- Did you have a problem with drug misuse before you came to prison?
- If yes, did you need a detox on arrival in prison?
- Have you self-harmed before?
- If yes, was this in prison, outside prison, or both?
- Are you close to your home area?
- Are you in contact by visits, letters or telephone?

Social networks outside prison

- In the last week before you came into prison, who were you living with?
- Who would you consider to be a close relative of yours?
- Who would you consider to be a close friend of yours?
- Out of all these people, who do you feel closest to?
- Have any of these people helped you out over the past week?
- How many friends would you say you have?

Semi-structured interview schedule

Below is a list of the core set of questions that I asked at each of the three interview stages. Depending on the responses given by each individual, I would then ask additional questions surrounding different topics.

- As prisoners described their experiences at each 'transition point', I asked about main activities, interactions with other prisoners, interactions with staff, core thoughts, feelings and any concerns.
- Concerns and willingness to seek support: What are your main concerns at the moment? How willing would you be to ask someone for help? How would you describe how you are feeling generally?
- Received social support: Have you been helped out by any prisoners since you've been here? If yes, in what way? How can prisoners help each other out here? Have you been helped out by any members of staff since you've been here? If yes, in what way? How can the staff help prisoners out here? Have you felt looked after since being here? If yes, in what way?
- Trust: Do you trust prisoners here? Why or why not? Do you trust the staff here? Why or why not? What does the word *trust* mean to you?
- Outside contact: Do you (expect to) get visits here? Do you (expect to) get letters? Have you written any letters? Have you made any phone calls?
- Further expectations and summing up: What do you expect to happen over the next week? What words would you use to sum up how you've been feeling over the past few days?

Additional questions within interview with individuals who had self-harmed

Listed below are some of the core questions I asked each individual. Depending on the responses given by each individual, I would then ask additional questions surrounding different topics.

- Can you describe how you were feeling just before you harmed yourself?
- What did you actually do?
- Why do you think you did it?
- What were you thinking about at the time? What were you feeling?
- How did the staff respond?
- Were you on an F2052SH form at time? What do you think of this form?
- Questions were also asked about prior self-harm and suicidal thoughts.

I also obtained information from the F213 form on the nature of the incident, the timing, the place, the medical seriousness and whether the prisoner was on an F2052SH form.

Index